INDIAN GENIUS

INDIAN GENIUS

THE METEORIC RISE OF INDIANS IN AMERICA

MEENAKSHI AHAMED

HarperCollins *Publishers* India

First published in India by HarperCollins *Publishers* 2024
4th Floor, Tower A, Building No. 10, DLF Cyber City,
DLF Phase II, Gurugram, Haryana—122002
www.harpercollins.co.in

2 4 6 8 10 9 7 5 3 1

P-ISBN: 978-93-6569-240-2
E-ISBN: 978-93-6569-916-6

Typeset in 12/18 Edita at
HarperCollins *Publishers* India

Printed and bound at
Replika Press Pvt Ltd

MIX
Paper | Supporting
responsible forestry
FSC™ C016779

This book is produced from independently certified FSC® paper
to ensure responsible forest management.

For
Shabnam & Tara
who light up my life

&

Liaquat

Contents

The Techies

Introduction

My first reaction to America when I arrived in 1970 was an acute sense of disappointment. I landed in Boston right before Christmas, just a few weeks after graduating from high school in India. As the car wound its way from Logan Airport to Brookline, I pressed my face against the glass, looking for the modern futuristic city I imagined all American cities to be. What were these quaint, old-fashioned houses doing in the land that had sent men and rocket ships to the moon? Where were the skyscrapers and network of highways depicted in the comics I had read? I saw a few high-rises in the distance, but it was nothing like the stunning Manhattan skyline that was emblematic of America, whose photographs I had seen in *Life* magazine. And where were the people? The silence was deafening.

Coming from a country teeming with humanity where much of life is lived outdoors, the silence was unsettling. In India, the streets are always full of people. Cars honk their horns gratuitously and music blares from roadside stalls. Life is noisy. The constant cacophony of sounds would get on my nerves once I got older, but in that moment, as the evening deepened, the cold, bleak weather and the pervasive stillness outside, made me feel suddenly homesick.

The academic year in India ran from January through December in alignment with the calendar year. College in the United States did not start until September, so I had nine months to fill. I was admitted to Beaver Country Day, a private girls' school in Brookline, to fill the gap and acclimatize.

I came from a world where uniforms were worn in school, students stood up when a teacher entered the classroom, and a great deal of formality governed the rules of conduct within the school walls. I entered Beaver as a senior, and when I walked into my homeroom, I was unable to distinguish the teacher from the students. The students sat on desks, casually exchanging cigarettes. Everyone was laughing and having a good time. *This was school?* I didn't know if I should love it or be appalled. Two girls had been caught smoking in my boarding school in India when I was a senior, and both had been expelled in disgrace. The atmosphere of my American high school was in equal parts intimidating and liberating.

Someone pointed out the teacher—a pretty, petite blonde sitting on a desk, dressed in jeans, and engaged in an animated conversation with a student. It was hard to distinguish her from the students that had gathered around her. Everyone was dressed alike. She greeted me with a hug and introduced me to everyone. That was the moment I fell in love with America, Americans, and American education. Everyone was warm, welcoming, and excited to invite me into their homes and teach me about their country. I was, for many, the first Indian they had ever met or seen. In turn, I loved my role as foreign student and unofficial ambassador, teaching my friends about life in India.

India may have been the world's largest democracy, but it barely registered in the American consciousness. Teaching geography, I discovered, was not a priority in American high schools, and the average American's knowledge of countries to the east of Europe was negligible. India was a country far away, one that the Beatles and hippies found fascinating and whose female prime minister, Indira Gandhi, continually clashed with American presidents. Nixon was president at the time, and the two leaders could not stand each other. The overwhelming impression that Americans had of India then, which persisted through the eighties was that it was a poor country teeming with people and in constant need of foreign aid.

My knowledge of American culture and history was equally deficient as it was not taught at my school in India. India's educational system was still based on the British system and was culturally biased toward European history and literature. I knew very little about the American war of independence and, though I had heard of Abraham Lincoln I did not know much about the Civil War. My only frame of reference was the fictional account I read in *Gone with the Wind*, which I found in the school library. I had spent the previous four years in a private boarding school in the Himalayas, cut off from news outlets. Television had only been introduced to a handful of cities in India in the sixties. There was no access to any television station in the mountains where my school was located, and we were not allowed to own radios. The local paper in the school library carried little national news, let alone international coverage.

I was familiar with Elvis, Louis Armstrong, Hollywood icons, and Dennis the Menace, but I was unaware of Kent State, the Black Panthers, or the anti-war movement that was consuming the conversations of young people around me in America. I had a lot to learn.

According to the United States Census, there were 51,000 Indians in the United States when I arrived.[1] When I began college a few months later, I discovered it was hard work meeting other Indian students—there weren't many of us and we were spread across the United States's many college campuses. There were very few women among us; most Indian families were reluctant to send girls far away to study with no means to communicate with them. Letters took weeks to go back and forth, and phone calls were prohibitively expensive if you were lucky enough to get a reasonable connection on the Indian end. American dorms usually had one communal phone per floor and there was no privacy. Computers, fax machines, cell phones and alternative ways to communicate did not yet exist.

After 18 months in Boston, I was homesick and desperate for Indian food. I wandered over to Central Square near MIT where I had heard there was an Indian restaurant. After the meal, best forgotten due to its abysmal quality, I walked over to MIT to see the campus. I ended up in the library, which seemed full of Chinese and Indian men. It was as though all the Indian students had come to the United States to become engineers and found their way to MIT. I saw no women in the library, and the students seemed surprised to see me there. After looking at me with some curiosity for a few minutes, they quickly went back to their books. Some of the students looked like they lived there. They kept their personal effects, including toothbrushes, in the cubicles, and a few appeared to have been sleeping there for days.

A decade after my arrival, the Indian American population had shot up. By 1980, there were 360,000 people living in the United States who identified as Indian. Almost every Indian I knew was a professional and had come to the United States on a student visa. Many had found well-paying jobs and remained in America but a group of us had returned to work in India, particularly those interested in public policy. Some of my friends took the very competitive civil service exam, which was the only entry to government service, but I had arranged an internship at a women's hospital in an urban slum in New Delhi to work on family planning and population control. My undergraduate degree in political science had trained me for very little. I learned more during my internship than I had during my classes. My supervisor suggested I get a degree in public health if I wanted to pursue working in the field and suggested I apply to a couple of well-known programs in the United States. I returned to the United States in 1976 and went to Johns Hopkins for a graduate degree. Shortly after I graduated and started working at the World Bank in Washington, D.C. I met my future husband who had joined the World Bank as an economist.

The World Bank was like the United Nations—employees were on diplomatic visas, you got "home leave" to your country, and we tended to socialize with the diplomatic crowd—essentially living an expatriate life. Washington only had one Indian restaurant that was as awful as the one in Central Square, just with better décor. The two enterprising young Indian students from Georgetown who started it said it was hard to find a good Indian chef. Most of the Indians in Washington were economists or doctors. A few engineers had started contracting with the defense industry, but technology was in its infancy in 1980. At some point in 1986, after my second child was in nursery school, I decided that I was not going back to India and that my husband and I needed to raise our children as Americans. My husband accepted a job in New York, we left the World Bank and the life we had been leading with one foot always ready to return to our country of origin, and we embraced our life as Indians Americans.

The first time I noticed Indians occupying non-professional jobs was when I moved to New York in 1988. It was raining hard one late spring morning that year as I was trying to hail a cab to return home from my daughter's school. I was getting soaked despite my raincoat. Suddenly, a cab stopped in front of me and opened its door, ushering me in and circumventing two other hailers who had pushed themselves ahead of me. I was so grateful. When I was safely inside, I saw that the cabdriver was Indian. It turned out that we were both Punjabi, and he wanted to speak in our native tongue. I asked him how he had come to the country, and he told me he had waited 20 years for his visa because he was not an engineer, doctor, or any other "desired" category. He missed India and his family, unsure if he wanted to stay in the United States. When I reached my destination, he refused to accept any money from me. He said talking to me had made him a little less homesick. I had been in the country for 18 years, but the Indian population was still sparse enough in 1988 that a fellow Indian was grateful to meet someone else from his country. I cannot imagine that happening today. There are so many Indians in the greater New York area—no Indian would blink at the sight of another Indian on the street.

According to the 2020 United States Census, there are 4.4 million Americans who identify as Indian, making us the fastest growing racial group in the United States. The greatest influx of Indian immigrants took place after 2000 during the tech boom, but between 2010 and 2020, the Indian American population almost doubled. I often think back to that day in 1988, when a homesick cabdriver gave me a free ride because I was a fellow Indian and it feels like another era. By the time my children were in high school almost everyone had encountered an Indian or heard of one. I am both a witness to and part of this demographic change in American society. I no longer need to look for Indian restaurants; they are as common as Chinese eateries. Thanks to cell phones and instant communication, I am in constant touch with loved ones in India.

Today, it is virtually impossible to turn on CNN, read the *Wall Street Journal*, go to a hospital, attend university, or browse a bookstore in America without encountering a sea of Indian names and faces. In the last decade, there has been an explosion of Fortune 500 companies headed by Indian CEOs, including Microsoft, Google, Mastercard, IBM, Gap, and Wayfair.

By 2000, dramatic articles the likes of "Indian Immigrants are Tech's New Titans" began to appear in the press. Today, a third of all start-ups in Silicon Valley are headed by Indians. Lyft, Instacart, Netscaler, Sandisk, and Zocdoc are just a few of the start-ups founded by Indian Americans. Although it was really the tech boom that created the opportunity for them to shine, Indians have found success across the board.

Indra Nooyi became CEO of Pepsi in 2006, having worked her way through the ranks. Vikram Pandit, who was running the equity group at Morgan Stanley, was made CEO of Citigroup in 2007, the same year that Shantanu Narayen became CEO of Adobe Systems. Ajay Banga became CEO of Mastercard in 2010 and currently serves as president of the World Bank. Satya Nadella and Sundar Pichai became CEO of Microsoft and Google in 2014 and 2015 respectively. All of them spent their early years in India and moved to the United States for graduate school.

According to AAPI, an organization representing the interests of more than 80,000 practicing physicians in the United States, as of 2019, Indians account for 8.5 percent of practicing physicians, making them an increasingly important and visible part of the United States medical community. During the COVID-19 pandemic, the face of Dr. Sanjay Gupta was everywhere on *CNN*, reassuring the nation, explaining the novel coronavirus to journalists and viewers, and sorting through President Trump's contradictory and often inflammatory statements. His bedside manner was soothing—he entered your living room during the day and comforted you before you went to sleep at night. Gupta effectively became America's doctor. He was the new Marcus Welby. They both reached their audiences via television, except Dr. Gupta was the real thing.

When Dr. Anthony Fauci was hindered from making statements on television because President Donald Trump thought he was too pessimistic[2], the networks turned to an Indian, Dr. Ashish Jha, at the Harvard School of Global Health, to provide us with scientific information on the virus that had virtually imprisoned us within our immediate communities.

Many of the doctors interviewed on TV were Indian, which is hardly surprising given the number of doctors currently practicing in the United States that are of Indian origin.

Several Indian physicians are also gifted writers. Siddhartha Mukherjee won a Pulitzer for his book on the history of cancer, *The Emperor of All Maladies*. Atul Gawande has written several bestselling books, including *The Checklist Manifesto*, a simple guide adopted across the industry that revolutionized hospital protocols and brought down infection rates dramatically. His book *Being Mortal*, about end-of-life care, has changed people's thinking on the subject and remained on the *New York Times*'s bestseller list for months. Abraham Verghese's *Cutting for Stone* perhaps holds the record, though, with two years on the bestseller list. While Deepak Chopra is often associated with alternative healing, he was a pioneer in getting Americans to consider holistic approaches to health. Championed by celebrities like Oprah, he has attained celebrity status himself and has authored several bestselling books on health and spirituality.

Indian Americans have also made a name for themselves in art and culture. From M. Night Shyamalan to Jhumpa Lahiri, Salman Rushdie, and Padma Lakshmi, their contributions are widely appreciated.

Fareed Zakaria, Preet Bharara, Neal Katyal, and Nikki Haley are all major influencers of public policy, and Kamala Harris is the first vice president whose mother was Indian. Ninety-nine Indian Americans ran for public office in 2020, which reflects their growing influence and acceptance as an integral part of American society. It is no wonder that upon the landing of the Mars rover Perseverance on March 4, 2021, President Biden exclaimed in a call to Swati Mohan, India-born lead scientist at NASA, "It's amazing. Indian-descent Americans are taking over the country—you, my vice president [Kamala Harris], my speechwriter [Vinay Reddy]. You guys are incredible."

My book is about the meteoric rise of Indians in the United States and the contributions they have made to American culture. The book begins with Indians who immigrated after 1965, when America's need for skilled labor led to the relaxation of immigration laws, replacing the quota system with a qualification system for non-white immigrants. During the tech boom of the 1990s and early 2000s, the demand for skilled workers dramatically increased immigration from India. By 2001, 50 percent of H-1B visas awarded to skilled workers with a specialization were awarded to Indians. By 2018, that proportion had skyrocketed to 75 percent. In 2023, 280,000 Indians were granted H-1B visas or had them renewed. By comparison, only 34,477 were awarded to Chinese nationals. That same year, people of Indian origin surpassed the Chinese as the second largest immigrant group in the United States, exceeded only by Mexicans. While the overall combined

Hispanic population is larger than the combined Asian population, according to research by Pew, Asians are expected to surpass Hispanics to become the largest immigrant group by 2055.

In order to understand the profound ways in which the cultures of America and India have influenced each other, I decided to focus on the three sectors where I feel Indians have had a transformational impact: tech, medicine, and public policy. I have profiled individuals from three demographic groups—the first wave includes people who came in the sixties and seventies, the second is made up of people who were part of the tech/STEM boom, and the third is the new generation, comprising those who were born here or came at a very young age. The profiles provide insight into each individual's path to success, the obstacles they encountered, and the source of their strength in their own words.

I acknowledge that there are many gifted Indian Americans in other fields. Some are accomplished writers as well as journalists—every time I open a newspaper or magazine, I see many Indian names, and the same goes for academia—but while their contributions are of immense value, I decided to focus on those three sectors where I felt their presence has significantly shaped their respective fields. Leaving people out was far more difficult than deciding who to put in.

There are many wealthy and successful Indians, but wealth and celebrity are not the only measures of genius or influence. There are several people I would have liked to include and who deserved to be in the book, but in order to provide the reader with some insight into how an individual found the path to their particular genius, I have limited it to five in each category. The profiles are not meant to be a critical evaluation of the individual. Instead, they are an opportunity for the reader to learn through a direct conversation with the subject how they charted their path to the top.

The Immigration Construct

There are two aspects of Indian immigrant that make them distinctive. Indians are among the most highly educated of any ethnic group in the United States, including whites. Seventy-two percent of Indian Americans are college graduates compared to 51 percent of other Asians and 30 percent of the rest of the population. Indians have also attained the highest per capita income of any ethnic group in the United States. According to a Pew research poll conducted in 2018, the median household income for Indians is $100,000 compared to other Asians at $75,000 and the general population at $53,600. Indians take great pride in these statistics, which they feel reflect well on their community, but it is important to acknowledge that the highly discriminatory immigration policies pursued by the United States—allowing some people into the country only if they were highly skilled—had the unintended impact of contributing to their success.

Prior to 1850, immigration to the United States was reasonably open. Anyone who made the effort to enter the United States was allowed to stay. But despite America being a land of immigrants, immigration policy in the United States quickly became burdened by discriminatory practices. The country was growing and needed cheap labor. Starting in the 1850s contract laborers from China were brought to work in the mines and on the railroads and on farms in California. The depression of 1876 turned people against them as the economy shrank and jobs became scarce and cries of "They're taking our jobs!" resulted in the Chinese Exclusion Act, passed by Congress in 1882, restricting Chinese immigration for the next sixty years. Cheap Japanese and Korean laborers came to take their place along with a few thousand Indians. They too encountered discrimination. The Barred Zone Act of 1917, essentially prevented Asian immigrants from attaining citizenship. It lumped all Asians, including the Indians, who were primarily Sikhs from the Punjab region, into the same category even though Asians spanned many countries from Pakistan and Sri Lanka to Indonesia and China and were culturally diverse.

Although we think of Indians as being one of the more recent additions to the demographic mix, they have a complicated history of race relations in the United States that reaches back to 1923—facing racism and being stripped of their citizenship, their land, and in some cases their wives because of the color of their skin.

After World War I, a small group of Indians had found their way to the west coast of the United States where the farming and logging industry was expanding.[3] India was still a British colony, and some enterprising Indians were looking for opportunities outside colonial India because their opportunities under British rule were limited. Bhagat Singh Thind had first come to the United States as a student and enrolled at Berkeley in 1913. He was recruited by the United States Army to fight in World War I, and after the war, he applied for and was granted United States citizenship in 1918. Just four days after being granted citizenship in Washington state, it was revoked on the grounds that he was not white. Between 1908 and 1923 at least 67 natives of India had been granted citizenship in 32 courts across 17 states. This should have indicated some concurrence on their status but that turned out not to be the case, as their eligibility for the category "Free White Persons," a qualification for naturalization, was called into doubt. Chinese and Japanese nationals were labeled "Mongoloid" and ineligible to apply.

United States laws recognized Caucasians as "white," which qualified them for citizenship. Thind, a North Indian Punjabi, argued that since he belonged to the Aryan race, he was technically Caucasian and eligible for citizenship. He reapplied to become a citizen in Oregon, where his argument was accepted by the court and he was granted citizenship for the second time in 1920. But the Bureau of Naturalization, a bastion of conservatism, appealed the decision and the case went to the Supreme Court, which in 1923, ruled against him in United States v. Thind—he was once again stripped of his citizenship and told that regardless of belonging to the Aryan race, only white people were considered Caucasian. The justices declared that he was not white.

To add insult to injury, they suggested that Thind's Indian lawyer, Sakharam Ganesh Pandit, a United States citizen since 1914, who had lived and practiced in the United States for many years, also be stripped of his citizenship along with his white American wife.

In 1907, a law had been passed that denied women their citizenship if they married an alien or anyone ineligible for United States citizenship. In one stroke, the whole family was rendered stateless. Land laws in those days were tied to citizenship, so Indians also lost the right to land ownership. It was not just discrimination but disinheritance as well.

Pandit challenged the court on the plea of res judicata. The government was denied a hearing by the supreme court and an appellate court agreed with Pandit and denied the government's request to revoke his citizenship. In 1928, all further attempts to revoke existing citizenships of Indians ended, when the supreme court took the case of an electrical engineer at General Electric—Shankar Laxman Gokhale and ruled in his favor. [4]

Still, Thind and the many Indians whose citizenship was revoked would have to wait nearly 20 years until the laws changed to regain their status. According to The Asia Society, "By 1924, all Asian immigrants, including Chinese, Japanese, Koreans and Indians were fully excluded by law, denied citizenship and naturalization, and prevented from marrying Caucasians or owning land."[5] People sympathetic to Indians like Senator David Reed of Pennsylvania tried to introduce a joint resolution in congress in 1928 to prevent future injustices, but others objected. It was only with passage of the Luce-Celler bill in 1946 that racial qualifications for naturalization were removed. Several Indians left the country after 1923, while some transferred their land to white friends, hoping they would hold them in trust until the laws changed. Thind eventually received his citizenship in 1936 based on his service record, married a white woman, and had two children.

It is estimated that only a few thousand Indians had come to the United States during this early period. They had not been allowed to bring their families or spouses and were subjected to the laws of miscegenation. Limited to marrying only brown people, a unique community of Mexican women married to Indian men came into existence in California. Names in the phonebook like Carlos Singh or restaurants with curry enchiladas were common, but once the laws changed and immigrants were allowed to bring their families, the Mexican Indian community died out.

Most of the Indians during the early years had come to work as laborers on the West Coast. The Western Pacific Railway in northern California recruited several hundred Indians and by 1907, the lumber mills of Bellingham in Washington State employed several hundred Indians as well.[6] A few, such as Thind, had come as students and it is worth noting that even in those early days some of them managed to excel despite the racial barriers. In 1914, Dhan Gopal Mukerji came to study at Stanford University. He won the Newbery Medal in 1928 and became a popular writer. Yellapragada Subbarao, who came to study at Harvard in 1922 from the state of Andhra Pradesh, was a scientist whose work on folic acid and the discovery of methotrexate formed the basis for some cancer treatments still in use today. Dalip Singh Saund was the first Indian American to be elected to Congress in 1956. He was elected from California, where the majority of Indian Americans lived. Har Gobind Khorana, along with two other scientists, won the Nobel Prize for physiology and medicine in 1968.

The United States went from a country that embraced immigrants to a xenophobic country with restrictive policies put in place to control both non-white immigration and "undesirable" immigrants from Europe. A fascination with the newly discovered field of eugenics that had gained adherents in Europe and America were influencing policymakers who were being influenced by peoples fear of racial assimilation. It would have catastrophic consequences in Europe, but in the United States, it resulted in declining levels of immigration.

In 1910, the foreign-born population in the United States was 14.7 percent. By 1960, it had dropped to 5.4 and would go down to 4.7 a decade later.

The Immigration Act of 1952 (also known as the McCarran-Walter Act) reversed the earlier racially biased policies but, even then, there was a quota that limited Asian migration to 100 people per country, per year. Immigration laws were further relaxed in 1965–driven by America's need for skilled labor–and the quota system was replaced, but skill requirements for certain nations simply replaced the quotas. Immigrants from Europe did not have to satisfy any professional criteria to be allowed into the country.

The color of the immigrants entering the United States began to change dramatically after 1965. Prior to 1960, Europeans accounted for 75 percent of immigrants. Until then, non-white foreigners were not viewed as a threat to the demographic balance of the country. By 2010, the numbers had been reversed. Europeans had slipped to just 15.8 percent. Most of the immigrants entering the United States were brown. The race reversal coincided with a rise in immigration levels to the double digits of the pre-war years. One in four children under 18 in the country were likely to have at least one foreign-born parent. As most of the immigrants were from Latin America or Asia, it pointed to a profound shift in the racial profile of the country. The change in racial composition was perceived as a threat to the status quo by some.

Fear of the changing complex of America represented by the new wave of immigrants has been at the heart of the immigration policy debate inflaming tensions on Capitol Hill for several decades, extending through both Republican and Democratic administrations without arriving at any comprehensive consensus. United States policymakers have fallen short of the poetic ideals inscribed on the plaque of the Statue of Liberty, a monument that is often pointed to as a symbol welcoming all immigrants. "Give me your tired, your poor, your huddled masses yearning to breathe free..." Despite the relaxation of immigration laws in 1965 to accommodate the growing demand in the United States for skilled workers, the change has been applied unevenly. Indians wishing to come to the United States to maximize their potential often have to overcome discriminatory visa restrictions. Holders of Indian passports are generally required to have certain skills, particularly in the STEM fields, to obtain entry to the United States unless they fulfill some other category. The United States is hardly the only country to impose tough visa requirements on Indian citizens, however. Europe, Australia, and Japan all had similar restrictions. To get a United States visa, you had to be talented enough to gain admission to a university, receive a job offer, or come as an investor. Otherwise, like my kind cabdriver in New York, you would have to wait in the queue for 20 years.

Despite the high bar that immigrants from India must reach to get into the country, most successful Indians have nothing but praise for their adopted homeland and the opportunities they were given. It's not that they didn't encounter discrimination, but that they found opportunities to succeed despite it. That credit is partially due to their own grit, but for many of them who came from a country where caste, class, and connections determined their growth, America still represented equal opportunity.

Population of
Indian Americans by Year[7]

YEAR	INDIAN BY RACE
1900	2,031
1910	2545
1920	2507
1930	3130
1940	2,405
1950	NA
1960	NA
1970	51,000
1980	361,531
1990	815,447
2000	1,678,765
2010	2,843,391
2020	4,460,000

The Techies

CHAPTER 1

Silicon Valley

The Valley of Heart's Delight

Until the sixties, San Jose was an unremarkable place. It first came to the world's attention in 1968 when Dionne Warwick won a Grammy for a song written for her by Burt Bacharach and Hal David called "Do You Know the Way to San Jose." It sold more than three million copies. San Jose was the place that young hopefuls left to find fame and fortune and where they returned when they were wounded, their dreams broken by places like Los Angeles and New York. Today, it is a destination—albeit for talented scientists and engineers.

Before Santa Clara County was nicknamed Silicon Valley after the silicon chip, it was called the "Valley of Heart's Delight," for the abundance of orchards that draped the undulating hillsides with breathtaking blossoms in the spring, producing most of the country's prunes. Canneries and dried fruit packing houses became big industries in the Valley. Both Del Monte and Sunsweet, two of the largest commercial dried fruit businesses originated in Santa Clara. The history of Santa Clara's fruit orchards dates back to a mission settlement in the 1880s, when the region produced walnuts, apricots, apples, and prunes. Until the war years, the existing population was primarily employed in agriculture or canning, but labor shortages combined with advances in technology spurred the businesses to become increasingly mechanized. As large companies like Del Monte took over the industry, controlling everything from growing and canning to marketing, the workforce gradually became dominated by Mexican Americans and immigrants from Central and South America.

World War II changed the economy of Santa Clara. The war absorbed many of the local people who had previously worked in agriculture. Some shipped off to war, while others moved into jobs being created by the War Department. Raytheon Lockheed Martin and Northrup Grumman established roots along the Pacific Coast, and the Moffett Field Naval Air Station became the newest big employer in the Bay Area. The Cold War and the Korean War expanded the Pentagon's presence in California as the United States was increasingly locked in fierce competition with the Soviet Union in its struggle to lead the world.

The United States military had invested heavily in research institutions since the Korean War. Initially, much of the money and resources went to the East Coast and institutions like Harvard, Princeton, and MIT, but substantial sums began to find their way to the Santa Clara corridor. Anchoring the tech revolution on the West Coast was Stanford University. The geographic footprint of San Jose expanded, and the population surged from 95,000 in 1950 to 459,000. By 1980 it had doubled to over 800,000.[8]

Many well-known scientists had made a name for themselves along Boston's Route 128 corridor, but by the 1970s they lost ground to Silicon Valley. Right from the beginning, Silicon Valley developed its own very distinctive style where creativity and the ability to think outside the box was admired.

Tech—The New Frontier

The invention of the computer, along with the Internet, became as significant to the twentieth century as the steam engine was to the eighteenth. The analytical engine, a machine that could calculate several mathematical tasks and would become the foundation of the modern computer, was invented in 1856 by the English engineer and math genius Charles Babbage. It would take almost a hundred years to get to ENIAC, the first programmable, electronic general purpose digital computer in 1945. The personal computer that we take for granted today was invented in 1973 by Xerox and copied and commercialized by Steve Jobs at Apple in 1977. There were many incremental contributions during the intervening years between 1856 and 1977 made by several brilliant, mostly white scientists that contributed to the computer revolution. There were also, however, some remarkable women whose contributions to the field advanced the development of software. In the 1940s, women were recruited to aid in the war effort and helped break German codes at Bletchley Park in England. In the United States, women were found useful as programmers for ENIAC, but they seldom got the credit they deserved even though they became indispensable to the smooth operation of computers. Ada Lovelace, Lord Byron's daughter, was a mathematician who was besotted with Babbage's work. She wrote a series of extensive notes on his analytical engine that both explored and explained functions that became the "core concept of the digital age: any piece of content, data, or information—music, text, pictures, numbers, symbols, sounds, video—could be addressed in digital form and manipulated by machines,"[9] according to the historian Walter Isaacson, Babbage's invention was a hundred years ahead of its time, Isaacson observed, but even Babbage had not understood it fully as he had been focused on the numbers. It was Ada who realized that the digits on the cogs could represent things other than mathematical quantities. She made the conceptual leap from machines that were mere calculators to what we know as computers.

The incremental accumulation of the advances related to the computer led to rapid technological changes that generated their own momentum. This pace accelerated after World War II in the United States thanks to massive investments from the military. From Alan Turing and Howard Aiken to Konrad Zuse, John von Neumann, and Vannevar Bush, discoveries were being added from across Europe and the United States that were propelling technology forward. The Advanced Research Projects Agency Network (ARPANET)—a precursor to the internet—was established by the Department of Defense in collaboration with universities and private corporations. Some of the most innovative work on personal computers was being done by private corporations and individuals in the Valley, and Stanford University was at the hub of it all. It had been established by the wealthy industrialist Leland Stanford and his wife, Jane to honor their only son who succumbed to typhoid at the age of 15 during a trip to Europe in 1884.

Stanford and the Regional Advantage

Frederick Terman, often referred to as the father of Silicon Valley, spent four decades building Stanford, and in particular its computer and engineering departments into the MIT of the west. He had studied chemistry as an undergraduate at Stanford and received his master's in engineering before going east to MIT for his Ph.D. He returned to Stanford in 1924 and recruited the brightest minds to come and teach at the university. He rejected the secretive and proprietorial approach of the East Coast where research was siloed, preventing the free flow of ideas. Terman promoted horizontal engagement between people and institutions and believed in keeping one foot in the real world. He developed relationships with businesses in the area and encouraged students and faculty to do the same. He famously lent his students William Hewlett and David Packard money to start Hewlett-Packard out of a garage in 1939–a story that has now become part of Silicon Valley legend. What was unusual about Stanford is how proactive the faculty and university was in helping its students to commercialize their ideas as well as assist West Coast businesses and defense-related industries. In order to advance these relationships, Terman established the Stanford Research Institute. Set over 8,100 acres, Terman also founded the Stanford Industrial Park and leased land to General Electric, Eastman Kodak, Lockheed, Hewlett-Packard, and several others. The proximity of the companies to the university led to a revolving door between academia and business that would both benefit and spur innovation. From the 1960s through the 1980s, 50,000 acres of agriculture were lost to the Central Valley and Santa Clara saw businesses, research parks, and housing developments proliferate. The tech revolution that would give Silicon Valley its name had permanently replaced the Valley of Heart's Delight.

Other East Coast transplants that gravitated to the Valley included William Shockley, the genius who won the Nobel prize in 1956. He developed the silicon transistor that revolutionized computers and contributed, famously, to Silicon Valley's name, referring to the main ingredient used in the semiconductor.[10] He brought in a brilliant team of engineers, including Gordon Moore, who became famous with "Moore's law", the observation that " the number of transistors in an integrated circuit doubles every two years." His predictions of a digital future where integrated circuits would one day lead to such wonders as home computers would prove to be accurate.

Shockley was notoriously difficult to work for—his team eventually rebelled and went to work for Fairchild. They were called the "traitorous eight" and several of them went on to start other companies. The Fairchild group of engineers and the companies they spawned liberated entrepreneurs. In the old days, workers were expected to stay with a company for life, rising through the ranks and retiring with the proverbial gold watch. By 2014, 70 percent of the publicly traded tech companies in the Valley could trace their roots to one of the "Fairchildren."[11]

Gordon Moore started Intel with Robert Noyce and was later joined by Andy Grove, a Hungarian immigrant whose success story was an inspiration for Vinod Khosla, who read about him in India. Eugene Kleiner, another Fairchild alumni, was well connected through his family to the financial world and would go on to form Kleiner Perkins Caufield and Byers, becoming one of the most powerful venture capital firms in the Valley.

Stanford University became, in the words of one Silicon Valley historian, a "bastion of innovation, helping to spawn nearly 6,000 highly innovative companies. Among the companies whose technology or business plan was developed during a student or researcher's time there, include—Atheros Communications, Charles Schwab & Co, Cisco Systems, Cypress Semiconductor, Dolby Laboratories, eBay, E*Trade, Electronic Arts, Gap, Google, Hewlett-Packard, IDEO, Intuit, Intuitive Surgical, Kiva, LinkedIn, Logitech, MathWorks, MIPS Technologies, Nanosolar Inc, Netflix, Nike, NVIDIA, Odwalla, Orbitz, Rambus, Silicon Graphics, Sun Microsystems, SunPower, Taiwan Semiconductor, Tensilica, Tesla Motors, Varian, VMware, Yahoo!, Zillow, Robinhood, Clubhouse and Instagram."[12]

By the 1960s, Xerox had opened its R&D entity Xerox PARC in Palo Alto and joined IBM and other established technology companies who saw the benefits of maintaining research labs where the latest innovations were taking place. On the East Coast, scientists and companies were proprietary about their discoveries. In the Bay Area, Stanford and the hacker community developed horizontally in ways where information was freely shared, equipment was borrowed back and forth, and ideas were eagerly discussed. It led to an explosion of innovation that quickly overtook the East Coast.

Another regional advantage that encouraged innovation was an 1870s California law that denied companies the right to impose non-compete agreements on their employees. This allowed people to move freely between jobs and gain new skills. Kanwal Rekhi, the first Indian entrepreneur to take his company public and be listed on NASDAQ, began his career in 1969 on the East Coast but quickly found himself constrained there before moving west. At the time, IBM dominated the world of computers and engineering. In 1969, Rekhi declined an offer from IBM and instead went to work for EAL, a small firm in New Jersey, and was laid off within eight months. He reapplied to IBM but discovered he had burnt his bridges. They sent him a letter that he has saved for almost 50 years. "They told me I was barred from working for IBM for life because I had turned them down without a satisfactory explanation!" This attitude was alien to California where talent moved easily between jobs and the pace of innovation was far more rapid.

The 1970 recession hit the East Coast at a time when Silicon Valley was hiring. Engineering firms were located all over the country, so to be laid off or fired often required moving—a major disruption to employees' lives. By the mid-seventies, the industry had consolidated and many engineering firms had relocated to Santa Clara County. If an individual moved jobs, their entire family was not adversely impacted; instead, they simply shifted to a different parking lot. This gave Silicon Valley a significant regional advantage.

CHAPTER 2

The IIT Supply Chain: Passage to America

The time has now come when the engineer
plays an infinitely greater role than anybody else.

JAWAHARLAL NEHRU

Ten thousand miles away, India was just finding her feet having gained independence from British colonial rule in 1947. Literacy rates were at an appalling 12 percent and the per capita income was $80. Over 80 percent of Indians were dependent on agriculture and lived in rural areas. Jawaharlal Nehru, India's first prime minister, a visionary, was ambitious. He firmly believed that education, particularly in the sciences, held the key to India's future and the path out of poverty. To accomplish his goals, he set up five world-class engineering institutions in collaboration with other countries called the Indian Institutes of Technology (IITs). The United States funded the IIT branch in Kanpur, the Soviets set up IIT Bombay (Mumbai), and the Germans and British helped establish other branches.

These were and remain highly selective institutions, with an acceptance rate of less than 1 percent from a pool of one million applicants each year.[13] They stood out for the quality of their student body and high standards of teaching, becoming fertile recruiting grounds for Silicon Valley.

Kanwal Rekhi, an IIT alumnus, who left for the United States after graduating, recalls it as a very competitive environment. "I was a very good student before I went to IIT Bombay, but competition was very tough. Just about everybody at IIT Bombay was at the top of his class before he got there. So, it meant that everybody at IIT Bombay was good. To get to the top there you had to be really sharp."[14]

Vinod Khosla, a venture capitalist and one of the original founders of Sun Microsystems, went to IIT a few years after Rekhi. He spoke about IIT as a great equalizer in a society where generations of people were prevented from advancing due to caste and class discrimination. Prime Minister Nehru had insisted the institution be meritocratic. Khosla explained, "Getting into IIT was the only way to escape whatever your lot was in society. Everyone knew it was a fair playing field—there was no ability to use influence or 'Who do you know?' and no one doubted that it was a totally performance-based institution. What happened once you got there? The best people strived to get in and reinforced each other. It was multi-way learning. I'm learning from my roommate, he's learning from me, and we are all learning from the institute. Your community determines how you develop, especially when you are 16 to 20 years old. Then it becomes this filter, a brand of excellence that you are associated with."

Although Nehru's dream of a new generation of educated scientists building a new India was ambitious it did eventually happen after 2000. In the fifties, sixties, and even the seventies, India was unable to absorb the talent that was graduating, particularly as additional IITs were added. The more ambitious and gifted students began to look for opportunities overseas just as the need for skilled engineers was increasing in the United States. Many talented graduates trained in India made their way to America as its tech sector began to take off.

Rekhi recalls the lack of opportunity in India for someone like himself, driven yet lacking the social connections or mentors that were essential to get ahead and compete for the few desirable jobs that might be available. "In India the job environment was very, very bad. India was a socialist country. They had set up these centers of excellence for education, but they had not allowed industry to be set up. Yeah, the government was still trying—they were following the Russian model of planning and licensing the businesses. And so most of us who came out in my generation had no suitable jobs in India. You could be hired as a sales engineer, you could be hired as support engineer for one of the overseas, foreign companies. There were no design jobs. No engineering jobs to speak of. So, 80 to 90 percent of my classmates left India back in 1967. In United States, you didn't worry about the jobs. By the late fifties, if you remember, the world was very excited. In the sixties, the space stuff was starting to happen. The transistor radio had arrived and the early computers from IBM were happening and so there was the sense that the science and technology is the future. … People were being sent away to Vietnam. There was a shortage of people for the jobs."[15]

Among the overseas investors in the IITs, none would benefit more than the United States. It was the biggest dividend that the United States would reap from the relatively modest investment they had made in one of Nehru's IITs when it was first set up.

Due to the lack of resources and opportunities in India, close to 40 percent of IIT graduates left to go overseas, with the majority going to the United States.[16] Social and policy changes in Washington combined to align the supply and demand of labor between India and the United States. It was a perfect match.

Kanwal Rekhi, Suhas Patil, and Vinod Khosla, all IIT graduates, were part of the first tech wave that helped to invent products and start successful tech companies in the United States. Rekhi founded Excelan in 1982 and sold it to Novell in 1989. Patil started Cirrus Logic and Khosla helped start Sun Microsystems in 1982 before becoming a venture capitalist.

Patil had gone to MIT and Rekhi started his life in the United States in Michigan, but they quickly discovered that the place to be and the heartbeat of innovation was Silicon Valley. When Rekhi arrived in Santa Clara County in 1971, computers were large, cumbersome machines that took up entire rooms. The personal computer as we know it did not exist—neither did cell phones or the internet—but Silicon Valley was incubating new technologies at institutions in and around Stanford and Xerox PARC as well as among the "hacker" community, a group of pot-smoking devotees of technology who believed in freely sharing their discoveries.

When the first wave of Indian engineers began to arrive in the sixties, there were fewer than 50,000 Indians living in the United States.[17] During the first 15 years after the 1965 immigration laws were relaxed, 93 percent of the immigrants that entered the United States from India were classified as professionals. The pace of immigration remained minimal, however; between 1971 and 1980, only 35,000 people from India became United States citizens.

Pitted against Americans' fears of new immigrants were the needs of the country. After President John F. Kennedy's assassination, the country was consumed by a sense of unrest and fear. The 1960s were a period of turmoil; the civil rights movement and the assassinations of Robert Kennedy and Martin Luther King Jr. added to this feeling of insecurity. Layered over this was the fear that the Soviet Union was ahead in the Space Race. When the Soviets sent the first satellite—Sputnik 1—into space, the United States military was stunned. Determined to catch up, it opened a spigot of funding for innovations in space and technology and galvanized the Department of Defense to pour resources into technology that could be applied to military purposes.

It was decided, that in order to compete with the Soviets, the United States needed to encourage highly skilled individuals in the STEM fields (science, technology, engineering and mathematics) to emigrate to the country. But it became increasingly difficult to recruit talent from Western Europe once the economy there had recovered after the war years. Eastern Europe was isolated behind the Iron Curtain, so the United States had to widen its outreach to include countries like India. The growing demand for trained engineers helped push Congress to pass the Immigration Act of 1965 (Hart-Celler) by a vote of 326 to 70. By 1980, the number of Indians living in the United States from India had shot up to 361,531 from 51,000 in 1970.[18] The American Dream still beckoned, but its glitter now attracted talented individuals largely from the developing world.

The Eight Dollar Exit

In December 1970, I boarded a Pan Am flight in New Delhi for Boston with just eight dollars in my pocket. It was the first time I was going overseas and the first time I had been on an aircraft. India was a poor country in those days, dependent on food aid and living between floods and famine with limited foreign reserves. The government had a strict policy of only allowing you to exchange the equivalent of just eight dollars officially, regardless of how wealthy you were. No one I knew had gone overseas as a tourist—it was an unheard-of luxury that only maharajas could indulge in. Since independence, it was rumored that even they had restraints and would have to stop at their jewelers in Europe to sell some fabulous gem in order to finance their trip.

I was hardly alone. All of the Indians who left for the United States during this first phase in the sixties and early seventies exited with the legally allowed eight dollars. Rekhi, Patil, and many of the immigrants who would go on to become tech millionaires were part of this eight-dollar club. Years later it became a badge of honor, but at the time it was nerve-wracking. You had to line up a scholarship, making sure someone would be there to meet you since the eight dollars would not get you from the airport to your campus. Some thoughtful colleges would have volunteers meet arriving students with a ride to campus and warm winter coats as they had become aware that winter clothes were not available in India. We all depended on the kindness of strangers for small things.

Patil had come to the United States in the mid-sixties after graduating from IIT like many others. He recounts his eight-dollar trauma and the anxiety of his first trip when he discovered he had been booked on Air India to go to Boston on the same flight as India's prime minister, Lal Bahadur Shastri. Excited at the possibility he might get to meet the prime minister, Patil panicked when he discovered that the flight could get detained if the prime minister's work delayed the scheduled departure time. Patil had a crucial connection in Frankfurt and was being received in Boston by a volunteer. With just eight dollars in his wallet, Patil had to make sure he did not miss his connection to Boston in order to meet his ride from Boston's Logan Airport to MIT. Patil changed his flight to Alitalia, not realizing that the transfer of planes involved a transfer of airports within Italy that required a transit visa he did not possess. Wild with anxiety and unable to communicate with the Italians, Patil was rescued by a sympathetic flight attendant who recognized him from his earlier flight and helped him get where he needed to go. When he finally arrived in Boston, his luggage was not at baggage claim. Worried about how he would replace his clothes with no money, he turned to Mrs. Smith, the volunteer from the foreign student office who had come to receive him. She located his bag, which had been mistakenly tagged to Philadelphia, and deposited a very grateful—if tired—first-time traveler to MIT.

A couple of the people who had come in the sixties told me of a special arrangement one of the airlines offered that they had taken advantage of, where the airline would overcharge on their ticket price and give the students the difference in fare in cash. It was usually a small amount in the region of a few hundred dollars, but it eased their start in America. Not everyone was aware of the arrangement. Suhas Patil, who would become a professor at MIT, the founder of Cirrus Logic, and a multi-millionaire, was unaware of this unusual arrangement. Neither of us flew out on that airline—and I'm not sure I would have dared to enter into such a questionable arrangement at the age of 16.

CHAPTER 3

Inventors and Founders

The goal of education is not to increase the amount of knowledge
but to create the possibilities for a child to invent and discover,
to create men who are capable of doing new things.

JEAN PIAGET

India suffered from an immature industrial base and a stagnant economy and despite 20 years of Independence it had become heavily dependent on foreign aid. Graduates of the various IITs who left India in the sixties and seventies and became successful in the United States, came from middle-class backgrounds, had little exposure to private entrepreneurship and had no money or capital of their own, but they learned to punch above their weight to thrive. This group, according to their own telling, had no mentors in America and yet managed to achieve great success. How did they do it?

In his book *Outliers*, Malcom Gladwell makes the argument that the often-heard stories of a hero born in modest circumstances and rising to greatness by virtue of his own grit and talent is unconvincing. He argues that successful people are the beneficiaries of hidden advantages, extraordinary opportunities, and cultural legacies that allow them to learn, work hard, and make sense of the world. He adds to the mix that where and when a person grew up has some bearing on their success.

I have selected two or three individuals from this first group and spoken to them about their path to success. I will return to discuss how their success or specific aspect of "genius" conforms to Gladwell's assertion that hidden privileges and cultural legacies enabled them. Their personalities and reflections on success are unique, but there is much in their backgrounds that is similar. This cohort seems to align with Malcom Gladwell's "10,000-hour theory" that an individual, by concentrating on their skills and honing them till they become experts in their particular area of expertise, do exceptionally well.

But there is another aspect to this group. They were creative, they were inventors, and they founded their own companies. Was this driven by necessity, a way to expand their opportunities, or were they just born inventors and founders?

Kanwal Rekhi: The Godfather

I think frugality drives innovation, just like other constraints do.
One of the only ways to get out of a tight box is to invent your way out.

JEFF BEZOS

Kanwal Rekhi is affectionately called the "godfather" of the Indian tech community in Silicon Valley. When he walks into a roomful of Indian businessmen, people quickly make sure he gets seated in the front row. There is a great deal of respect for his achievements and contributions. Many Indian Americans recognize that he paved the way for them, breaking several glass ceilings to achieve success. Along the way he had to endure cultural biases and professional inequity. His company, Excelan, was the first fully Indian American-owned company to go public when it was listed on Nasdaq in 1987. "Indians in the Valley did not look at Bill Gates and imagine they could become him, but when they saw me, another Indian, run a company and go public with it, it inspired them. They felt, 'If he can do it, why not me?'"

The genuine regard that the Indian community feels for Rekhi is due to his lack of affectations and the role he played in mentoring many of the Indian entrepreneurs that sought his help, a role he took on after he left Excelan in 1995 to establish The Indus Entrepreneurs (TiE), an organization that fostered many Indian start-ups.

Rekhi, a Punjabi of the Sikh faith, grew up poor in a crowded home without a running toilet. He was the third of seven brothers with a father who was employed by the Indian military in the lower ranks. He suffered from severe sleep apnea for most of his life and would doze off in the middle of classes and chores during the day. His medical condition went untreated and his tendency to fall asleep was mistaken for laziness. His father thought he would amount to nothing and beat him often, but Rekhi credits his mother with finding ways of making him feel special despite her burdens of looking after a large extended family. When Rekhi applied and was accepted to IIT, his father, who wanted his sons to attend the military academy, had no appreciation for the enormity of his son's achievement until his commanding officer told him his own son had tried to get in but had been rejected. Once Rekhi achieved economic security in America, he would bring his family over and help them get settled.

According to Rekhi's younger brother, who now owns a vineyard in California and credits his brother for helping him get established, his older sibling stood out from the rest of them even as a child. He was serious, academically gifted, and kept to himself, helping their mother with chores when their father was away. He seemed destined even then to break away from the economic hardships that engulfed his family and find a different path driven by interests alien to the people surrounding him. He finished high school early, but IIT did not accept students until they were at least 16 years old, so he briefly attended a local college. He aced the standardized examinations and topped the list of the state university that administered the exams, making his local college famous for a brief period. The star quality of Kanwal Rekhi had begun to shine.

After IIT, he made up his mind to go to the United States, but his poor financial circumstances forced him to zero in on Michigan Tech, the least expensive engineering school he could find that offered the best financial package. He graduated with his master's degree in 1969, but with no one to guide him he made a series of blunders as he began work on the East Coast. He turned down an offer from IBM, who at the time dominated tech and was a leader in computer mainframes. Rekhi took jobs with companies that laid him off in quick succession. After the third time he was laid off in two years, he decided it was time to try his luck in Silicon Valley.

When Rekhi arrived in San Jose in 1971 to work for Singer Link designing flight simulators and complex algorithms in hardware systems, it would take him three years to rid himself of the scars of being constantly laid off. He had come with his wife, and they planned to start a family. He could not risk instability and unemployment. Rekhi continued to send out job applications as a backup plan despite getting promotions. "It took me two years. It was around 1974 before I stopped looking over my shoulder. By then I had become pretty indispensable to Singer Link. Singer Link builds flight simulators to train pilots on. I developed massive hardware systems for Singer Link with tens of thousands of functions built in. Most of the designs had to be debugged and had flaws. I became indispensable because my designs were highly accurate with hardly any flaws, and my designs always worked the first time, so my turn around time was faster than anyone else's. They began calling me 'the magician.'"

But Rekhi quickly hit a glass ceiling at Singer Link. "I was a really good engineer and had become critical to Singer Link's work, but people I had trained were becoming managers over me. I asked my boss if he had considered promoting me to management and he said I was too good an engineer."

Rekhi knew his boss was being disingenuous. Managers were better compensated than engineers and although he was well paid, it was clear they preferred him in the bowels of the company rather than as one of its representatives. He had been with Singer Link for over a decade, and yet a British immigrant who he had trained had been promoted over him. When he left to start his own company, it unsettled Rekhi; he said he couldn't sleep and became restless. "I began to ask myself why I was still with Singer and dissatisfaction set in and I told Ann I was going to quit." Rekhi's wife didn't stop him but reminded him he had a family to support and a mortgage to pay, but by now he was being driven by his internal ambitions and felt he had to try.

This was not the first time Rekhi had encountered discrimination. Sitting in his sprawling home in the wealthy suburb of Los Gatos just outside San Jose with Ann, his wife of 55 years beside him, it is hard to believe that in 1971 they had difficulty finding someone to marry them in Florida. Loving v. Virginia, the Supreme Court decision that removed all barriers to interracial marriage, had been decided just four years earlier in 1967. But when Ann, who is white, wanted to be married by a priest in a church, they had trouble finding someone in Florida to agree to marry them and were turned down several times. Finally, they discovered that an occasional tennis partner of Rekhi's was a minister and he eventually acquiesced. Ann's stepfather and grandfather disapproved of her marrying someone who was non-white and refused to attend the wedding.

In 1980, Rekhi took a pay cut to move to a company called Zilog. He had been a defense engineer using military spec chips and technology that was a few years behind and felt he wasn't ready for the commercial world. "The defense industry is cost insensitive, so you don't learn commercial values working for them. Their stuff also has to work in harsh environments such as the battlefield, so they use military spec chips which are always three to five years behind commercially available chips, so I was using old technology and it was clear to me that I wasn't ready for the commercial world just yet, and Zilog was a good place to hone my skills."

At Zilog, Rekhi acquired commercial skills and a set of partners for his future business. "When I came to Zilog, which was a start-up owned by Exxon, it was highly dysfunctional. Computers didn't work, customers were unhappy, and within six months I fixed everything for them. They were very happy with me. I had learnt the new technology, I was using the latest chips which were new to me, and I could still make all the designs work perfectly. I now felt confident that my magic touch was not a one-off and that I had a gift with logic and network systems. Working there and picking up commercial skills gave me the self-confidence I needed and within a few months we left to start our own company."

A couple of other Indians in the Valley had just started their own companies that appeared to be doing well. Suhas Patil moved west from MIT and co-founded Cirrus Logic, the first fabless semi-conductor company, while Vinod Khosla co-founded Sun Microsystems in 1982 with his fellow students from Stanford. Patil had run into trouble raising money until one of his mentors and a venture capitalist suggested he find a partner who was a "marketing guy" and they identified Michael Hackworth. Patil remembers Hackworth asking him if he could really build the design he had and he said he could. He then asked Hackworth that once he built it, could Hackworth sell it? And Hackworth said yes, thus their partnership and Cirrus Logic was born. Patil was the inventor and Hackworth operated as the marketing face of the company.

Although he didn't have any white American partners, Rekhi decided that this was the moment to risk it all. In 1982 he took the plunge and teamed up with two Indians to start a company called Excelan. They specialized in connecting hardware to networks, with solutions as visionary as they were commercially astute. "I did the math," Rekhi said. "If you have a VAX and a few UNIX machines and PCs, you need me, because besides me, there's no easy way to transfer files between the systems. I pioneered the technology that enabled different hardware systems to communicate. The internet and ethernet had been introduced, Intel and Digital had said chips were in development and three to five years away. I studied their specifications and worked out a system where you could install it into your hardware. I was able to design an Ethernet board using commercially available chips and do it in four weeks. I suppose that was my genius!" It was cutting-edge technology for the time, and he was just 36, but there was one glaring problem. None of them had any money, and if people had been unwilling to promote Indians to management, who was going to trust three Indian guys with no track record to start a new company and risk their money?

Securing a bank loan proved difficult, so initially he raised money the old-fashioned way: from family and friends. He recalls that all the venture capitalists they approached had more or less the same response. "'We love what you guys are doing, but you guys are engineers. There is no business guy on your team.' The implication was there was no white person representing us as managers." Surely they weren't thinking of running a company themselves?

Looking back on those early days, Rekhi admits he did not look like a buttoned-up CEO, but this was Silicon Valley—his somewhat disheveled outward appearance, T-shirts with logos and casual clothes wasn't that different from other computer geeks in the Valley like Steve Jobs and Steve Wozniak, who were part of the hacker community.

During the seventies, Jobs was infamous for not bathing and smelled bad due to the weird fruitarian diet he was on. After returning from a trip to India in 1975, he showed up at Atari, where he had previously worked, barefoot, wearing a saffron robe, sporting a shaved head, and carrying a Baba Ram Dass book. He wanted his old job back. Nolan Bushnell, the young, six-foot-four, easy-going founder of Atari, indulged his eccentricities and hired the young Jobs, although he put him on the night shift to prevent complaints from the other employees.[19] Unlike some of his contemporaries who were white, Rekhi repeatedly faced discrimination.

Many of the people we think of as tech geniuses—such as Jobs, Wozniak, and Bill Gates—were all sloppy dressers, but Jobs pushed the limit when he tried to raise money from Atari in 1976 and showed up for the meeting barefoot, proceeding to put his feet up on company president Joe Keenan's desk. Atari embraced a fairly alternative culture, with meetings conducted in hot tubs and an accounting system that would have given a straitlaced company like IBM heartburn. Keenan, a more conservative businessman, famously threw Jobs out of the office, turning down his offer for part of Apple and telling him, "Get your feet off my desk, get out of here, you stink, and we're not going to buy your product."

Despite this rough start, Wozniak and Jobs, who were still in their twenties and had no bank accounts or references, found people to help them get started. Bushnell, who later regretted not investing in Apple, liked Jobs and was instrumental in connecting him to Mike Markkula, an Intel engineer who became an angel investor despite his reservations about their appearance. "They were bearded, they didn't smell good. They dressed funny. Young. Naïve." While everyone commented on their unprofessional appearance, the doors kept opening for Jobs and Wozniak. If you were talented, you were given a chance—life was easier if you were white. Wozniak and Jobs had started Apple Computer and Bill Gates was revolutionizing software. Rekhi realized that the world of computers had changed after the PC and recognized that developing network connectivity was going to be the next step forward.

"The Intel guys who came from Fairchild—they were a generation ahead of me, they were really impressive," Rekhi recalled. But Apple was as simple a computer as you can imagine. There was no magic in the early stuff. They were doing one board; I was designing a system with a thousand boards in them. They were doing simple functions; mine were complex functions for massive computer systems, for me theirs was Mickey Mouse stuff. I met them and Bill Gates when I was at Excelan."

All it took was one VC to believe in them and they finally got their break. John Bosch of Bay Partners decided to take a risk and bet on them. Rekhi still beams when he recounts his first breakthrough. "John offered me two million dollars for half the company and gave me 15 minutes to decide. I was overjoyed. It took me under 15 seconds to say yes! He also told me to go out and hire some businesspeople. John, by the way did very very well. He made over one hundred times his money, and liked to brag that he discovered the Indians in Silicon Valley."

Rekhi was not just an inventor; he was a real entrepreneur. A few years into his partnership he realized they were not making headway with clients. He made some tough decisions, pushed his Yale-educated, suave Indian partner out and took over marketing while retaining the engineering component to save the company from going under and turned it around. "My real genius turned out to be marketing, not design engineering. Everybody was giving up on the company. We were running out of cash. I had seven months of operating expenditures left, and no one wanted to put more money in. I had to do something to make it happen. I transitioned from being an engineer to becoming a CEO. I led a targeted marketing campaign with precise messaging about what I could deliver. I understood our products, so it helped. The response was immediate. If you are a company with a main computer and lots of PCs like a bank, you need us. Wall Street ended up signing on as they were heavily computerized. They became 40 percent of our business. So did factories, General Motors; within six months of my taking over we had taken off."

In 1987, Rekhi decided to take the company public and once again, despite now having an outstanding track record as a manager running a successful company, the board insisted that he bring in a white, CEO from outside. Rekhi was told it was to reassure the market. He was furious and found it demeaning. Rekhi had made his investors rich. He was running a successful company and had proved he was a good manager. His employees trusted him. He had shaved his beard, started wearing business suits and white shirts, and had even taken speech therapy to overcome a childhood stammer. This time everything was supposed to be different—Excelan was different—and it was *his* company. He had developed a solid reputation, but he could not change the fact that he was Indian. He saw no justification for the board's decision.

But the board may have had other reasons for concern. After a high in 1983, the IPO market had declined; tech companies had underperformed and the promise of artificial intelligence that had been in the works for years had failed to materialize. The board was looking at the bottom line and told Rekhi to choose if he wanted to run the company or make money on the IPO.

Dick Moore, a white Hewlett-Packard veteran, was brought in to replace Rekhi as CEO, and although the IPO was a success, the management arrangement was a failure. Rekhi was the brains behind the company, while Moore did not understand Excelan and departed after the IPO. Rekhi took back the firm's management until it was acquired by Novell in 1989 for $210 million.

John Dougery, an Excelan investor and board member, later expressed regret at the way Rekhi had been treated but tried to explain away the board's decision. "Back then, Indians weren't perceived as winning CEOs," he said. "We didn't know if people would trust them as managers." The discrimination that stemmed from racial prejudice was similar to what other minority-group executives faced at the time. Rekhi was now a wealthy man, yet one final humiliation remained.

When he joined Novell, Rekhi felt he had finally earned a seat at the high table. Ray Noorda, the CEO, was on his way out. Rekhi had analyzed the business mistakes Noorda had made and felt he was qualified to replace him, but once again he was passed over for a more traditional pick. The firm's stock sank, and by 1995 he was fed up and left.

Eric Schmidt, who is now a legendary figure in Silicon Valley and would eventually become CEO of Google, joined Novell as CEO in 1997 after Rekhi's departure. He credits Rekhi with the smooth transition and holds him in high regard. I asked if he thought discrimination played a part in Rekhi being passed over for management and board positions, but he diplomatically deflected. "Kanwal was very, very good. I was not part of that process, so I can't really comment on it. He recruited me to Novell and helped make my job work. He also introduced me to the still nascent Indian community, where I learned about the IITs and the breadth of Indian capabilities." Schmidt had come from Sun Microsystems, where another Indian, Vinod Khosla, and a co-founder had decided to part ways. Rekhi believed that Khosla was brilliant, but as an Indian with an accent, he didn't fit the image of what Kleiner Perkins and the investors wanted as CEO and moved him over to Kleiner.

Kanwal Rekhi was finished trying to run companies. He decided to use his experience to mentor other South Asians and provide them with a support system so they would not have to struggle the way he had. A handful of other Indians had started successful companies that were now, like Rekhi, in a position to help other start-ups. In 1992, several of them, including Prabu Goel, the founder of Gateway, Suhas Patil of Cirrus Logic, and Rekhi had set up an organization called The Indus Entrepreneurs (TiE) to help advise, incubate, and occasionally fund start-ups by young South Asian entrepreneurs. TiE was transformational for aspiring Indian entrepreneurs who now moved to the Valley in droves. Eventually, Rekhi's investments in these start-ups would make him more money than he did from the sale of his company.

Suhas Patil: The Inventor

Although it wasn't obvious during his maiden voyage in what felt like the journey from hell, Suhas Patil possessed what Indians call "jugaad," an ingenuity or genius. Patil founded Cirrus Logic, a fabless semiconductor company.[20] "The conventional wisdom in the semiconductor industry in the eighties was that you had to manufacture your product in a facility you owned. I did not have the necessary resources or access to a fabricator when I started out, so I developed a different business model. I was able to design the semiconductor chips in months not years, because I did not have to spend money to build and operate a fabrication plant. I outsourced that to established semiconductor manufacturers. I was able to invest the money I saved, on developing the intellectual property needed to develop advanced and unique application-specific products. My company was called the Fabless Semiconductor company and I began to supply the fast developing electronic product companies making personal computers and disk drives. I became the leader of low-cost graphic chips for PCs. Today it is quite routine. Nvidia and AMD are also fabless semiconductor companies."

As a young child Patil was obsessed with how things worked—sewing machines, phones, steam engines; his curiosity was insatiable. "My father was the eldest of eight children," he recalled. He came from a small town off the Bombay-Poona highway. There was not enough money for the college education of his siblings, so initially just he and one of his brothers were educated. "My father did very well and became a material scientist. In those days women sold their gold to help pay for their education. His other brother joined the army to get an education and the two became the wage earners in the family. The money was not enough to support everyone, so my father started a radio repair shop on the side. When I was old enough to recognize things around me, I became mesmerized by the tools. My uncle gave me a textbook for an amateur scientist and that, combined with the tools in the repair shop, taught me how to build things."

Patil built projects from cardboard, metal scraps, wood, leather—anything he could lay his hands on. He found a way to power his projects using his bike headlamp and wheel rotations. In the summer, he repaired his neighbor's radios, adding to his skills along the way. "I had an insight while I was in high school that electronics had legs and as a field had room for growth, so I decided to apply to college in engineering, but I was too young to attend, so I went to St. Xavier's where I learned English. The fathers who taught me were a great influence on me at the time and taught me self-reliance and gave me confidence, but IIT made me who I am. I became friends with Professor Donald Bitzer, a visiting professor from the United States who had a big influence on me and left me all his transistors when he returned to America, so I built an electronic counter (pulses) from scratch. It was a versatile instrument that could calculate frequencies. Until then, I had only encountered vacuum tubes, as transistors were not readily available. But thanks to Professor Bitzer, I now had transistors. I designed the whole thing, the chassis, circuit board, and the innovative display. By the time I graduated I was the top student, so someone paid my application fee for MIT and I was accepted based on my thesis. Had I not gone to the United States, I would still have had a comparable product out of the bits and pieces that I had created in India that worked."

Hardware people were designing computers that required a process of debugging unlike software, which was expected to work right away. Patil's insight was to apply computer architecture in a new way and make the logic array flat so that the hardware would work as well as the software. "I was wondering how one could design hardware to make it work right away, just like software without having to debug it, so what I invented at MIT was a 'clockless array,' a process that eliminated the need for debugging."

He accomplished this by 1974, but his invention needed to be built in silicon. Without the professional connections that would give him access to a fabricator, he hit a wall. He was forced to leave his coveted position at MIT and moved to Utah, where General Instruments offered to let him use their fabrication facilities and conduct his research there. "My introduction to entrepreneurship came from Professor Amar Gopal Bose at MIT. I was his intern and he had just started the Bose corporation and he gave a seminar demystifying how you start a company and how the ecosystem works. I was learning that a professor could start a company." Convincing people that he had a unique product was another story and proved challenging. "No one believed in my ideas as it was not an incremental improvement. It was revolutionary as opposed to evolutionary. A silicon compiler was too much of a leap. The industry is fine with incremental improvements but negative if it's revolutionary. In those days, everything was funded by ARPA. I had no 'in' or access. I had no network despite being a professor at MIT. It took four years to build the chip based on my methods in Utah and of course it worked the first time. I moved to Silicon Valley in 1984 and started my own company. I had the best design automation software in the industry. No one was even close. Not Intel, not IBM. We became famous for our graphic chip. IBM became our client, as did many others."

Patil became a highly respected inventor and entrepreneur in the valley. He joined forces with Rekhi to found TiE, so others like him, engineers with good ideas, would not have to struggle due to a lack of professional support. The Indian network would develop into a powerful group.

Sanjay Mehrotra and Vinod Dham

I would be remiss not to include Sanjay Mehrotra and Vinod Dham among the stars of the first generation of Indian engineers who had an impact on Silicon Valley. Neither had the imprimatur of the famous IIT, but their contributions as inventors and founders have added to the legend of the Indian "genius" brand in the tech industry. Like Rekhi and Khosla, they were ethnic Punjabis. Dham's father was also a military man, like Rekhi's father. Both arrived towards the tail end of the first wave in the late seventies. Mehrotra initially attended the Birla Institute of Technology and Science, Pilani (BITS)—he was at the cusp of change, where a handful of engineering colleges in India had opened as an alternative to the impossibly hard to get into IITs. BITS has become a very competitive institution today, but in the seventies, it was relatively new and did not yet have the cache that IIT possessed both in India and overseas. Mehrotra chose to transfer to Berkeley to complete his studies.

Mehrotra, the current CEO of Micron Technology, started Sandisk in 1988 with Jack Yuan and Eli Harari. They sold the company to Western Digital in 2016 for $19 billion. He continued his studies at Stanford University's graduate school for business executives and graduated in 2009. Aside from his degrees, Mehrotra holds 70 patents. In 2022, the National Academy of Engineering elected Mehrotra as a member for his contributions to non-volatile memory design and architecture-enabling multilevel cell NAND flash products. Mehrotra took over as CEO of Micron Technology in 2017. Like many of the first-wave immigrant Indians, Mehrotra was both an inventor and founder of companies.

Vinod Dham, the inventor of the Pentium chip, was another member of the eight-dollar club. In India, Dham had been more interested in physics than engineering, but his brother persuaded him that studying to be an engineer was more practical. He switched from studying physics to engineering in Delhi and, once again, his brother helped him get his first job at a semiconductor manufacturing company called Continental Devices India Limited. His exposure to work in semiconductors reignited his interest in physics and he decided to go to the United States in 1975 for further studies.

His financial security in America rested on a scholarship and a job as a research assistant. Immediately upon his arrival at the University of Cincinnati, he needed $75 for his first month's rent, $15 for his health insurance, and money for food. Moved by his plight, the counsellor at the foreign students' office used the distress fund to help him out. Dham was struck by the support he received from the faculty and the ease of working in America. He started work at Intel in 1979 and co-invented Intel's first flash drive memory, ultimately being put in charge of the team that developed the Pentium chip. It made Intel the dominant leader in the market for years. In 1995, he left Intel and joined NextGen—a start-up—and became an entrepreneur and investor.

The South Asian Network—The Dot Com Boom/TiE

Indians were growing up in a more connected world by the 1980s and the students heading to the United States were far savvier than the previous generation. The eight-dollar restriction had been raised and travel had become more common. Indians who were settling down in America were sending money home and bringing family members over to visit or live. American films, music, and pop culture dominated youth culture all over the world, and India was no exception.

The country had undergone a green revolution in the eighties and become self-sufficient in food, but the economy remained stagnant. Per capita income had risen from $112 in 1970 to a mere $442 in 2000. A glaring indicator was the state of its television industry. Black and white television had arrived in India in 1965 but its penetration progressed at a glacial pace. By 1975 it had only advanced to seven cities, and color television and programming directed at entertainment rather than education only began in 1982. India still had a long way to go in meeting the aspirations of its growing population.

If you were an ambitious IIT graduate and wished to pursue post-graduate studies, you still went overseas. Despite its outstanding undergraduate education, most of the scientific universities in India—even the IITs—were under-resourced at the graduate level. IIT had become an active recruiting ground for United States companies looking for cheap engineers and a fourth of its graduating class left for the United States each year.

Between 1980 and 1990, the annual growth rate of Indian Americans in the Valley was 8.5 percent. By 1990, immigration policy in the United States had eased considerably to accommodate the United States expansion in tech. In the decade between 1990 and 2000, the population of Indian scientists and engineers in Santa Clara County grew by 646 percent, while the rest of the population grew by 103 percent.

As the year 2000 approached, a near hysteria gripped United States companies who worried that their computers would get paralyzed. To address their anxiety, companies went on a hiring spree. The dot com boom was hitting its peak the same year and the Indian population in the United States had surged to 1.71 million. The job expansion in tech led to the largest expansion of H-1B visas being granted to people of Indian origin. The visa is granted for a period of six years to highly skilled foreigners with advanced degrees. Although the world crossed into the new century seamlessly without the catastrophic computer glitches that people were predicting, the growth in hiring continued. According to NPR, 72 percent of the H-1B visas designated for immigrants that contribute special skills to the United States were awarded to Indians last year; 280,000 Indians were granted H-1B visas or renewed them.

The mid-nineties were a heady time for start-ups in Silicon Valley. Amazon was founded by Jeff Bezos in 1994, Pierre Omidyar started eBay in 1995, and Hotmail was founded by Sabeer Bhatia in 1996. For a budding entrepreneur in India, the lack of available capital and infrastructure to support start-ups at home, made Silicon Valley the ultimate destination and the success of Indian entrepreneurs like Rekhi and Patil and Khosla inspired others to follow in their footsteps. A new organization called The Indus Entrepreneurs TiE had been set up to mentor new immigrants and the word had got around.

The idea of TiE started out when a group led by Rekhi, Suhas Patil, and AJ Patel got together to discuss ways in which they could give back. As immigrants with no cushion or people to guide them, they had all achieved success the hard way—through grit and perseverance—Helping the next generation seemed like a no-brainer. Rekhi, who became the first president of TiE, explained, "Ours was a pretty lonely journey. We didn't have mentors or advisors, so we had this desire to make it easier for the next generation."

Rekhi decided to devote his time to TiE after he sold his company and physically moved to the TiE offices on Democracy Boulevard in the heart of Silicon Valley. The office was in an unassuming office block resembling a warehouse more than a corporate suite. The sparse furnishings and modest conference rooms did not deter the many supplicants who quickly began to form lines around the office when they discovered Rekhi and other Indian CEOs were making themselves available as mentors. Networks like TiE would become central to entrepreneurs from the Indian subcontinent starting out during this early period. They began stopping by for advice, funding, or just to try out an idea. If you were an Indian entrepreneur, you were no longer adrift and alone in the way that the eight-dollar men had been. Many of them who had struggled in isolation now came together to support the next generation of aspiring entrepreneurs.

Rekhi would listen patiently, ask questions, critique their projects, and help them develop their ideas if he felt they had merit. Eventually, in addition to giving advice he began to actively invest in projects he felt were worthy. Over the course of his presidency, he invested in over 45 start-ups, many of them owned by IIT graduates.

According to Rekhi, Indians account for over a third of the start-ups in Silicon Valley. Under his guidance, TiE began to expand its network, opening several chapters across the country. The press began to carry stories about the contribution of the new immigrant group and TiE conferences became sell out events. In 2000, the TiE conference in San Jose's Fairmont Hotel attracted 2,000 participants.

One of the early successes of a TiE-supported start-up was a company called Exodus. Rekhi thought it had great potential, but it was all over the map and lacked direction. Though Exodus was a pioneer in constructing server farms, it was disorganized, working out of cramped offices with servers stacked on tables, and about to run out of money. Rekhi bailed them out with a check for $200,000 so they could meet payroll. He joined the board, helped round up other investors, and reorganized the company. His eventual $1 million investment became $130 million. Co-investors Ed Shay and John Dougery, angel investors grew to trust Rekhi's judgement and invested with him on other deals. Indian entrepreneurs were gaining recognition in the Valley.

Rekhi was trusted because he was honest. When his classmate from IIT, Jay Karmarkar, came to Rekhi with an idea for a network computer that would run on a stripped-down Unix operating system and be compatible with Linux applications, he was not spared from Rekhi's laser-sharp critique. This particular model, involving the Unix operating system was Rekhi's specialty. Before Karmarkar could finish his presentation, Rekhi made it clear that he found the project without merit, pointing out all its flaws. He told his disheartened classmate that he could not support his project.

Rekhi sometimes received six or seven presentations a day at the office and would get cornered when he went out to restaurants or grocery stores.

I asked Rekhi how he decided on what companies to back and if he focused on the idea or the person.

KR: There are two schools of thought. What's more important? The jockey or the horse for the race? Who wins the race? An entrepreneur is the jockey, and the business idea is the horse. I always invest in people, but you need to have a nose for it and it's important to mentor them. My partners in my current fund are both successful entrepreneurs who launched successful start-ups. Thirty years ago, they came to TiE looking for help. I invested in them and mentored them and they did very well. Today we are partners.

MA: During the dot com boom which Indian did you miss?

KR: Hotmail. I met Sabeer Bhatia but I did not see how the business plan would work. I was wrong. But on the other hand, he has not been able to repeat his success.

Sabeer Bhatia had come during the second wave and caused a sensation by starting Hotmail in 1996 with Jack Smith and selling it two years later to Microsoft for $400 million during the height of the dot com boom. His star fizzled out after that as his later ventures failed to gain traction.

MA: Is there a way to mitigate risk?

KR: You can't remove the risk, so you need to diversify the portfolio. Most of the companies will fail but you count on two or three making it big. Ninety percent of the VCs don't make money, period. Of the 10 percent that do, they do extremely well. The secret of this industry is that many of the funds lose, but one or two will do well.

MA: Are you saying that most VC companies don't make money? So, all the pension money coming into big venture funds lose?

KR: Many don't make money. You have guys with MBAs investing who have never run a company. Then you have the giants like Sequoia or Kleiner, but these are often closed funds. They are experienced people. But you have a lot of people that lack expertise opening venture companies and when these new funds form, they often lose money. It's a risky business. They fail because most of the employees are MBAs who have never run a start-up. But I can talk about myself—my partners, we have all had experience running start-ups. We know the risks, the pitfalls. We actively mentor companies we invest in, we guide them because we understand how to run companies. We still anticipate that most of the companies will fail, but we hope that a few will make it big. We try to improve our odds by picking the right person and then helping him become an entrepreneur.

MA: How worried are you about AI disrupting tech?

KR: Every new technology disrupts. The Internet disrupted publishing, music, retail, but it also creates opportunities. It's a power tool. It should be used wisely. I keep hearing they will take over the world. I understand programming. I don't believe that will happen. I have created logic designs for massive systems. Think NASA and Boeing. Everything has flaws. We can stop that. We can also always pull the plug.

As TiE's reputation grew, other chapters were created. Today, TiE has 61 chapters across 14 countries and 15,000 charter members. Within 10 years, companies like Goldman Sachs, Morgan Stanley, McKinsey and Co., and KPMG were lining up to sponsor TiE's annual conference. They have grown into one of the most enviable professional networking groups among the immigrant communities.

Venktesh Shukla of Monta Vista Capital, who became president of TiE in 2016, said, "TiE captured the imagination of successful, ambitious Indians worldwide, but particularly in Silicon Valley. Once *Forbes* and *Fortune* magazine started writing about TiE around 2000, it got recognition and grew into a worldwide network. It was the only non-profit organization who had a mandate to foster entrepreneurs, and successfully launched hundreds of start-ups. Now there is Y Combinator and the Kaufman Foundation and others, but in 1996 there was no one but us."

In the early 1990s there was a small coterie of Indian engineers who had founded their own companies and become immensely rich as a result of the technology boom. Between them, they were worth close to $8 billion by 2000. The ones that survived the dot com boom and bust and the Y2K fallout established themselves as important players and became significant financiers and advisors to start-ups in Silicon Valley. Shukla is very open about the pitfalls of being an entrepreneur and talks about being a victim of the dot com bust. "I suffered during the dot com collapse. My company Ambit Design Systems sold for $260 million in 1998. That would be the equivalent of a billion today. It was a lot of money back then. I started another company that provided mobile access to the internet. I raised a lot of money and many big clients signed on, but I got caught in the dot com bust. Clients pulled out or delayed orders and it was the kiss of death. This was before the iPhone when the compulsion to have mobile access wasn't entrenched and I had to shut down. Later I joined another start up that was very successful."

Shukla would be instrumental in setting up the angel investors arm of TiE that provided funding as well as mentoring to start-ups.

After 2000, things began to change in the Valley. The frustration of encountering the glass ceiling when Indians were viewed as the "brains of the back office," not suited to represent the face of the corporation during the seventies and eighties, had been dispelled. The first generation of Indian engineers had proved that they could start and run substantial companies. This had opened up enormous opportunities for Indian immigrants with aspirations as now the path had been paved and a successful track record established.

CHAPTER 4

Venture Capital

New industries are created by entrepreneurs
who don't necessarily have subject matter expertise when they get started
yet they are still responsible for most of the innovation we see in society.

VINOD KHOSLA

While inventors and start-ups were proliferating in Silicon Valley during the seventies and eighties, so were venture capitalists looking for the next Steve Jobs or Bill Gates. Silicon Valley would not have expanded as rapidly as it did unless the many inventors and start-ups had been able to raise the capital to turn their dreams into reality. Sequoia and Kleiner Perkins, two legendary venture capital firms, were founded in 1972. The United States passed two laws that were responsible for the massive injection of funds into venture capital markets that, until the seventies, had been developing at a modest pace. In 1974, Congress passed ERISA, which removed the constraints that had previously prevented pension funds from investing in risky assets, including start-ups and venture capital, and in 1978 the Department of Labor relaxed the rules further. This had a giant impact—the funds going into venture capital increased from less than $40 million in 1977 to $6 billion in 1982.

Venture funds chased young people and their ideas. Throughout the 1980's and 90's investments by venture capital companies kept growing steadily until the late 90's when investment spiked to above $50 billion for a couple of years during the ill-fated dot-com bubble. Following the bust in 2000, it collapsed to less than $25 billion a year for the next 12 years. From the 2010's with the growth of social media, the venture business had a dramatic revival, rising above $100 billion in 2018 and peaking at $300 billion in 2021. Through all its ups and downs, the venture business was concentrated in California. See graph below.[21]

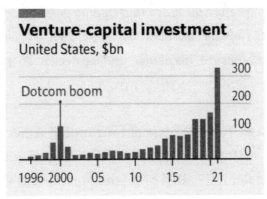

Venture-capital investment
United States, $bn

The Economist

More than half of all venture investments went into technology, and a further quarter went into biotech. As a result, California in general and Silicon Valley in particular, dominate the venture industry accounting for over 60 percent of investments, followed by New York and Massachusetts who share 30 percent.

The tech sector has gone through a retrenchment, sending shockwaves through Silicon Valley in an industry that got used to constant expansion. In 2022, venture capital investments went down by 35 percent to $200 billion and continued to slide to $100 million the following year.

It was compounded by the sudden collapse of the Silicon Valley Bank in March 2023. For a while it looked as though the contagion would spread to other regional banks, but it became the dog that didn't bark, and the government bailed out the depositors. Venture capital will likely see a slowdown, but if history is any guide, money and talent will continue to seek each other out even if it occurs at a more cautionary pace. Start-ups like OpenAI and ChatGPT have injected new energy into the Valley, a place which is continually on the frontier of the next big thing that promises to transform our lives.

Vinod Khosla: Driven to change the world

Is it 10 years, 20, 50 before we reach that tipping point where climate change becomes irreversible? Nobody can know. There's clearly a probability distribution. We need to ensure this planet, and we need to do it quickly

VINOD KHOSLA

Vinod Khosla, listed by *Forbes* as one of four Indian American billionaires, is one of the most successful and consequential venture capitalists in the Valley. Salesforce CEO Marc Benioff called him "the preeminent venture capitalist of our time" and Bill Gates said, "he has a rare combination of being a visionary who possesses deep technical acumen."[22] His firm Khosla Ventures ranks among the top 50 venture capital firms and was an early investor in OpenAI, the disrupter that accelerated the race to dominate artificial intelligence on steroids.

Khosla Ventures occupies an office building on Sand Hill Road, otherwise known as venture capital row, just down the road from Stanford University. When I called to make an appointment to meet Khosla at his office, I was asked to come in at 12:30 p.m. and assumed we would be meeting over lunch. No, I was firmly informed. Mr. Khosla does not eat lunch. I discovered that he believes eating during the day slows him down. With no Indian hospitality expected, I made sure I grabbed a Frappuccino before my meeting. Khosla is tall, trim, and elegant. He entered dressed in black knit top and dark slacks, reminding me of the late Steve Jobs in his stylish phase during the last years of his life.

Khosla believes that technology can solve almost all the world's problems. Two quotes that he repeats often when he gives talks—the first, "All progress depends on the unreasonable man," by George Bernard Shaw, and the second, "Human salvation lies in the hands of the creatively maladjusted," by Martin Luther King Jr.—encapsulate his approach to life and seem to have not only influenced his own conduct but have provided him with a philosophy for investing. He believes that human progress is brought about by unreasonable people.

In his various interviews over the years, he has made several disparaging remarks about journalists, English majors, and people who have non-technical jobs, implying that they weren't "real jobs." Although he loves to quote George Bernard Shaw, the value of writers that so enrich our lives through literature and poetry, and whose work he likes to quote, seems to have eluded him.

We were off to an awkward start while I fumbled with the voice recording app on my iPad and apologetically admitted I wasn't tech savvy, and weakly offering that perhaps there could be an advantage to my deficiency. He said, not unkindly, "I hope it's not to anyone's advantage not to be up to speed on tech." I later read somewhere that he said technology was his religion. I had not made a good start.

What is inspiring and exciting about Khosla is that he is truly an out-of-the-box thinker willing to place big bets on transformational ideas to benefit society. He views his investments as a form of philanthropy. He bet $3 million on Impossible Foods in the hope that a delicious plant-based alternative to meat would help sustain the health of the planet. He invests in green technology and is convinced that fusion is the future.

Contradicting his altruistic investing philosophy are his occasional personal decisions. He has pursued a long legal battle with the state of California over land-use rights. In 2008 he purchased prime beachfront property for $32 million along the California coast with 47 cottages on it. The land came with a path with direct access to the beach which the previous owners, who had owned the property for 100 years, had allowed the public to use. Khosla blocked the path and denied the public access to the beach via his property, bringing him into conflict with just about everyone, ranging from the public to environmental activists as well as the state of California, who sued him. He ended up in legal battles that lasted over 12 years. The saga, which he tried to take to the Supreme Court, garnered him a great deal of adverse publicity in a case that he eventually lost.[23] It pitted his purported environmentally friendly idealism and his do-good image against the reality of a wealthy businessman using his money to deny the public an environmental resource.

So who is Vinod Khosla? Where did he come from? How did he achieve such dazzling success?

Khosla's wealth is entirely self-made. He comes from a middle-class family in India of modest means—his career in the United States and meteoric success is the embodiment of the American dream.

Khosla's father like Rekhi's, worked for the Indian army and had hoped his son would enter India's military academy and become an officer. Both families are ethnic Punjabis who take pride in themselves as a martial race. The Indian army is a highly respected institution and considered a steady employer at a time when the country's future was uncertain in the decades following independence. Khosla grew up in somewhat more comfortable circumstances than Rekhi since his father was a senior officer, but Khosla admits that growing up surrounded by military families, he had little exposure to entrepreneurs, business, or, for that matter, scientists. While most kids his age were reading comic books, Khosla came across some technical journals and was hooked. After that, he would take a bus to the old city in Delhi to find copies of technical periodicals in second-hand book shops. He read about Andy Grove's life from Hungarian immigrant to Intel in the Electronic Engineering Times and was inspired. In the fifties and sixties, Nehru, India's first prime minister, exhorted the country's youth to help develop the country by studying science engineering and medicine. The newly established IITs gave young people options. Khosla was a good student, academically bright, and applied to study engineering at the prestigious IIT in Delhi that had been set up in collaboration with the United States government.

Khosla was driven and displayed leadership at an early age. When the operations staff at the school's computer center went on strike, he took over its operation and started the first computer club at IIT. A budding entrepreneur, in 1975 he came up with a project to distribute soy milk that didn't require refrigeration, as only a small fraction of the consumers in India owned a refrigerator. In the seventies, India was not a place where young people with adventurous ideas were supported, and Khosla was discouraged when he discovered it would take seven years just to get a landline for his business. Impatient to start living out his dreams, he decided to leave for the United States. Khosla had gained admission to Carnegie Mellon who had offered him a stipend to attend. He graduated with a master's in biomedical engineering but had his eyes on Stanford. Rejected twice for the MBA program as he lacked work experience, he persisted, working two jobs simultaneously and staying in touch with the admissions office in case a place opened up. His persistence paid off—someone dropped out and he made sure he was offered his place.

Khosla was driven by ambition from the start. He started three companies in three years. In 1980, the same year he graduated from Stanford, he started Daisy. The following year, he started Data Dump with fellow student Scott McNealy, which did not succeed; undeterred, in 1982 he started Sun Microsystems. He was young, had nothing to lose, and was brimming with self-confidence. Setting up a business with a marketable team is helpful, but you still need to prove yourself. Luckily, Sun Microsystems was a success and Khosla, as CEO, was a rising star.

Stanford has been the launching pad for many successful partnerships, and it is where Khosla met Andy Bechtolsheim and Scott G. McNealy. Together, they founded Sun Microsystems and were joined by Bill Joy from Berkeley, who developed the Java script that is still used by programmers today. Khosla became president and Bechtolsheim developed the workstation and was the brains behind the hardware while Joy headed up software. Sun Microsystems became profitable within a few months and the company went public in 1986. Between 1985 and 1989, Sun was the fastest growing company in the United States with a compound annual growth rate of 145 percent.

Khosla could also be aggressive in the pursuit of a goal. When he was at Sun, he discovered that a potential client had signed with a competitor. Unwilling to take no for an answer, Khosla flew to the East Coast to meet the client, parking himself in his lobby until the executive agreed to meet with him and reconsider. They arranged to meet the following day in Chicago with their respective teams. Khosla persuaded them to sign on by offering terms that were so favorable he couldn't refuse. While telling the story to students at Stanford Business School, he gleefully said, "The customer is not always right."

Khosla left Sun Microsystems in 1984 after just two years. When I asked him the reason for his premature departure, he did not answer. There is very little information available that one can directly attribute to him regarding his short tenure at Sun, but a couple of references have implied that his management style rubbed people the wrong way. Despite his early departure from Sun, Khosla had become wealthy and was invited to join Kleiner Perkins, an offer that would shape the rest of his life.

Khosla's transition to venture capital began in fits and starts. He joined Kleiner Perkins in 1986 as a general partner. He initially began part-time and some of his early investments such as DynaBook and Go Computing did not do well, but things began to turn around and he discovered he had a talent when it came to mentoring start-ups. Among his successes were Nexgen, which was sold to AMD for 28 percent of its market cap. He helped Excite adapt its search engine and the company was eventually sold for $7 billion, but his largest return was on Juniper Networks which he incubated and earned Kleiner Perkins $7 billion on a $3 million investment.

On another occasion when he was at Kleiner Perkins in the early nineties, he was convinced that the Internet, still in its nascent days in the early nineties, would grow exponentially. He was nurturing a company called Cerent and invited the dominant router giant Cisco to co-invest with him: Among other things, Cerent would facilitate the handling of voice data. Cisco refused, calling Cerent too much of a long shot, so Khosla went ahead alone and invested $8 million, recruiting the first engineers and serving as its chief executive. The technology proved workable, and Cisco changed its mind and offered him $300 million in December 1998, but Khosla turned them down. Four months later, Cisco raised their offer to $700 million. Khosla decided to play hardball and held out. He didn't have to wait long—four months later while vacationing at Machu Picchu, he was told that an offer had been made for $7 billion. Khosla got off the mountain! He took a helicopter, then a plane, and shook hands on the deal over breakfast in San Jose the next morning.

In 2004 he left to start Khosla Ventures. By then Khosla was a billionaire and had established his bona fides as a venture capitalist.

Khosla and Rekhi were among the first wave of immigrant engineers that arrived in the United States, although Khosla arrived almost a decade after Rekhi. Both men have accents that linger to this day and come from similar backgrounds in India, but Khosla seemed to have had a much smoother ride to the top. Khosla went to the prestigious Carnegie Mellon University, but most importantly ended up at Stanford—the center of it all. He not only had the regional advantage, but he won the cultural lottery. Khosla had Bechtolsheim and McNealy on his letterhead; they had the imprimatur of being Stanford grads. Everyone was ready to listen to their ideas.

Rekhi, with no one to guide him, had picked the least expensive graduate school that gave him the best scholarship. He applied to the Michigan Technological Institute in 1967 for a master's degree in electrical engineering. The tuition was just $200 a quarter. When asked why he chose Michigan Tech, he replied, "The schools all had nice brochures that I found in the library. You couldn't tell them apart a whole lot. But Michigan Tech offered financial aid. It was cheap." Rekhi had spent a difficult three years after graduating from Michigan Tech in 1969. He had been laid off three times in three years before making his way west to Silicon Valley in 1971.

He had arrived in California with a family to support and continued to keep an eye out for job listings even though his position at Singer Link was secure. His experience of being laid off on the East Coast had made him anxious—it would take three years before the ghosts of that unhappy experience wore off. It would take time and feeling underappreciated that would push him to start his own company.

Family is a high priority for Khosla. Deeply in love with his girlfriend when he left India in 1976, he insisted on marrying her in 1980 despite coming from a tradition where parents picked your life partner and arranged marriages. After leaving Sun Microsystems, he moved his wife and four children to India in 1992 for three years so they could get to know their grandparents and learn about their heritage. His belief that human progress depends on people doing unreasonable things extended to the way he raised his children. An example he likes to give is throwing food around and at them when they were young because they were being too "proper." He keeps a baby rhinoceros on his desk: it is a present from his four children as a reminder of how bruising he can be. Khosla has his soft side and admits he enjoyed taking his daughters shopping for clothes and hearing them talk. He makes an effort to have dinner with his family several times a week. These rather sentimental attachments provide a different insight into someone who is generally regarded by many as cold and cerebral.

In a lecture he gave at a school, he encouraged children to disobey their parents, color outside the lines, and not listen to their teachers. One of the children said his mom told him he needed to improve his handwriting, and so he asked Khosla if he should practice—Khosla said not if he had something more important to do. You can always convince yourself not to do something. It's uncomfortable trying to do things that haven't been done if you're smart.

Khosla can be brutally blunt. Some people find him difficult to work with, but in his defense, Jack Dorsey, who founded Twitter, said Khosla—who had been a mentor and advisor to him—was a deeply principled person and cares deeply about what he does. Heavily influenced by Sam Harris's book *Lying*, Khosla refuses to lie and doesn't seem to be willing to soften his responses to accommodate even ordinary sentiments. He says he finds it liberating, although he admits it can alienate people on the receiving end. It's an indulgence he treasures and applies it equally to all aspects of his life, big and small. He is straightforward when he thinks a company he has invested is on the wrong track and lets them know his views, but he also makes no allowances for people's feelings. He refuses to tell people a gift they have given him is wonderful if it isn't. "When somebody sends me a gift—I get a lot of gifts—I ask Ruthie [his assistant] to not say, 'That was wonderful,'" he says. "If it wasn't, I have her send a nice note back saying, 'Thank you, that was very interesting.'"

Khosla likes to read and posts his reading list online. It includes 45 books, most of them on technology, investing strategies, or self-improvement. *Lying* was No. 13 on the list. I presented him with my recent book, *A Matter of Trust: India-United States Relations from Truman to Trump*, partly because it had been well-received and I wanted to reassure him about my credentials, and partly because—well, what else do you take to a billionaire's office? I was disappointed when he said he only read books on audio, as my book would not be on audio for a few months, but he kept the book, which I thought was a hopeful sign. Two months later, I noticed that a book I had recommended by my friend David Epstein called *Range* had been added to his reading list, but mine had not made the cut!

The following conversation provides some insights into his journey and path to success.

MA: You were among the early wave of Indian Engineers that came to the United States and found success here. There were a handful of you that became successful, although not everyone did as well as you. Were you smarter than everyone else?

VK: In the seventies, a whole bunch of Indians, very smart people, very qualified, were graduating from IIT and leaving the country, leaving their family to pursue a vision. It takes a certain kind of personality; smarts are not enough. Education is not enough. You had to have a risk-taking entrepreneurial culture to leave the comfort of home and come to this country not knowing anybody. There wasn't anybody I knew here. There was no mentor. But this willingness to take risks along with lots of capability is a combination that really works well for Indians in Silicon Valley. Silicon Valley is about performance and it's not just a place, it's a mindset.

MA: How much credit do you owe to IIT for your success? Many successful engineers in Silicon Valley, including several CEOs, are graduates of IIT.

VK: There are a billion-plus Indians now and bright people everywhere, but even in my day it was really hard to get into IIT. It was stunning that the results of the entrance exam were published in the *Times of India*. That would be unthinkable in the United States—to have admission results published in the *New York Times*—but it's important to understand why it was culturally important. Because the IIT students are so deeply selected, more even that MIT, that schools like Carnegie Mellon paid for me to come here with a stipend, without which I couldn't have come. IIT students became a brand that were known for being smart with a good work ethic. When I came to the United States to pursue graduate studies at Carnegie Mellon, the work was a breeze after IIT. I was able to work full-time jobs while carrying a full load of classes. My roommate from college is still here and we remain friends to this day.

MA: Have you ever worked for anyone else, or have you always known you wanted to be your own boss?

VK: I was clear I was coming to the United States to start a company. I was never coming here to just get a job. What makes me happy are the things I've pursued. It's this internal drive to do things that motivates me, not what others expect of me, which is titles, promotions, income, cars, and bigger houses. Sundar [Pichai] has the same personality if you know him. I have never taken a job that I wouldn't do for free.

MA: Your career seems to have had a smoother path than say Kanwal Rekhi, who worked for various companies like RCA and Singer Link and started on the East Coast and ran into discrimination.

VK: Corporations have cultures with institutional rules. If you joined RCA or IBM, you were in a hierarchy that followed a set of internal rules. Performance was important but probably ranked four, especially in the senior ranks, after whether you played golf or looked the same or had the same accent.

MA: What qualities do you have that contributed to your success?

VK: I'm willing to work in extreme ambiguity. Most people are not. I'm willing to take risks. Most people aren't. When I started Daisy, my first company out of Stanford before Sun, I had no material expectations. When I left India, I'd never had a TV or even a telephone at home, I just had a desire to work on interesting technology, which I still do. There are two things that motivate me—technology and science. Science is my religion. There is also the element of luck, and I wouldn't underestimate its contribution to my success. Luck is a big element in all our careers. Having said that, I'm willing to give myself a chance to win which opens me up to also lose. It is my willingness to fail that has given me the ability to succeed. Before I started Sun, I started a company with Scott McNealy called Data Dump that did not work out, but few people remember it. People don't remember your failures. It's your successes that matter.

MA: You view failure as a learning experience. Could you explain how it helps you?

VK: Failure is allowable but not desirable. One should use it as a tool to succeed. I have a collection of failures that I have learnt from. Edison had multiple failures before succeeding, but with each failure he learnt and built on his knowledge till he finally succeeded. There are many examples in history like his. I don't wish to romanticize failure. It's not fun. It's never easy, it's not a party, but the freedom to fail is extremely liberating. People's fear of failure restricts them from trying. Most people are limited by what they are willing to try, not by what they are capable of. I don't mind failing, but if I succeed, it better be consequential.

MA: What are the key characteristics you look for in a person to assess if they will be successful? Given the rate of failure of start-ups, how do you decide who to back?

VK: I gave a lecture at Stanford Business School in 2015. There were 400 people in the audience and I said, "I'm not trying to speak to all of you. I'm trying to speak to the five percent who will be internally driven." High IQ and training, while important, are not the only thing that matters. You need to be curious and to be driven by your internal engine, not because you pursue goals due to external pressures. Most CEOs of Fortune 500 companies lack that internal belief system.

Experience can be a bias. It can be good if you are trying to extrapolate the past into the future, but when you are trying to invent a new future, it can be a real hindrance. No large societal innovation that I know of in the last 40 years was done by anybody who was an expert in the area they were innovating. When I talk to the government about energy, and they tell me to talk to GE, there is not a person at GE I'll even take a phone call from that's relevant to energy transformation. They just extrapolate the past. Not everyone thinks from first principals. In Silicon Valley people try to do away with assumptions and work with first principals. There's no chance anybody at Hilton or Hyatt would have come up with Airbnb. No chance. Retail innovation did not come from Walmart; it came from Amazon. Space innovation did not come from Boeing and Lockheed; it came from Elon Musk's Space X. Next generation cars did not come from GM and Volkswagen; they came from another Musk company, Tesla. Nobody in media could do Google or Facebook or YouTube or Twitter or Netflix. Nobody, and Rupert Murdoch tried. I spent a lot of time with him in the early 2000s. He bought Myspace—he was very curious about it, but there is too much traditional thinking to go far enough and innovate. Innovation depends on first principals thinking and the courage to say, "I might not be able to pay my mortgage or to fund my kid's education." A perfect example is Larry Page. Innovators and disrupters do not come from the establishment.

MA: What role will AI play in our future and your strategic investing?

VK: AI in half a dozen areas will be the single most important and nonlinear innovation which by 2050 I believe will eliminate the need for human labor. The notion of labor will disappear, and people will work because they want to, not because they need to. This I am very clear about. How soon will this happen? I am not sure, but sooner than you might think. You can replicate China's $2 an hour labor in every neighborhood. The most creative music will be done by AI, the most creative graphics and entertainment. Even tutoring.

MA: What are your concerns about the future?

VK: For the next 25 years we will be engaged in a techno-economic war between China and the West, mostly led by the United States, mostly probably led by Silicon Valley. It will be driven by technology which will determine economic influence across the world—in Asia, in Africa. I am very clear that we are at war with China on technology and it will get worse. There is no compromising in this regard. It will determine the basis of all economic and political activity. AI-based cyber warfare will become much more important. You will be able to fight wars without losing a single person. In the 1800s, people fought wars over scarce resources like salt. In the 1960s it was oil; now people are talking about lithium-ion batteries and metals. We are looking at non-linear solutions to fight that war. We will need cheap energy, but all these problems are trivial if we make better use of fusion technology.

MA: There are major issues facing us—the water shortage, energy shortage—

VK: I have a philosophy in life that whatever I believe I should make happen. I have a very clear plan for the next 20 years. I am internally driven by how to combine science to produce technology in ways that others think is impossible. That is why I don't plan to retire. At 60 I went to my business school reunion; everyone was talking about retirement. I thought: Golf seems like a terrible way to spend my time and I can't imagine sailing. I wrote a 50-page document called reinventing societal infrastructure with technology. For the next 20 years I have identified several issues I can work on. Fusion, for example, solves the world's power production problem, natural gas problem, nuclear and coal problem, and by 2030 we should be able to prove that fusion can replace every source of power on the planet. I talked to a team at MIT and said it's too important not to work on.

I'm building a new public transit system. People think it's crazy for start-ups to work on that. I believe I can play a role in the United States winning the war against China on the technology front and hence on the economic front.

I often get criticized for saying a 90 percent chance of failure is fine with me if there is a 10 percent chance of changing the world, and so I decided to work on all these problems.

At the energy summit that took place in Seattle in April 2023, Khosla admitted that the breakthrough technology needed to combat climate change by 2030 just wasn't there—2040 was a more realistic timeline. Khosla and other investors like his friend John Doerr, had started investing in clean energy in the early 2000s but had seen several clean tech start-ups fail. Collectively, venture capital firms invested more than $25 billion in climate tech companies between 2006 and 2011 and ended up losing half their money, according to a paper from MIT. President Biden, climate activists, and the UN have used 2030 as a time frame against which it has set goals to reduce emissions and the earth's warming, but Khosla warns that focusing on short-term goals will force us to use suboptimal technology.

Nuclear fusion occurs when two light atomic nuclei merge to form a heavier one, releasing vast amounts of energy. The relatively low levels of carbon emissions and radioactivity make it a very attractive clean energy alternative. Khosla's bet on fusion technology will not be commercialized by 2030. He said, "Every single technology at scale has to achieve unsubsidized market competitiveness. And if it doesn't do that, it's the wrong technology."

Three months after I interviewed him, a *Wall Street Journal* article validated Khosla's claims regarding the importance of fusion in our future. Khosla, along with Jeff Bezos of Amazon, Bill Gates, Sam Altman—who galvanized the AI community with ChatGPT—and a few other prominent investors have all, according to the article, invested in fusion that now seems within years of becoming a reality.

In 2016, Khosla produced a thought-provoking paper on the future of medicine titled "20 Percent Doctor Included." It pointed out the inaccuracies in scientific research, the misdiagnoses due to human shortcomings, and the compromised state of medicine in the way it is currently practiced. Khosla predicted a future where the use of artificial intelligence in medicine will lead to far fewer mistakes in diagnoses and vastly expanded research capacity in the genesis and treatment of diseases as well as drug discovery. Khosla's paper was thoroughly researched and cited, but I wondered if medical research was as flawed as he claimed. The National Institute of Health and universities like Harvard Medical School and Johns Hopkins Medical School are renowned, trusted institutions where so much of the medical research was conducted. We had been conditioned to trust them. By sheer coincidence, the morning after I had watched the slide show and viewed his talk, I opened my inbox to a news item in *Semafor* titled "How Science is Broken." The article, written in April 2023—seven years after Mr. Khosla gave his talk—went on to confirm many of the points he had made, such as the fact that an astonishing number of scientific studies, particularly in medicine, are not only wrong, but sometimes outrightly fraudulent. Khosla was not only a step ahead of everyone else, but he had also already come up with solutions. It was another illustration of his genius.

No one had described Khosla as a warm and cuddly guy, but there was a kindness in his eyes and a drive to do good that mitigated his brusque manner and cold angularity. What makes Khosla so unique is his high capacity for risk, combined with an agile mind that is always curious and forward thinking, ready to contemplate the unimaginable.

CHAPTER 5

The Company Men

The fast pace of tech innovation was becoming the defining characteristic of Silicon Valley as the world stepped into a new century. Big companies that had dominated tech through the eighties—Bell Labs, Xerox, and IBM—had been the crucibles of innovation until disruptors began to change the world.

Five big tech companies—Apple, Microsoft, Google, Facebook, and Adobe—started out as disruptors run by 20-somethings but have overtaken in size, impact, and market cap even the IBMs and AT&Ts of their day. The original founders of Adobe, Microsoft, and Google have all chosen Indian CEOs to take their place while they have left to pursue other interests. None of them invented products or founded the companies they now run, and they didn't all graduate from IIT either. I call them the "company men."

The new generation of CEOs, in particular the big three—Shantanu Narayen, Satya Nadella and Sundar Pichai—are "company men." After finishing their education and a short stint getting some job experience, they spent most of their career working up the ladder of the companies they now head. With the exception of Narayen, who briefly tried his hand at a start-up and holds a couple of patents, the others are neither inventors nor entrepreneurs.

The first Indian to be appointed CEO was Shantanu Narayen at Adobe in 2007. Satya Nadella and Sundar Pichai took over as CEO of Microsoft and Google in 2014 and 2015 respectively. They each inherited companies that had become large corporations but whose self-image was still wrapped up in the cloak of a start-up.

This presented the new leaders with a toxic combination of proprietary turf battles, and a culture of insubordination that was admired among innovators and start-ups—but this wasn't always helpful in a large company whose management needed to balance the needs of large departments in a vast company which also had to create opportunities for everyone and to be seen as fair.

All three CEOs transformed their companies into friendly work environments and inspired loyalty among their employees who gave their respective bosses high marks on their management style.

The tech industry is dominated by men, which gave rise to a "bro culture" in the valley.

Microsoft was a tough work environment under Bill Gates, who had no hesitation yelling at employees and sometimes even clients when he ran Microsoft. Though he is a soft-spoken philanthropist today, he admits that he was harsh as a manager: "When I was at Microsoft, I was tough on people I worked with. Some of it helped us be successful, but I'm sure some of it was over the top." Joel Spolsky, a former program manager assigned to Microsoft's Excel product line, remembers Gates frequently using the "F" word. He said, "Bill doesn't really want to review your spec, he just wants to make sure you've got it under control. His standard M.O. is to ask harder and harder questions until you admit you don't know, and then he can yell at you for being unprepared."[24] As CEO, Nadella removed the yelling and confrontational style from meetings, and treated people with respect.

Google and its parent company Alphabet had been accused of discriminatory hiring practices over the years, and issues of sexual harassment within the company, reaching to the highest levels, had begun to spill into the open. In 2018 Google employees staged a walk-out in protest of a culture they felt had become toxic, and co-founders Larry Paige and Sergey Brin stepped down and Sundar Pichai became CEO.[25] The *New York Times* interviewed several executives who acknowledged that Pichai is a thoughtful and caring leader and that Google is a far more disciplined and organized place since he took over. While some people expressed frustration with Pichai's indecisiveness and predilection for mulling over things at length, he tamped down some of the toxicity that had built up on the personnel side.[26]

Indians are taught at an early age to respect their elders, teachers, and superiors. Showing up for an official meeting in your pajamas, as Mark Zuckerberg did, would be unthinkable for most Indians unless they had no other clothes. Narayen, Nadella, and Pichai transformed the management style in their organizations once they became CEO and found ways to extract the best from their employees by creating a more inclusive and collaborative atmosphere. Respect and inclusion, like any lofty principle, is not always universally applied in India, as the less fortunate are often mistreated, along with complicating factors like caste prejudice.

Shantanu Narayen, Sundar Pichai, Satya Nadella, and Arvind Krishna of IBM are all South Indians that belong to the privileged Brahmin caste. Narayen, Nadella, and Krishna grew up in Hyderabad and attended the same school. The two Indian CEOs of Microsoft and Google, despite their shared ethnicity, are now at war with each other in their race to dominate AI. Nadella has publicly goaded Pichai in the media with taunts like "I want to see Google dance," but without any yelling, as was the case between Steve Jobs and Bill Gates, as famously reported in the press when Gates was developing software in the early days of Microsoft and Jobs accused him of stealing ideas from Apple.

While a handful of Indians who moved to America have become CEOs of large companies, Narayen and Nadella have distinguished themselves as exceptional leaders and have had a transformational impact on their companies by changing the existing models they were being run on and developing a vision for their futures. They stand out as truly visionary CEOs who have grasped the new frontier that is changing the world with artificial intelligence and are well positioned to lead their companies to the next phase of growth. Nikesh Arora, a newcomer to the C-Suite, is trying to chart a similar path in cybersecurity, an increasingly critical area of technology.

Although Narayen and Nadella came from the same city, knew each other in school, and have been invited to family weddings, they do not seem to be part of each other's inner circle of advisors. The two companies have business interests in common but are also competitive. It is their mutual love of cricket, India's national obsession that has brought them together on more than one occasion. When Nadella was young, he was convinced that his future happiness lay in pursuing a career in cricket. He later decided it was an unrealistic aspiration and is a part owner of the Seattle Orcas, a professional T20 cricket team that participates in major league cricket.

Narayen confesses that he sometimes stays up late at night to watch a game being played halfway across the world.

In 2022 Nadella and Narayen got together to start a United States Major Cricket League, securing an investment of $120 million to popularize the game in America. If the success of the Men's T-20 Cricket World Cup co-hosted by the United States for the first time in June 2024 is any indicator, they have exceeded all expectations and may have put cricket on the path to becoming a mainstream sport in the United States More than 34,000 fans paid up to $1300 per ticket to attend the match in East Meadow New York. The atmosphere was as highly charged as any major baseball or football game and when the United States team in a stunning upset beat Pakistan, one of the world's established teams, the spectators went wild. The star player on the American team, Saurabh Netravalkar, is a 32-year-old bowler, born and raised in India who works at Oracle as an engineer. He has been known to bring his laptop to practice so he can code in between matches. He cemented his reputation when his team played against India—one of the world's top cricket teams and he knocked out their captain Rohit Sharma, and one of their best players, Virat Kohli.

When Los Angeles hosts the 2028 summer Olympics, cricket will be included as a new sport and investors are already looking for ways to cash in on this latest addition to professional American sport with a readymade global fanbase.

Narayen and Nadella followed slightly different paths starting in Hyderabad, India, and moving to Silicon Valley and Seattle. They both reached the top of their professions and each in their own way along with newer CEOs like Arora, are now making their contributions to the evolving American tech story.

The careers I found most compelling among the Indian CEOs of the tech companies were Narayen, Nadella and Arora. Narayen has displayed immense strategic skills and combined it with effective management to propel Adobe into the big leagues. Although the Europeans put brakes on his expansion plans by preventing Adobe from acquiring Figma, Narayen has fortitude and is playing the long game. Nadella had shown extraordinary vision and made Microsoft the pre-eminent company in the world, a feat not accomplished by Bill Gates. Arora is ambitious and dogged and cybersecurity along with AI is bound to dominate our future. The person I decided to omit profiling is Sundar Pichai of Google. Although he is known for his management skills, he has fallen short. When Google felt threatened by Open AI, Pichai seemed to panic and called on the founders to return and help him out.[27] He has not presented a convincing strategic vision for taking Google forward to meet the recent challenges.

CHAPTER 6

Shantanu Narayen

Adobe is consistently ranked as one of the pre-eminent places to work and Shantanu Narayen is ranked as one of the finest CEOs to work for. *Barron's* magazine named Narayen as one of the world's best CEOs in 2018, 2019, and 2023. *Fortune* included Adobe among the 100 best companies to work for in the United States for 24 years.

Before joining Adobe in 1998 as vice president and general manager of its engineering technology group, Narayen had worked at Apple on product development from 1989 to 1995. While at Apple, he met another Indian American engineer, Gursharan Sidhu, who became one of his mentors. "Gursharan was a huge inspiration at Apple." Narayen recalls, "He always pushed me to do more. He saw in me things I didn't see in myself and challenged me to excel." Sidhu taught Narayen to be uncompromising when it came to product design, and during his time at Apple he even held a couple of patents. Narayen's time at Apple was challenging. His wife had just given birth to their first son, he was enrolled in Berkeley's Haas School of Business evening program, and was juggling a job, classes, and family commitments. It taught him how to prioritize what was most important and to use his time efficiently, a skill he would draw on later as CEO of Adobe.

Hoping to become an entrepreneur, Narayen co-founded Pictra, a photo sharing start-up in 1996 that was ahead of its time. Pictra was not a commercial success and Narayen joined Adobe as head of engineering in a division that became very successful, and six months later he was running all engineering at Adobe. His rise within the company was smooth; he became COO in 2005, and in 2007 he became the first Indian American to become CEO of a major global tech company.

Adobe has transformed digital media, from PDFs—how documents are shared across devices electronically—to automating business processes including signatures. More than 90 percent of the world's creative professionals use Photoshop.

Adobe had posted record growth and revenues in 2007 when Narayen had taken over, but when the 2008 recession hit, Narayen faced his first major challenge as CEO. The 2008 recession put pressure on earnings. The share price fell by 50 percent but by January 2024 Adobe's stock price was up thirty-fold.

Narayen recognized that Adobe products were a discretionary purchase and that the business model needed to be changed. "There is always a silver lining, even in adversity, if one uses it as a learning experience. One can either be paralyzed by what's happening in the macro-economic environment, or you innovate." Narayen and his team changed the business model of Adobe to one that was subscription-based in 2012. Initially his revenues went down, but they recovered. Having weathered the financial crisis of 2008 and navigated their way through a new business model, prepared them to handle the global pandemic of 2020 a decade later, a global challenge no one could have predicted would have lasted as long as it did, with such enormous global consequences.

Narayen's investments in the cloud and AI, and resistance to lay off his staff, have earned him the loyalty of his clients and employees.

Narayen likes to surround himself by smart people. He sees his job as creating a vision for the group and being the coach or team leader. "You need to build successful teams. My job is to clarify the direction; the company and the people will self-select. Surround yourself by people smarter than you and tap into the wisdom, and if you remove the obstacles in their way, you multiply the impact. Some people dominate and it's important to hear everyone. Cast your net wide and get as much data as possible. The more you listen to people, the more you can put the puzzle together. You don't always make the right decision, but you have to be comfortable making a decision and change it if it's wrong. Preserving the status quo is not a strategy—one should stay paranoid. Business schools do a good job emphasizing that." The Andy Grove adage: "Only the paranoid survive."

Narayen readily admits he was the academic slouch in the family and he was less academically inclined when he was young. It took a while for him to focus on his studies. His mother has a PhD in American literature, and his father, an engineer and gold medalist, attended the University of Illinois.

His older brother had followed in his parents' footsteps. He had not only attended every prestigious school but had also graduated at the top of his class in India. One of the schools, Mayo College—which was actually an Indian boarding school and not a college—was reserved for the British elite and the sons of the maharajas during colonial times. Princes would arrive with a retinue of staff, and the school allowed them to bring their horses, dogs, and stable hands. That all changed after independence in 1947, when it became a boarding school for India's elite, not unlike Andover and Exeter in the United States. Narayen was due to follow his brother to Mayo, but in 1971 India was at war with Pakistan and his parents decided not to send him, bringing his brother home for safety as well. Narayen's brother, a gold medallist in high school, graduated from IIT before making his way to the United States.

Narayen was proud of his family's intellectual achievements but dreamed of a different life for himself. He was passionate about sports and wanted to pursue a career as a journalist. But his parents were big believers in education. In an interview that he gave to Paul Merrill in November 2021 to CEO *Magazine*, Narayen said that when he was a teenager, his parents talked him out of being a journalist and advised him to study engineering. He took their advice.

He credits his parents with instilling a sense of ambition and drive in him and says that going to engineering college was the best thing that happened to him. His interest in journalism did not match his passion for sports as he seemed easily persuaded to abandon his interest in journalism, but sports remained a lifelong obsession. Even after a long day, he often unwinds late at night by watching sports.

SN: I wake up in the middle of the night to follow cricket in India or Australia or the World Cup. I wasn't good at playing it in school, but growing up, it was a religion!

MA: Did you play sports when you were young?

SN: I grew up in Hyderabad and my parents were members of the Secunderabad

Sailing Club, so I had access to boats. I sailed in local competitions in the regattas and represented India in the nationals once. I love all sports. I love playing, watching, observing. I enjoy golf as well, but cricket is a passion.

MA: To what do you attribute your success?

SN: Every parent in India believes their child is capable of incredible things. Education and investing in yourself is a way out of poverty and the path to opportunity and fundamentally positive. This is regardless of your social status and income level. I am unbelievably grateful for where I grew up. I always look at the positive side. We learn to be resourceful in India. There is a word for it. *Jugaad*. My school was miles away. If I missed my bus, I didn't run home, I figured out how to get to school. We don't take no for an answer. We're inventive. We figure out how to get things done. All this teaches self-confidence. You develop a tool chest that you call on when required. The ability to be resourceful, start from scratch, and above all, invest in an education.

In the 1990s, the country adopted massive economic reforms, stepping away from its socialist orientation and towards a free market one. India began to crawl out of its economic malaise and began to emerge as a global economy. Although poverty persisted, call centers, back offices, and tech hubs had sprung up in India, transforming the economy and culture.

Microsoft and Apple were now established companies and Bill Gates was the new celebrity. Driving through the crowded streets of Mumbai in 1995, I saw aspirational billboards advertising computer classes with Bill Gates's picture plastered across it saying, "You too can become Bill Gates!" Employment in the tech sector in India was expanding rapidly as well, but it was at the lower level of skills.

When Narayen recounts his story, it is clear that his brother has been very influential in his life—when he speaks of him, he talks with love and genuine admiration.

SN: My brother was three years older than me and was always academically significantly better than me. He used to ace everything. I had these different interests. I like to sail, I like to play tennis. When I didn't get into IIT, I was like, "Wow!" I was in a little bit of shock, but I didn't study. Now when I look back on it, I recognize I didn't put in the effort, right? So, you learn from it. Engineering college was the best thing that happened to me. My brother was incredibly supportive. He probably thought I was capable of good stuff but didn't necessarily apply myself, and in my first year in the United States, I remember him telling me—he said, "If you get a B in graduate school, they may deport you!" So when I did my masters in computer science I buckled down. My brother called me every day to make sure I was okay.

MA: Adobe was once a start-up disrupter. Can you describe the genesis of its innovation?

SN: Our two founders started the company coming out of Xerox because they felt like Xerox wasn't reinventing themselves. The world's most seminal innovations came out of there. Networking as we know it today, which is the ability to connect two computers. Your ethernet, the user experience, the first graphical user interface. At one point Xerox attracted the smartest people in the world. They hired incredibly smart PhDs and posed ambitious problems for them to find creative solutions to. John Warnock and Chuck Geschke, the founders of Adobe, were part of that. They created the graphics and imaging lab at Xerox. PCs were coming out and they were focused on the ability for people to print. That was their fundamental innovation. People talk about black swan events. Desktop publishing was one of those. Canon had come out with the laser printer, Apple had come out with the Macintosh; the ability to use a PC to create content was happening. The timing was right. They went to Xerox, but it just wasn't a priority for Xerox, so they went and started their own company.

MA: Adobe was a disrupter, but now it's a major corporation. How do you avoid the pitfalls that Xerox and big companies suffer from and not lose your ability to innovate and remain competitive?

SN: We are foremost a creative company. Everyone has a story to tell, and if we can help them tell that story we are filling a societal need. The easier you make it, the more you democratize the process, and you can really enlarge your footprint and make it inclusive. Digital technology is changing the world whether you are making a video or creating packaging for a bottle of water. Technology has evolved since Gutenberg, when technology was only available to a few.

MA: How do you make sure you remain on the cutting edge of innovation? Is Kickbox the creative space you're providing inventors within your company to come up with new technologies?

SN: It's evolving. The question is how do you promote entrepreneurship within the company and are you sufficiently paranoid? Are we looking around the corner enough and experimenting? Software and tech products have an S-curve. You have the start, followed by explosive growth, then comes maturity. You need to incubate a portfolio of products that are in different stages in their life cycles. We tend to artificially limit our own aspirations. The entrepreneurial genes have always been a part of who I am. Working at Apple taught me to think big. Apple wanted to have an impact. Their mantra was "the journey is the reward." In a small company I learnt how not to take no for an answer. I hope that's the hallmark of how I manage. When you work for a small company, you have to overcome every single adversity. I still try to instill in people an "everything is possible" attitude. What makes the Valley such a special place is no one cares where you went to school, or if you were successful in your company, but what tools you acquired. I believe you should expose yourself to a whole lot of diverse experiences.

MA: Have you drawn any lessons from the venture companies to see if their culture of encouraging innovation can be applied to a big company like Adobe?

SN: The venture community is generally focused on the incubation at the start. Companies our size have to look at the whole spectrum. The one lesson I've learnt from the venture community is that they always bet on the person first. The other lesson I've learned from the venture community which we try to promote within Adobe is that ideas don't conform to annual planning cycles the way companies build their strategic plans. If you are an entrepreneur with an idea and you go up and down Sand Hill Road, you just need one sponsor to back you and you're off and running. In a company, to get an idea off the ground, everyone needs to sign off. If one person says no and the idea gets killed, it's not a good way to encourage incubation. You need to change the culture so that all you need is one sponsor. There are so many lessons to be learned. There are two philosophies and if we let 1,000 flowers bloom within a company and say, "Hey, whoever has an idea, go do it. We'll give you a little money, come back with your next milestone and let's see how much progress you've made and then let's ramp up." There is something very powerful about that. That's what the venture community does. Incubation can come in increments rather than a yes or no and if you see progress, you can determine funding. Here are the areas that are of significance for us, go apply your ingenuity. It's more top down.

MA: Have you had any success using this method?

SN: Huge, huge successes. We have something called the Adobe experience platform. It's technical but it's called the customer data platform. We are seeing dramatic success with customer engagement. The evolutionary innovation is never perceived to be astounding and that's a mistake. To be successful as a company you need to recognize your true value. Your true value is your people. You have to have a north star and then you need the flag planters—they know what hill you want to climb. You need the road builders, who say, "Hey, this is how we get there." The magic is when you make it aspirational enough when you can't completely see your way there today but have a vision for the future.

MA: Adobe has close to 30,000 employees. How do you stay connected to them and know them well enough to recognize who the most gifted people are and make sure they thrive? CEOs of large multinational corporations are prone to getting isolated from the trenches and are surrounded by "palace guards" who limit access to them. Last year you spent 96 days traveling. That is a further impediment to cohesiveness. Michael Bloomberg was a pioneer in the open plan office—perhaps influenced by his days on the Salomon Brothers trading floor. I once heard him explain that by placing his desk in the middle of the open plan office he could always work out who the critical people in his company were because there was always a line in front of their desk of people going up to them for help.

SN: As the company scales, it's become harder for me. When you grow up in a company you get to know the people and sort of know who the thought leaders are. I think for the most part people I would say I'm accessible. Sometimes I go around and have lunch with people. We had open floors but then went back to closed floors, but anyone can use the office. There are always stories that emerge in a company which says, "Oh we would never do that," or, "You could never do that." I would argue at times it's harder to find those.

MA: How do you approach management so the scale is not counterproductive?

SN: The way to think about it is that I just manage eight people. You could have 35,000 people in the company, but how many do you actually manage? Just eight. Then you amplify it through the 64 that report to them, you could get really caught up in the numbers and get overwhelmed. Oh my god! The company is so large... I'm fortunate that I've grown up in the company and there are people who've been here for 20 to 25 years that will shoot me an email if they see something they don't like and they know I'll respond. That's just the culture we have inculcated.

MA: If you have a problem, management or product, do you ever call up Satya Nadella or Sundar Pichai as fellow Indian Americans who are running major tech companies to see if you can solve problems together? Is there a camaraderie among you? A friendship? Or is it too competitive?

SN: Satya and I have known each other a long time. He and I went to the same high school in Hyderabad in India. It's probably fair to say that Microsoft and Adobe partnered a lot more on the big move to the cloud. Satya and I signed a deal on Azure. It's a very professional and good relationship with Satya and with Sundar, but it's a more personal relationship with Satya, no question about that. He came to my son's wedding, and I consider him a close friend. But when I have a problem, would I go to him? It depends on the problem. It's more about, "Hey, how can we do business together and solve things?" If it's a management issue, maybe I'd reach out to him. When you're at this level, you have to be very careful because you have business interests to protect—it cannot be perceived as two companies colluding to do anything, so we are incredibly, incredibly careful about that. But I do have a self-help group. There are four or five CEOs that I've talked about before. I have tremendous respect for them, people who have gone through similar experiences. John Donahoe, the CEO of Nike, is one. He was the CEO of eBay and PayPal and we were in YPO together. George Roberts at KKR is another who I have great respect for. I feel very fortunate to have their skills to call on. I also have some very deep, close friends. That's all one needs really. I'm not a connector.

When I ask Narayen about who he is close to, who his circle is, his reference point is his family. He has tremendous admiration for his parents and speaks to them every day. He compiled a book for his father that contains his dad's writings and spoke admiringly about his father's eloquence with words and masterful storytelling. He also relies on his wife Reni as a sounding board and trusts her counsel.

MA: Can you share some of your favorite books?

SN: We read a lot growing up. My favorites are P.G. Wodehouse and *Sherlock Holmes*. I also like *Atlas Shrugged*; it speaks to the power of the individual. John Galt. Francisco D'Anconia is one of my favorite characters. That the individual can accomplish whatever they want. What I took out of this was this fundamental belief that people are capable of doing a lot.

MA: Companies like Google and Apple have all tried to create worker-friendly environments for their employees. To what do you attribute your high rankings and did you model yourself after them?

SN: We were one of the first. If you go back to your founding principles that people are the critical factor, then you say that the environment in which people work is important.

MA: How do you identify creativity?

SN: We have a Photoshop floor where you can observe creativity in motion. People can customize it to be a place that they want to work in; that's such an important part of inspiration.

MA: Indians like yourself have risen to the top in Silicon Valley and the tech world, like Microsoft and Google. How had this "Indian genius" been allowed to prosper?

SN: I don't think one can do justice to the idea of Indian genius as it relates to Silicon Valley without appreciating the environment that enables it. The United States has been this incredible sandbox—the fact that we're all welcomed, and the color of our skin is not a criteria. I'm one of the first tech CEOs in software. It's been 17 years. When you fail in India, it's held against you. In Silicon Valley, if you fail, you look at it and say, what are you learning? If you're successful here, great, you gain experience, but here, if you fail, you also get experience. It's considered okay. It's how you create a culture where disrupting yourself is acceptable. Luck has a huge role in my success. People do their best work when they do something they are passionate about. I love building products and I like engineering. I always took initiative. If you do the right thing for the company when they need it, it pays off. Put the company first.

These were sentiments that any CEO of Exxon or Haliburton or a big multinational would approve of. It seemed a little out of place for Silicon Valley, but perhaps Silicon Valley has changed.

CHAPTER 7

Satya Nadella

Our industry does not respect tradition.
What it respects is innovation.

SATYA NADELLA

When the prime minister of India, Narasimha Rao, discovered that the children of two of his most senior ministers were getting married and had not invited him to the wedding, he decided to attend anyway. B.N. Yugandhar's son, Satya Nadella, was marrying the daughter of his principal secretary, K.R. Venugopal. Nadella's father had also served at secretary to the prime minister, a cabinet-level position. Usually, well-connected members of the elite consider it a status symbol to have the head of state show up at a family wedding. Nadella's family and his in-laws were different. Similarly inclined, they shunned the limelight. Despite their privileged status Nadella said that his father had Marxist leanings. Yugandhar was known among his peers for his dedication to reducing poverty. At the time of the wedding, he was a minister in the department of rural development. He worked on improving the lives of the poor and marginalized well into his retirement. He was brilliant and well read, and his house was always full of books.

Nadella was an average student, mostly obsessed with cricket when he was young. His father, who had excelled academically and "aced all his exams," worried about his son's lackluster academic achievements. Nadella adored his mother and unequivocally admits being his mother's son. She was a classics scholar and taught Sanskrit, literature, and Indian philosophy, but put no academic pressure on him. "She, my mother, cared deeply about my being happy, confident and living in the moment without regrets," Nadella recalled. His love for her came through whenever he mentioned her. He says she was the opposite of a tiger mom, and he appreciated that she just wanted him to be happy. "Unlike most of my peers at that time, whose high achieving parents applied tremendous pressure to achieve, I didn't face any of that."[28]

Growing up in a home surrounded by books, he attributed his intellectual curiosity to his father, whose disposition toward intellectual pursuits rubbed off on his son. As Nadella achieved success, he would drop literary references to Cicero, Nitze, and the *Mahabharata* in meetings, conversation, and in his writing.

Nadella's father had entered the Indian Administrative Service, one of the most coveted jobs in the country. Thousands apply but only 100 are selected each year. The family moved constantly, as civil servants like his father were posted to different districts during their career. His father's job required a great deal of travel, and it was Nadella's mother who provided stability and was the constant fixture in his life. When Nadella was six, his five-month-old sister died. The tragedy hit the family hard. His mother stopped working, and the loss and grief cast a shadow over them.

In 1982, the family had settled in Hyderabad, a sleepy town that used to be the center of Muslim power in the south before India gained independence in 1947. Mosques, minarets, and old bazaars were strewn across the city, and when Nadella was in school, the city bore little resemblance to today's bustling metropolis of 10 million people. It is now known as India's tech capital, with Google, Amazon, Microsoft, and Salesforce all headquartered there.

Nadella attended Hyderabad Public School; a boarding school that later became well known for its famous alumni. Ajay Banga, president of the World Bank and former CEO of Mastercard, and Shantanu Narayen of Adobe both went there, along with the sons of ministers, movie stars, and writers. The school had a diverse student body with a mixture of religions and regions represented. It would influence Nadella's inclusive hiring approach at Microsoft.

Nadella's first love at school was cricket, a game introduced by the British that was enthusiastically embraced by Indians as the national sport. His enthusiasm for the game remained even after he moved to America, where it was relatively unknown. It was a passion he shared with Shantanu Narayen, and the two alumni of HPS invested in setting up a cricket league in the United States in 2023.

In 1982, when Nadella turned 15, his father bought him a birthday present that changed his life forever: a computer. He was instantly hooked. It quickly became his second passion after cricket, and he decided that he had found his vocation in life. "When I first learned to write a few lines of BASIC code for the Z80 computer my dad bought for me, the lightbulb went off... I had discovered software. It was like lightning in a bottle."[29] Nadella's newfound love of computers did not boost his academic skills at this stage. His father had high expectations for his son and put pressure on him to leave the comforts of home and work harder on building his career. Nadella took the notoriously difficult IIT exam but failed to make it. Rejected by IIT, he was admitted to a second-tier engineering school in Manipal, but it was a step in the right direction and put him on the path that eventually led to his extraordinary success.

Nadella's friends at college were resourceful and entrepreneurial. Many ended up in California, where they reunited and briefly lived together again. Nadella was captivated by computers and technology in college and decided to continue his studies in electrical engineering in the United States, leaving for the University of Wisconsin–Milwaukee in 1988 to pursue a master's degree. He had no idea what Milwaukee was like, but at 21 he was ready for anything. In his memoir, he recalls the winters as bitterly cold and said he stopped smoking because he couldn't bear to step outside to do so and conform to the new smoking rules. He remembers many of the international students quit smoking due to the inclement weather except for the Russians, who were used to below-freezing temperatures. Cold weather never seemed to bother them.

Nadella was expanding his skills in Wisconsin, including graphic coloring, image processing, and coding. He was particularly fascinated by the theoretical aspects of computer science. It not only showed him the limitations in what today's computers were capable of, but allowed him to explore quantum computing, machine learning, and artificial intelligence.

His exposure and exploration of ideas would become the repositories of knowledge that he would draw on when making critical decisions that redirected the future of Microsoft, transforming it into the leading tech company. In 1990, Nadella left Milwaukee for his first job at Sun Microsystems in Silicon Valley. It had been co-founded by a fellow Indian immigrant, Vinod Khosla in 1982. Although Khosla had left a while back and was now a venture capitalist, his partners Scott McNealy and Bill Joy were still around, as well as the intrepid Eric Schmidt, who was vice president of software development before he left to join Google. Sun was going through a rocky phase when Nadella joined, and after two years there, it was no longer a fulfilling place for him to work. 1992 was a pivotal year for Nadella. He wanted to change his life and decided that one way to enhance his prospects was to go to business school. Nadella had been accepted to the business program at the University of Chicago when he was offered a position at Microsoft which was taking off. His decision to accept the job that year would prove to be the best decision he ever made for his career.

Bill Gates and Paul Allen had founded Microsoft 16 years earlier in 1976. Gates was 20 years old when he quit his studies at Harvard to start the company, an intense risk-taker and taskmaster who worked round the clock when he was engaged in a project and expected others to do so as well. He liked to call his group "hard core," people who breathed, ate, and slept their work. Gates was a demanding boss.[30] People who worked at Microsoft were used to getting emails from him at all hours, but in 2014 he stepped away from being chairman to devote his time to public health and philanthropy. By then, Microsoft was the world's leading software company and its revenues had grown to $86 billion. (Revenues had been $7.5 million in 1980.) Gates was listed by *Forbes* as the richest man in the world.

Gates, Allen, and Jobs had helped put a computer on every desk, and by making it user-friendly, accessible, and fun, they had democratized technology. But by the late nineties, Microsoft had gone from being a disrupter pushing frontiers to becoming the status quo. It had ceased to be a leader in technological innovation and had fallen into the rut of the innovator's dilemma.[31]

Nadella had found his passion by the time he joined Microsoft and was fully focused on becoming the best he could be. He decided to accept the offer from the University of Chicago to study business and began commuting between Redmond,

Chicago, and his other business trips. He had to move his studies to the part-time program to accommodate work, finishing his MBA in two years. He credits his interactions with some of the renowned professors at the school as having a long-lasting impact on his thinking. Nadella may have felt he was his mother's son, but he was now fulfilling his father's aspirations for him.

In 1992, Nadella proposed to his childhood sweetheart during a visit to India. Two months later they were married in Delhi in the presence of the prime minister, who, determined to give the couple his blessings, famously gatecrashed the wedding. Nadella and Anu were childhood friends, their social circles overlapped, and their families were close. Anu was an architecture student and they planned for her to move to Washington state as soon as she graduated, but complex United States immigration rules put a spanner in the works. Nadella had a coveted green card, but it created problems for her visa application, which was ultimately rejected. Nadella would end up renouncing his green card and moving to an H-1B visa, which allowed highly skilled workers to bring their spouses with them while they were contracted to work in the United States. In his book *Hit Refresh*, Nadella recounts the story and how immigration laws hurt the United States when they become obstacles to talented people remaining in the country. He cites the example of another Indian Microsoft employee who quit when his H-1B visa expired rather than remain in the country illegally as his green card had not yet arrived. He ended up returning to India and starting Snapdeal, which is worth over $1 billion—a loss of talent for the United States.

Nadella swiftly climbed up the ranks after he joined Microsoft in 1992. He experienced the innovator's dilemma firsthand when he began to work with a new advanced technology group within Microsoft as a product manager for a video-on-demand service, but as the internet developed, the product became obsolete. He went on to work on an emerging business within Microsoft called Dynamics, run by Douglas Burgum. When Burgum left to start his own business (he would later be elected governor of North Dakota), Nadella took his place. It was the first time he had been given the responsibility of managing a business from start to finish.

Gates had decided to leave in 2000 to spend time on his foundation and other interests, just as the market was changing. Microsoft had missed the handheld mobile ecosystem. Smartphones and tablets were the newest innovation, and their sales were skyrocketing while personal computers were stagnant. A sluggish PC market did not bode well for Microsoft's profit margins as PCs are a lucrative revenue stream—Microsoft makes money on every PC that is loaded with its software.

Steve Ballmer, who took over from Gates in 2000 as CEO, was trying to steady the ship, but several people had left the company when Gates departed. Ballmer was falling behind the curve on the tech front, so he recruited Nadella to become head of engineering for what would become Bing, Microsoft's search engine. He hoped to challenge Google, but Google had the first mover advantage on search engines and its revenues were over $100 billion. Nadella was in a new area and wrote, "I was entering a new world, and the move proved to be fortuitous. Little did I know it would be my proving ground for future leadership and the future of the company."[32] But by 2008, things were not going well at the company.

The 2008 recession hit Microsoft hard, and the stock price began to slide. Google with its search engine and Amazon with the launch of its web services looked energetic by comparison, while Microsoft was increasingly looking like the sick man in tech. Morale within the company was at an all-time low. "Our annual employee poll revealed that most employees didn't think we were headed in the right direction and questioned our ability to innovate... Employees were tired. They were frustrated. They were fed up with losing and falling behind despite their grand plans and great ideas. They came to Microsoft with big dreams, but it felt like all they really did was deal with upper management, execute taxing processes and bicker in meetings."[33]

Nadella was given additional responsibilities for Bing, a search engine that Microsoft launched in 2009. He hired Dr. Qi Lu from Yahoo. Yahoo had made a deal with Microsoft to make Bing its default search engine, and together they captured a quarter of the search market—although in 2024 Bing held just 9.19 percent to Google's dominant share of 83.49 percent.

According to some sources, Jeff Bezos tried to hire Nadella away from Microsoft. Amazon was the up-and-coming company at the time and was one of the first to invest in the cloud. Doug Burgum said it was his job to convince Nadella to stay. Nadella was promoted with a mandate to take the company's investments in its new technologies to the next level. In typical Microsoft fashion, he was told by Ballmer that if he failed there was no parachute that could save him, and it could well be his last job at the company. Nadella has an ego and is driven to prove himself, and the challenge was one that he relished. His approach impressed Gates and Ballmer enough to convince them that he had the leadership qualities as its next CEO.

Nadella understood right away that Microsoft needed to focus on the cloud. It was Nadella's big insight and one that would turn Microsoft around. "The emergence of cloud services fundamentally shifted the economics of computing. It standardized and pooled computing resources and automated maintenance tasks once done manually... Cloud providers invested in enormous data centers around the world and then rented them out at a lower cost per user. This was the Cloud Revolution."[34]

Nadella was determined to catch up with Amazon, who was already ahead. By 2010, Nadella was asked to lead STB, Microsoft's precursor to its cloud and enterprise business. Not everyone at Microsoft was as intrigued by the potential of the cloud as Ballmer and Nadella. People were still locked into Microsoft being a server-driven company. Nadella would become the driving force behind convincing people that the cloud was the future and putting Microsoft on course to becoming a leader in providing cloud services. By 2021 almost 70 percent of organizations use Microsoft Azure for their cloud services worldwide.[35]

In 2014, Ballmer left the company and Nadella was appointed as CEO. There had been a great deal of speculation about who Ballmer's successor would be. The names of Tony Bates of Skype and Stephen Elop of Nokia were bandied about. Ballmer had just concluded a $7.2 billion deal with Nokia, so it was not surprising that his name was in the mix.

Nadella, like Sundar Pichai of Google and Shantanu Narayen, the first Indian American to become CEO of a major Fortune 500 company in 2006, was one of the company men in the tradition of the old school, where people rose through the ranks and spent the better part of their careers in the same company. Except for a brief stint at Sun, Nadella has worked at Microsoft for most of his career and will be completing 32 years there in 2024. Gates and Allen started Microsoft in 1976 and Ballmer took over the helm for just four years before Nadella stepped in, becoming the third CEO in its 38-year history. He recently celebrated his first decade as CEO of Microsoft.

Nadella had grown up in the culture of Microsoft and understood it well by the time he took over. Meetings at Microsoft were often contentious affairs. Gates was an intimidating boss whose management style was top-down.[36] The atmosphere was far from collegial, and Nadella knew that Microsoft would continue to hemorrhage its best talent if morale remained low. Right from the start, he let it be known that his approach to management was going to be different. Nadella believes that a leader needs to bring out the best in people.

Nadella learned a lot from cricket and applied those lessons to the way he conducted himself. He likes to come up with rules of three. His first principle is to compete with passion and to respect your opponent but not be intimidated by them. Putting the team before oneself and one's own desire for recognition is crucial. Otherwise, he feels you destroy the team. Knowing when to lead and building people's confidence was another. In his book *The Future Leader*, Jacob Morgan describes how Nadella put these beliefs into practice. "Satya begins his weekly senior leadership team meetings with a segment he calls 'Researcher of the Amazing' that showcases employee success from around the world. On many occasions, employee teams join the meeting via video to demonstrate their developments and inspire the leadership team. Instead of putting himself first, Satya steps aside to share his employees' successes as a way to inspire the rest of the company before they jump into hard numbers."[37] Nadella was determined to shift the culture of the firm where people were siloed in their own expertise, ultra-competitive, and would argue rather than support each other. He cites several instances in his book which allude to the pernicious atmosphere in the company. Nadella was on a mission to reclaim the soul of the company. He was in receive mode, and wanted to not just hear but listen to the feedback he was getting. Shifting the atmosphere away from personal ego-driven competitiveness to teamwork, communication, and recognition of the talents of various employees changed the toxicity that had seeped into the system. Nadella's efforts seem to have paid off. Morgan found Nadella consistently had approval ratings of 98 percent.

Teamwork and cooperation were core principles that Nadella insisted on and extended to include external business practices. A company recognized as a corporate bully now went out of its way to accommodate its customers and made Microsoft applications available for competing platforms like Google's Android operating system and Apple's iOS. He wanted Microsoft to become universal, and that meant cooperation—when a customer bought an iPhone, it would come preloaded with Microsoft apps.

Another one of Nadella's three principles had to do with leadership. He believes you need to bring clarity to concepts you are trying to communicate. That requires developing the ability to synthesize a great deal of information. The second mark of good leadership is the ability to energize team members—not just your own, but across the company—with a shared sense of optimism and, finally, driving innovations that resonate with the people you are trying to service.

Nadella, Pichai of Google, and Narayen of Adobe all receive high marks for their management style, which has been called "gentle management." The performance of all three companies surged under the Indian American CEOs and employees were responding positively.

We are all products of our experiences. Nadella, for all the success and wealth he had accumulated along the way, had suffered through personal tragedy that would shape and impact him as a human being.

In 1996, Zain, their first child, a son, suffered from asphyxia in utero and was born with cerebral palsy, had spastic quadriplegia, and was legally blind. He weighed just three pounds at birth and would be dependent on a wheelchair for most of his 25 years. Nadella credits his son with teaching him to value diversity and people with special needs. His empathy deepened as he juggled taking his son to medical appointments and his ever-growing responsibilities at Microsoft. He was awed by the technology, including computers and Microsoft software, that was employed by the various medical devices that helped his son. This observation hovered in his subconscious as he strove to get the product perfect as they advanced their systems. Nadella's son died when he was 26 years old in March 2022. He and his wife Anupama, have a daughter, Tara, who also had mild learning disabilities and attended a special education school in Vancouver, Canada until one opened in Washington state with their help. Anyone who has had to encounter any serious medical treatments for themselves or a loved one is aware of the teamwork required to restore a patient to health. Nadella applied his observations, along with the empathy he encountered, to the way he approached management.

In 2014, he made a rare misstep when attending a conference for women in tech. Addressing the issue of gender pay disparities, Nadella suggested that women should not ask for a raise but trust in the system and in karma. Given that the system had treated women unfairly for generations, it reeked of a chauvinistic mindset. The response was swift and critical. He had displayed the opposite of empathy. He quickly apologized and reversed himself, but the damage was done, and it would take some time to reset his reputation. Microsoft at the time had a 71-29 percent split between men and women in the workplace. It was widely acknowledged that the bro-culture dominated tech and Silicon Valley in particular.

Nadella immediately tried to control the damage and apologized to his staff. His efforts seem to have mitigated his faux pas and regained people's respect because, in 2019, *Financial Times* named him person of the year and *Fortune* named him businessperson of the year. He was regularly invited to state dinners at the White House and Microsoft has seen stunning growth under his leadership.

When he took over as CEO in 2014, *Bloomberg* magazine said Microsoft was at risk of technological irrelevance. Although its market cap was $300 million and revenues were respectable at $86.8 billion, Nadella managed to turn the company around, outperforming everyone's projected expectations. In 2023, its revenues rose to $211.91 billion and in 2024, for the first time, Microsoft's market cap surpassed a trillion dollars, making it the world's most valuable company. In February of the same year, its share price went to a high of $420, outperforming its rivals including Apple, who reported lackluster third quarter earnings. For a company that was not a member of the exclusive FAANG grouping—Facebook (Meta), Amazon, Apple, Netflix, and Google (Alphabet)—he not only outdid them, but he has made Microsoft the most valuable company on the planet. In the process, he has become the most powerful CEO today.

What sets Nadella apart from his predecessor and other CEOs is that he has two invaluable qualities. In addition to being a good manager, he has vision. By this I mean he has the gift of being able to look around the corner and recognize what the next big thing is. The PC market contracted from 341 million in 2021 to 241 million in 2023. [38] The smartphone market has also steadily declined since 2022. Nadella decided to make games that were exclusive to Microsoft's Xbox available across all platforms, including rivals like PlayStation and Nintendo. He said, "We believe we can play a leading role in democratizing gaming and defining that future of interactive entertainment."[39] Was Nadella trying to be inclusive and make things easier for the customer? Or was he trying to expand and save his gaming business in an increasingly competitive space? Competition generally benefits the consumer, so overall this was a good thing.

Nadella's most important insight that would become a critical component of Microsoft's success was to quickly focus on the importance of cloud computing, which now contributes close to half the company's revenue. Today, 70 percent of organizations use Microsoft's Azure for their cloud services worldwide. Four out of five Fortune 500 companies use Microsoft Office 365, and they control half of the office productivity software market.

Brad Smith, Microsoft's president, credits Nadella with understanding the cloud better than anyone. He was always cognizant that the information stored in their data centers did not belong to them but to their clients, and that transparency, privacy, security, and compliance were of utmost importance if they were to be trusted. This sometimes put them in a complicated position when it was the government who requested the data. He also admired his management skills, both as a problem solver and when it came to dealing with the government. He attributes this to the lessons Nadella absorbed growing up as the son of a senior civil servant in India. He felt his exposure gave him an intuitive feel for how governments worked. This would come in useful when Microsoft was hit with anti-trust suits.[40]

Nadella believes that artificial intelligence is the next big innovation with Big Data, massive computing power, and increasingly sophisticated algorithms accelerating AI from science fiction to reality. Data is power, and whoever controls the most data will be the most powerful player tomorrow especially with the rise of AI. Data is being collected at exponential rates and is an essential ingredient for AI to learn from. Data centers, which require massive amounts of power, are looking at locations outside urban areas to be able to cope with the space and power they need, particularly as the chips for AI become more common. At the end of March 2024, the tech world was rocked by yet another bold announcement—Microsoft and OpenAI were planning an ambitious $100 billion data center project. It dwarfs anything that other companies are doing.

Stephanie Palazzolo who reports on AI wrote "I never thought I'd say this about a nearly 50-year-old company, but Microsoft is turning out to be a trendsetter."[41] It is Microsoft's AI products that are defining the direction that industry players like Google, Amazon and Meta are incorporating. Microsoft is also finding innovative ways in which to expand that avoid running afoul of government regulations that others are watching with interest .

Many companies in the tech sector recognize the potential of AI and have been working on it for years. Google's Deep Mind is a division that has been dedicated to its development for some time, so how did Nadella and Microsoft upstage Pichai and Google's years of investment in the development of AI?

Microsoft has noted that the percentage of growth that is generated from the demand for "AI services" in its own company has steadily increased and views this as one of its biggest growth areas for the future. The competition for the best AI engineers has become fierce. Meta has poached people from Google and in March 2024 which turned out to be a big month for bold moves by Microsoft, Nadella hired Mustafa Suleyman who helped co-found DeepMind with Demis Hassabis and Shane Legg and was acquired by Google in 2014. In a coup for Google, Hassabis was awarded the Nobel Prize in 2024. Suleyman left Google in 2022 and started his own company called Inflection but moved to Microsoft en masse with 70 of Inflection's employees. He will not only add a great geal of depth to Microsoft's AI base but in what must feel like a stab to Google, as a key creator of DeepMind he can transfer all Google's AI advantage over to Microsoft.

That brings us to Nadella's management skills-his other gift, which is the ability to execute effectively and make the right decisions. Google may have invested far more in developing its AI capability and for far longer, but Nadella decided that Microsoft needed to integrate artificial intelligence into its structure and made a massive investment in OpenAI—a company started by Elon Musk, Sam Altman, Ilya Sutskever, and nine others in a San Francisco lab ostensibly to benefit humankind. It was an unusual structure as it was established as a nonprofit and a board was selected to make sure it adhered to that principle. The larger-than-life personalities had conflicts from the start, and Musk departed in 2018. Altman created a for-profit subsidiary and raised some initial funding from Microsoft, but some members of the board were unhappy with the departure from the nonprofit ideas and left.

In early 2023, it became apparent that they had a successful product with ChatGPT, and Nadella made the decision to throw his lot in with them and invested $13 billion in OpenAI. It was a rather novel arrangement where they did not give outside investors a board seat. Vinod Khosla was another initial seed investor who put in $50 million without a board seat. Microsoft began to integrate OpenAI technology in its offerings; they resell OpenAI's large language models and retain much of the revenue for themselves. In keeping with Nadella's philosophy of accessibility, he also likes to promote Microsoft's small language models as a more affordable option for price-sensitive customers.[42] Google, having been upstaged, began to consider how they could bring their AI capabilities to the forefront of the competition. A turbulent few months followed, making headlines across the tech community, with Geoffrey Hinton, the father of artificial intelligence who worked at Google and several other companies, warning against the technology being released to the public as downright dangerous and irresponsible. He quit Google so he could speak out. He was awarded the Nobel Prize in Physics in 2024.

In the middle of the controversy, Altman was abruptly fired by his board without giving him or the investors any warning or any say in the matter. Nadella immediately made the decision to stabilize things by offering Altman and any other employees who wanted to leave a place at Microsoft. With head-spinning speed, heads rolled, and with Microsoft and Nadella backing him, Altman was reinstated at OpenAI. For the time being, it seems as though things have stabilized. Microsoft came across as the big player with Nadella as a decisive leader who had the courage to make bold decisions, rescuing what could have become a disaster for Microsoft's investment in OpenAI. Microsoft joined the board as a non-voting member, but at least from now on they would not be taken by surprise. Calls to regulate AI continue, and Elon Musk, one of the original founders of Open AI who left in 2018 has threatened to sue them for breach of their original mission.

Microsoft has exclusive rights to sell OpenAI's software and provide its computing power. For now, this is mutually beneficial, but Altman is ambitious and has been busy raising trillions of dollars internationally to ostensibly develop and manufacture AI chips while also retaining his financial independence. Despite the fact that Nadella stepped in to save him and his company, Altman's ambitions and the agreement with Microsoft that constrains him may pose a challenge to the future of the relationship, especially if the two companies end up competing in the same area for the some of the same customers. Nadella has decided that AI is the future and is not just courting OpenAI. Microsoft has made deals with other AI developers as well as tried to invest in its own in-house capabilities.

So far, Microsoft has been outperforming Google in AI, its biggest rival in the field. Nadella challenged Pichai, the India-born CEO of Google, early in 2023, saying he was going to make Google dance.[43] When OpenAI shook the tech world in early 2023 with ChatGPT, a potential alternative way to search for information, it shook Google, and Pichai declared a code red. Google—for now—continues to dominate the search engine market. It recently introduced Gemini Ultra, an AI-powered answer to ChatGPT, in an attempt to maintain its market position, but it botched its launch in February 2024 and had to recall it, adding to Google's image of having lost its way. As AI gets more sophisticated and its application improves,

Google's search monopoly could well come under threat not just from Microsoft and OpenAI but other start-ups like Perplexity. Its search engine and Gmail were all creations of its original founders, Sergey Brin and Larry Paige, and it was to them that Pichai turned when it seemed that Google had fallen behind on AI. The founders had left the company in 2019 but returned to help find a path forward through the AI crisis. Pichai is genuinely liked by his employees, but he has not displayed the bold vision of Nadella that has made Microsoft the leader in tech. Pichai has not managed to make Google cloud-competitive and Waymo, its self-driving cars, that were supposed to be the wave of the future, was slow to take off, plagued with recalls and accidents early on. Recently there has been open speculation about his ability to lead Google.

Is Nadella right to view Pichai and Google as his primary competition? Microsoft is far ahead in its cloud business and, for now, its main competitor in that area is Amazon. Microsoft has gone on to become the world's number one company while Alphabet (Google) continues to disappoint, overtaken by Invidia in 2024. Eric Schmidt, an ex-CEO of Google, believes that "both Sundar and Satya are extremely smart and also very detail oriented. They are personally very kind to everyone. This is the best of India in my opinion. Google is the inventor of much of the AI technology, and Satya did a very clever deal with OpenAI to buy the technology. My view is that the competition is great for everyone."

CHAPTER 8

Nikesh Arora

*Being a genius is not just about having one big idea. I think there is a whole
lesson to be learned from Indians who have been successful by their tremendous
ability to adapt and be prepared. Culturally, growing up in India, we always
had to make do with less and try to make the most of it. Some call it jugaad.
There are so many people chasing the same dream—if you are not relentless
and disciplined, you are not going to get anywhere. There are so many things
that are culturally ingrained in us in India, that it sets us up much better in this
environment [the United States] to succeed.*

NIKESH ARORA

Nikesh Arora made headlines in 2023 when his compensation as the CEO of Palo
Alto Networks catapulted him into the billionaire club. It was unusual for a non-
founder to achieve that level of wealth, but Arora had gained a reputation for
his ability to negotiate lucrative employment contracts for himself. In 2018, he
received $128 million in stocks and options when he joined Palo Alto Networks,
a global cyber security company specializing in advanced firewalls and cloud-
based offerings to protect enterprises from cyber threats. In 2023, he exercised
some of his stock options and sold $300 million in shares, while also receiving up
to $750,000 in stock awards subject to performance, bringing his overall wealth
close to $1.5 billion.[44]

When he was being interviewed for the position of CEO of Palo Alto in 2018,
the board initially balked at his price tag. "The board felt they could not afford
me," Arora recalled, "but I offered to structure a pay package where I would make
money only if I doubled or tripled the value of the company. They agreed and we
wrote a deal." Arora not only met all the targets, but under his leadership, Palo Alto

Networks has effectively pushed out several competitors, acquiring 19 companies, and significantly made its mark with its strategy of offering comprehensive security. The share price went from $66 when he joined the company to $371 in February 2024. His personal stake was estimated at the time to be worth $830 million.

Eric Schmidt, the former CEO of Google and a legendary figure in tech, said that Arora was the finest analytical businessman that he had ever worked with. "Nikesh ran businesses not like a VP of sales but like an investor, where he measured productivity and generated billions of profits where no one else could find them," Schmidt said. As CEO, Arora is determined to make Palo Alto the undisputed leader in cyber security.

An ethnic Punjabi, Arora grew up in a modest, middle-class Indian family. His father, whom he admired, worked for the military and the family moved constantly. Arora puts a great deal of emphasis on integrity—a quality he felt defined his father.

NA: My father was a lawyer in the Indian Air Force. They switched him back and forth between the finance and legal department. His last job was serving as the Judge Advocate General. They could not promote him any further as that was the highest he could go. He was handing down decisions and commensurate punishments as a judge. Arguing the cases was done by other officers who were the prosecutors or defending lawyers. We had a lot of people in and out of our house. He made some unpopular decisions that invoked the ire of his superiors and was summarily removed from Delhi overnight and sent to Shillong, a remote assignment, as a punishment. He stuck to his principles and paid the price, but growing up, it was ingrained in us that integrity matters.

I was a normal kid, but I was diligent and conscientious, so my parents never had to push me to do my homework or study harder. I wasn't a nerd who studied all the time, but I got my work done. Later, I discovered that I might be smarter than some of my friends when we sat for the National Talent Search exam. It is an all-India award based on aptitude, given to 200 finalists. The award pays your tuition for the rest of your academic career in India. A couple of my friends were taking the exam, so I decided to take it. You are given a free bus pass and a stipend and spend the summer preparing for the exam. I'm the only person who made it among my friends. The scholarship paid all my fees. I was able to change schools and attend the Air Force School, which was better than where I was. Then I took the IIT exam. I managed to get my preferred major, electrical engineering—but it was in the Benares IIT, not Delhi. I probably graduated among the top 10 percent of my class, but I was never driven to be the topper.

One of my goals is to encourage education in India and alleviate deserving students from financial impediments so they can follow their dreams. To be able to attend an IIT is a gamechanger. I donated $2 million to IIT BHU, my alma mater, to be able to provide free education for future students. It was by far the largest donation they had ever received. I called on other alumni to join the effort. The fund has now grown to just under $3 million.

Arora was interested in more than just academics. When he was 17, he began directing plays in school and took teams to different colleges to compete. He participated in public speaking and at IIT, he ran the college festival.

MA: The Indian educational system is not known to foster creativity. You went to the prestigious Indian Institute of Technology. Did it produce creative thinkers or outstanding engineers who were the cogs in the machine?

NA: I would push back on that. Don't short the Indians who are outstanding executors and have gone on to build the dreams of other people into big, successful businesses. Executors can also have a dream—you can be a creative thinker, but if you can't deliver the dream, it doesn't matter what your dream is. What's the difference between two great founders where one gets it done and the other can't get it done? Very often you will find that a bunch of Indians are the ones who get it done, so maybe that is the Indian genius. The ability to deliver. Let's take the example of Satya Nadella of Microsoft. He didn't have a big idea. He looked at everything he had in front of him and said, "Okay, here's the best I can do with this." He saw where things were going 10 years from now. He saw the cloud was going to be transformational and had Microsoft invest heavily in the cloud, and now it's a leader. Steve Ballmer, who led Microsoft after Bill Gates, was there for 20 years and couldn't turn the company around because he lacked the vision to see 15 years ahead. Elon Musk is a different type of genius because he can see 50 years ahead; he has the ideas and is able to get it done.

MA: India has not produced an Elon Musk. That sort of creative genius is not what the Indian system produces.

NA: Elon wants to put people on Mars and make autonomous cars. Is an Indian going to do that? Maybe not. But if an Indian was told to take that car and make sure people can drive it without anybody touching it except for the computer, they could, given enough time. We are taught how to get stuff done. Indians don't get credit in India for thinking great thoughts. They get credit for getting things done. There is nothing in our educational system that says, "Think great thoughts and good stuff will come." They don't teach philosophy in engineering school.

Our society is conditioned to minimize risk. From the day we are born, we are taught to avoid risk. Our parents tell us not to walk on the street. To look right and left—do this, don't do that. It is all risk management because your parents are trying to avoid adverse outcomes. Shantanu, Sundar, and Satya, we all landed in America with no money. We didn't have the luxury to sit around and think big thoughts. We all had lofty ideals, but the environment pushes you to maximize your opportunities.

MA: What about the younger generation? Are the Indians coming to Silicon Valley now any different?

NA: Things have changed in India now. There are more opportunities. There are close to 100 unicorns there. That did not exist 15 years ago. It's hard to fathom, but 30 years ago there was no internet, you had no access to information, cell phones and personal computers were rare. Now we have perfect information. It's revolutionized everything. This explosion of information and growth is a global phenomenon. The world is a different place. Information is power and the right to information has been a great equalizer. In the old days, if I wanted to learn about Apple or Steve Jobs, I had to go to a library and look for a book. Today, information is easily available on the internet. I can learn about any company or CEO and study how they took risks. I had no role models of entrepreneurs growing up. There was Ambani, but it was a family enterprise like a lot of businesses in India. Family-owned businesses dominate the corporate world in India and pose a barrier to personal ambition. The most disruptive thing you could do was break the mold and try to change your economic prospects by going west. You had the potential to improve your economic outcome by one hundred times. My first job paid me $26,000. Two years later it jumped to $45,000. That was a 20 times improvement in two years. I have no family legacy that I have to protect and nobody that I owe. This is my house; every dollar of this house is mine. I have taken care of my parents, my sisters, my family. I can and have walked out of lucrative jobs. It's liberating.

We were sitting in Arora's sprawling mansion, an artistic combination of glass and concrete nestled in lush landscaping with luxurious views of the Santa Clara hillsides. It looked like it belonged in *Architectural Digest*. The house was tastefully decorated with contemporary Indian paintings, expensive modern Italian furniture, and beautiful rugs. A large TV dominated the study where Arora likes to work. His large desk was neat and uncluttered, and the enormous seating area next to it, where we were sitting during this interview, was decorated in soft tones of grey and stone.

Arora is tall and was stylishly casual in his choice of clothes. *Fortune* magazine ran a profile of him and dubbed him the "Elvis of India." He married a Delhi entrepreneur and socialite, Ayesha Thapar, in 2014. It was a second marriage for both. The wedding, which took place over several days in Italy, was a lavish affair attended by several tech luminaries including Larry Paige, Sundar Pichai, Eric Schmidt, and Barry Diller. A sprinkling of Hollywood actors like Ashton Kutcher and Mila Kunis added a touch of glamour to the event.

Ayesha, stunningly beautiful, lived up to her online pictures. She dropped by to say hello and later took me for a tour of the house. The casual clutter of children's toys and books added a welcome dose of warmth to the architectural showpiece.

Arora has a reputation in the tech community as a brilliant businessman, but a tough negotiator with a big ego. Jim Goetz, a former partner at Sequoia Capital and a board member of Palo Alto Networks had been involved in the decision to hire Arora as CEO, met with several of Arora's former colleagues before hiring him at Palo Alto. He agreed that not everyone had been a fan. Arora had been both feared and loved at Google, but he pointed out that what impressed him was that even Arora's critics respected his abilities and there were far more people that had followed Arora. "Arora has incredible followship. Several of his former colleagues from Google followed him to Palo Alto. It's extraordinary. They all had lots of alternatives and attractive options. I think loyalty is one of his traits and the magnetism runs in both directions. He has built up an incredible team at Palo Alto."

During our conversation, Arora occasionally revealed a degree of arrogance when he described his recruitment to various jobs during his career, but he had a great deal to be proud of. He speaks quickly in a low voice but is thoughtful when asked questions. AI and cyber security are the new frontiers in tech, and I was excited to find an Indian American who was a leader in the area. I had been following Palo Alto's rise for a couple of years, as news of hacker activity began to affect people's lives when a bank or Walmart was compromised. More worrying was the potential to take war to a new paradigm. I was also struck by Arora's capacity for risk—his willingness to quit jobs and try something new. In each case he seemed to land on his feet. His path to wealth showed a particular tenacity and genius in negotiating increasingly lucrative employment contracts.

I have tried to capture his path to the billionaire's club by following his unusual career.

MA: Did your parents encourage you to move to the United States to study?

NA: My parents relied on me to tell them what direction I planned to take. I got to Boston with the help of my dad. When I was accepted at Northeastern for graduate school, I needed $10,000. I borrowed money from my dad. He could only manage $3,000, but I told him I'd figure out the rest. I was idealistic or foolhardy, perhaps, and returned to India after a year. In 1991 I got married and returned to Boston with my first wife. I moved out of the apartment I was sharing with five guys with one bathroom between us. I had a scholarship my second year, but the money was enough for a single person, not the two of us, so I got a job teaching night school at Northeastern's Burlington campus. There was no easy way to get from Brighton to Burlington. I had to take a combination of bus and train and walk the last one and a half mile. It was a winter job that lasted from December to March, and I had to trudge through snow with an inadequate coat. At that point it felt like hell, but now it feels like a character-building event in my life.

In 1992, Arora joined Fidelity Investments after graduating from Northeastern with a degree in business administration. He wasn't satisfied with one graduate degree. He attended night school and received an MS from Boston College while he was rising through the ranks at Fidelity. He became vice president of finance and took the Certified Financial Analyst exam, the largest exam in the world. It is a notoriously difficult three-part exam that is considered a career enhancing qualification for executives in finance. Not everyone passes or manages to take all three parts, but Arora did, and got a part-time job teaching it. It would lead to his next job.

NA: I was teaching a CFA class and one of the students was a fund manager at Putnam. When he discovered I did not teach for a living, and this was a side job, he questioned what qualified me to teach him. I told him that I had taken the CFA and completed it and since he was trying to take it, I was there to show him how. He decided I should be interviewed by Putnam. I joined Putnam as a regional analyst and shot to number one for two years by beating everybody else. You were judged by a relative index. I had to beat the telecom index, but I also had to outdo everyone else's performance. I'd never been an analyst before 1997, and it wasn't a good fit for me. I was bored sitting in a room analyzing numbers and trying to predict people's psychology. I quit shortly after two years, packed my two suitcases, and decamped to Germany to work with Deutche Telekom. I had no idea what I was going to do, but the CEO offered me a reasonable contract for $1,000,000. I doubled it. My daughter was two months old. I then decided to join a start-up and moved to London.

MA: Google was the longest that you have spent at a company. You were there for 10 years. When you left, you were the fourth most senior executive there and one of the highest paid. Was it a positive experience?

NA: I joined Google in December 2004. I was working in London where I was the chief brand officer in marketing for Deutsche Telekom, commuting between London and Germany every week. I was 34 years old, and I was trying to decide my next career move. I was looking at start-ups when a friend told me that a new company in the United States called Google was looking to head their operations in Europe. I was interviewed by Omid Khordestani who suggested I meet the five people in London who would work for me. I explained that I preferred to first meet the people I would be working for. Coincidentally, Larry Paige and Sergey Brin stopped in London on their way to Spain two weeks later, and they interviewed me at the British Museum. Then I met the people in London and flew to California to meet with Eric Schmidt. This process extended over a few months, and I decided to join Google on December 14. At first, the people there felt I was not "Googly" enough. I was a business guy. They didn't think I would fit their culture. When I joined Google, they were 450 people in London earning $800 million in revenue and Europe was a quarter of Google's business. When I walked in, I said, "Okay, show me your plans." They didn't have one. They were used to following California's lead. I told them that if you are going to run Germany or Australia, they had to have a plan about what we needed to deliver and how many people we needed. We spent quite a bit of effort putting systems and plans into place and understanding the levers that drove the business. I went to California and told Larry and Serge that we could grow to $4 billion in five years and showed them a plan. I wanted to hire 3,000 people and I was told, "Good luck getting to $4 billion," but hiring 3,000 additional people was too ambitious. I learned that it was because Larry Paige approved every hire and looked at each person to see if they were a fit for the company's culture and reviewed every package. It was tremendous quality control. I was told that because of this, I would not be able to hire fast enough as the people had to pass through Larry's filters. I manage to work out a system and we hired over 3,000 people.

MA: How did you do it?

NA: I told them I was going to send them the employment packages and we could keep track of who was hired and who was rejected. The HR teams in California kept track of the rejections and acceptances for six months to see how close we came to what Larry wanted in a hire. They were looking for a 95 percent correlation. Eventually Larry told us we had earned the right mathematically to hire, but he reserved the right to fire anyone if he decided they were not right. I agreed and he never stopped us for five years. By 2009, Europe represented 47 percent of Google's revenues at $5 billion. We had doubled our share. When I arrived at Google, overall revenues were at $18 billion. When I left in 2014, it had shot to $63 billion. Now it is $200 billion. Larry was obsessed with product and his view was that in Silicon Valley, companies die if their products fail over time. We fixed all the products. It's a lesson I have carried with me throughout my life. The first thing I always try to do is fix the products. Larry used to give us a talk every quarter about "products are the company." I would joke that if you followed the Google principle of the four "P's," product is all that matters. Pricing doesn't matter, positioning doesn't matter, promotion doesn't matter. I learned a lot at Google. It was a phenomenal place to work and I'm still friends with everyone there.

Arora was the chief business officer at Google when Masayoshi Son (Masa) recruited him to be his successor at SoftBank and brought him on as vice chairman. Arora, who was 47, negotiated an unprecedented $123 million as his compensation. For Japan, it was a record for a new executive. As a show of loyalty and commitment to the company, Arora bought a substantial number of shares worth close to $500 million. In the middle of 2015, nine months after he started at SoftBank, Son handed over the title of president to Arora, who also held the position of chief operating officer. Arora felt close to Son, and initially they had all their meals together and played golf together. He was fully invested in the relationship.

Being a foreigner in Japan was challenging, as gaining people's trust and confidence was a high bar. The share purchase was a grand gesture that Arora could barely afford at the time, despite the wealth he had accumulated at Google. Things started to go wrong when Son decided that he wasn't ready to retire. Arora had crossed oceans and moved countries based on Son's promise to make him his successor. Arora was not prepared to wait another 10 years to run the company. He sold his stock in the company and in 2016 decided to move on. In retrospect, he had been wise to drive a hard bargain on his compensation package. By the time he left, some estimate he was $200 million richer.

Arora was now a wealthy man. In addition to the $123 million he had been paid, in 2012, he had earned the title of highest paid executive at Google after the two founders and Eric Schmidt. His compensation was valued at $51 million, and he had received stocks worth $200 million before he left. Although he refused to speculate, I wondered whether he might have been running Google instead of Sundar Pichai had he not left for SoftBank.

MA: There was a two-year gap between when you left SoftBank and when you became CEO of Palo Alto Networks. Did it take that long to find the next job?

NA: I spent a few months winding down my SoftBank life. I took some time off to travel with my family and was looking at investment opportunities. I met with 50 founders to see if I wanted to invest with them or work with them and then I was approached by Palo Alto.

Arora is a risk-taker. He has guts and has walked away from secure and highly paid jobs without looking back. Each time, he landed on his feet and climbed the management ladder to reach the next level. Now he had made it to that rarified space at the top of the pyramid where top jobs become scarce. As the number four at Google and Masayoshi Son's presumptive heir, his next executive position—if he was to continue his upward climb—was to head a company.

According to Arora, at the time the Palo Alto position came up, he knew nothing about cyber security. He said that Israeli prime minister Benjamin Netanyahu was the first person that had spoken to him at length about cyber security at the World Economic Forum conference in Davos, when he was still at Google. Arora liked that Palo Alto Networks was a small, primarily public company and a category leader with the potential to grow. Its founder Nir Zuk, who was the technical brain behind the business, owns just 1 percent of the company. Zuk is the company's chief technical officer and lives in Israel, and Arora is the CEO, based in Silicon Valley. The two men seem to have worked out a compatible formula that allows them to work together.

Most cyber security firms had specialized in different areas, from firewalls to perimeter or cloud protection. They all had their own specialties. Arora pushed to build Palo Alto into a comprehensive cyber security company offering different services and becoming the market leader. Under him, the company embarked on an aggressive series of acquisitions. Of the 19 companies that Palo Alto has acquired, most of them driven by Arora, seven are Israeli. Arora and Zuk "cracked the formula of buying a startup at the right stage—when the product had already proven itself and there were sales. From the moment of purchase, Palo Alto puts the products into its well-oiled vending machine."[45] He has built out the company's capabilities around endpoint, cloud, and security management that have allowed the company to deliver superior products in five different security fields. His compensation last year was valued at $220 million—enormous by any standards, it was an acknowledgement by the board and Zuk of his contribution to the company. They have seen the value of Palo Alto increase by 300 percent under Arora's leadership and hoped to retain him, as they viewed him as critical to the company's future growth. It seemed to have worked. Arora signed up to stay through 2028.

MA: Why did Palo Alto hire you?

NA: You have to ask them, but I came to Palo Alto with no prior experience in security. They interviewed 17 people about me before hiring me. From my perspective it was because I had run large businesses and I'm a capable leader. But it's a highly innovative industry and given the structure of boards in the world and their appetite for risk, it was a big move for them. Boards get fired for making bad decisions.

Goetz, who was involved in hiring Arora said the board was very committed to recruiting him as CEO. "We thought it was going to take a high-end market package to attract him. The interest level from lots of other companies to retain Nikesh as an executive was high. He had an impressive track record at Google and SoftBank. We spoke to a number of individuals there including the founders who would include him in strategy sessions because Nikesh was often the person with the most important questions that a group of engineers and product people may not have raised. His references were astonishing, and it was clear that his best work was still ahead of him."

MA: Is Palo Alto a big enough platform for you?

NA: Everyone's becoming more technical. To be big, you have to be the market leader in your space, and in cyber security, Palo Alto is. I'm always trying to figure out the next big thing. I'm not trying to work out how to get to Mars—that's too much of a leap for me—but I am trying to stay ahead. Google went from being on the web to becoming the web. You have to be a market leader in your space. Palo Alto is.

MA: Do you attribute your success there to being the businessperson rather than part of the technical side?

NA: You need people who can execute. Most tech companies in Silicon Valley have died. Yahoo got the internet but missed mobility. Google transitioned from the internet to mobility. So did Facebook. They have WhatsApp and Instagram. You can afford to miss the one next big thing in technology, but if you miss two, you're done. You're obsolete. Half the companies that started in Silicon Valley are dead because they missed the internet. Google is a large platform, and the company does multiple things. It is huge in the way that Amazon is huge. They are expanding into everything from health care to space. I walked away from Google and was fine, but you are only lucky once. After that you have to have what it takes.

MA: How do you stay ahead of your competitors?

NA: Focusing on the competition is a bad thing. I try to focus on the problem I'm trying to solve. It doesn't mean you should not be cognizant about who's running against you and how fast they are running. If you spend your life trying to outdo them, you always run the risk of a disrupter overtaking you from left field who was not in your rearview mirror and has come up with a whole new way of doing things. By focusing on a competitor, you've taken your eye off the problem you are trying to solve and now you are left in the dust.

MA: What is the secret to your success? Do you have a secret strategy?

NA: When I came to Palo Alto, the company was amazing at a technology called firewalls. It's a way of protecting networks and making sure that malware or bad things don't happen in your network. But there are other areas of technology and cyber security which are sold by other companies, which are in slightly different swim lanes. It's cumbersome for the customer to attempt to understand them and incorporate the many swim lanes, as they don't talk to each other. We spend a lot of time thinking about how to make the customer more secure by stitching the different swim lanes together for them. A trillion dollars were spent last year with companies selling those different products to the customer. My insight was to overhaul the system from a fragmented set of products to a comprehensive one. I'll give you an example: When the iPhone and the Android phone came about, there were 200 different types of phones in the world. They have all disappeared. You don't remember them anymore. You either have an Android phone or an iPhone. The industry went from 200 phones to two. There are so many companies that tried to normalize things but lost the plot.

MA: Are you saying you want to be the one left standing? Do you have a plan?

NA: There was a time not so long ago when I used to log in from home and the modem said beep, beep, beep and you got connected and sent an email and it seemed magical and you said, "Wow, my email's gone today." You can watch videos while somebody else is watching a video in the other room and it's on the same wire that goes from your house that once just carried your phone connection. Access speeds are going to get faster and faster. The ability to store large amounts of data will become easier and easier. We are now in that iPhone moment. If you ask where the world is headed, I believe the world is going to the cloud. Why? Because it offers a very inexpensive way to collect large amounts of data. And you can collect large amounts of data and access it very quickly because overtime latency has only gone down. The ones who will win are sitting and looking at the lay of the land, asking what the land will look like in 10 years, 20 years, 30 years. What's the art of the possible? How do we maximize for 10 or 20 to 30 years? ChatGPT and AI are currently disrupting and changing the dynamics. We are not maximizing for the unknown 50 years from now or 100 years. Others send people to Mars or let's have cars that drive each other. But we're saying, given what we can see, how far we can see, what's going to happen at the end of what we can see. So that's what you do. You keep reassessing every 10 years.

MA: How can you use AI at Palo Alto to prevent security breaches?

NA: What you're seeing is a window into how a large-scale computing effort on the basis of ample training data can put together a series of cogent arguments and series of cogent answers. It is not yet in the predictive world of AI. It is still in the synthesis of information world of AI, but it's going to get predictive. The best example of predictive AI today is a self-driving car or a Tesla. Self-drive requires it to anticipate its move incrementally. If this car has been driving at 50 miles an hour in this lane and there are no other indicators you can see, there is a 99.9 percent probability this car will *not* go from 50 to 75 miles in three seconds. Nor will it spit up an indicator in the next sub-second to make it turn left. That's all it's doing. It predicts the next step, then the next step and so on. That's predictive AI. How's it doing that? It's got so much training data that it knows what the most likely outcome is going to be with a high degree of accuracy. Now you take that concept and apply it to security. When you see a bad act, you say, "Well, that's unpredictable. That shouldn't have happened. That's anomalous." All we have to do is to make sure that based on watching everything around us, we can predict if the next act is going to be a bad act. Right now, people are still stopping things as they happen. Security is about stopping things before they happen. If you can collect all the right data, you can analyze it the way Tesla analyzes predictive behavior or ChatGPT analyzes behavior to come. That's how we solve global security.

MA: How can Palo Alto help with concrete security threats? You participated in an interview with Suzanne Spaulding, a senior advisor from Homeland Security, discussing threats and the role that PA could play in their prevention.

NA: Cyber attacks are on the rise, even though the entities that are attacked don't go public with the information. As the world gets increasingly connected and data-enabled, it becomes a new type of warfare. So many things are now operated via computers. Why would I put people at risk and fly them 6,000 miles to fight you if I can cripple your entire technology remotely? You can create chaos in countries by pressing a button. You won't have to sacrifice human life to extract an outcome you want. You can instigate an economic war or fiscal war to achieve malicious goals. Take the example of Colonial Pipeline, which was hacked. The hackers said they would unblock the pipeline for $50 million. It was a ransom. Now if I said we will not unblock the pipe, what are your options? You could shut down for several months, sending the price of oil shooting up. Let's say Fidelity—which [is] $3 trillion of people's assets—or the New York Stock Exchange were hacked. It would upend the economy. If Bank of America was unable to dispense money for a week, it would undermine the banking system and people would keep their money under their mattress. The ramifications are endless. 2,300 companies were declared as held up for ransom in 2022. We try to stop this from happening. Today, cyber security is being used in the Ukraine to detect troop movements, track logistics, and prevent hacking of their infrastructure. The uses have grown exponentially. Twenty years ago, the Chinese made sure that no Chinese data come out of China. They built a great firewall. Google can't operate there and take data out. The Chinese limited Google because they understood that data is power. They saw an opportunity in vulnerable countries who did not understand how all this works and tried to embed themselves. The scandal was exposed when the Chinese decided they wanted infrastructure and expanded Huawei. It gave them the ability to go in and out and listen in to any conversations. It's one thing to breach data and hack, but collecting data and having it forever is another level of espionage. The implications of this are enormous. Western countries are aware of the implications and their antennae is up, but small countries don't have the ability to protect themselves.

MA: How do you identify who the most critical employees are in your office? Is retention a problem in Silicon Valley?

NA: When I walked into Palo Alto, everybody spoke a different language. I inherited 5,000 people. They had their own philosophy. I wrote a word document with 30 to 40 management principles [that] came to mind and distributed it. I like to use the analogy of building a house. Businesses fail because we hire people and expect them to be superhuman. We tell them they are going to be the architect, builder, and maintenance person. My architect could not have done the building part. There is no such thing in life or in business. You hire good people with first understanding if it's an architecture problem, or a building problem. Are you trying to come up with something new? Or are you trying to get them to build something? Now in business we have a lot of value for builders. You can have an architect who is a wonderful architect but couldn't build shit. Sometimes people try to build with the architect and it fails, and you say, "My god, this guy's an idiot because he or she failed." Well, they failed not because they had [a] bad idea or a bad plan, they just didn't know how to execute on the plan. If you work as long as all of us have worked, you realize that eventually the best people have to move. The question becomes, how do you harness the intelligence of the best people and codify it in such a way that nobody becomes a single point of failure? If you have genius like Elon Musk, you can change the world, but everybody else can't, so it goes back to an execution question, right? I have a lot of people who have great ideas. I have fewer people

[who] can take those great ideas and turn them into real insights and outcomes. Genius has two parts. One is implicit in our understanding of genius because it got done. You don't know about the geniuses who didn't get things done. We over-index the creative genius and under index the ability to make it happen. Madame Curie or Einstein can discover things. And that's genius because they can sit and come up with large equations and figure something out. They don't need anybody else's help. You know, I'm using Elon as a proxy, but he needs thousands of people to send a rocket to Mars. The retention of good people is always a challenge but given our performance and the strong value of our stock, not only are employees staying for the rise, but some who left to join start-ups have returned.

MA: In Silicon Valley, failure is sort of like a badge of honor, right?

NA: The reasons for failure are very hard to discern. Was it a failure of the idea, or its execution? If you look at the last five years, many bad ideas have survived for too long because people threw a lot of money at it. If you execute into a bad idea, eventually you say, "Oh shit, it's bad," and realize you've burned a lot of money. Take the example of those electric scooters people are driving around. I don't think they are around much more, but for a while they were a really good idea, right? There was a $40 billion company called WeWork; it was a good idea, but it was only worth $3 billion.

MA: How do you manage failure?

NA: If we all remember the most miserable things that happened to us, we'd be in a horrible state. We'd be in a depressive state. I'm 54. Bad things happen. You have family crisis, you have personal crisis, you have confidence crisis. You have insecurities. You make bad decisions. None of us is perfect. But what's amazing is that if you have the right attitude over time, you either learn from them, you build on them, and you romanticize your life away. You go back and say yes, you know, that was a tough time but this amazing thing that happened out of it, so. That's how you deal with failure.

MA: Do you follow a daily routine?

NA: I wake up between 5 to 6 a.m. and get a cup of coffee and watch CNBC. I try to get to the gym or go for a three-mile walk and then spend some time with my seven-year-old son, who is obsessed with his dad. He finds me and comes over to spend time with me. If I have to run for a meeting and am in a hurry to shower, he will hop in the shower with me. He's still half asleep. Sometimes I can spend a little time with him before school. If I have meetings, he feels disappointed. Once my day starts, it's non-stop.

MA: How important is India in your life?

NA: It's important. I have family in India, so I visit frequently, but my life and friends are here.

In 2024 Arora turned 56 years old, still young enough to continue to have an impact on the industry. He likes to keep up with technology and is constantly thinking of ways to improve both products and management. Making sure that products are the best they can be, is a mantra he has carried over from his years at Google and is central to his focus. He recently sent out a six-page memo to his employees outlining his management principles. They include items like:

- What can you be the best in the world at (lead in), what are you passionate about, what can drive a great economic engine.
- Winning ideas have a high standard deviation; high standard deviation ideas win spectacularly and fail spectacularly.
- You can't get everything right, get what's "important" right—understanding what's important and overprioritizing it over all else is genius.
- Don't stack yourself with people from the industry you are trying to disrupt. If you have to wait for a performance review to see what your manager thinks of you, you don't need to wait.
- Product obsession is key; great products help build great companies. As products lose their shine, competitors come up as products

get behind—companies get behind. Each rejuvenation attempt in
technology has required a product reboot—iPhone, Azure, Adobe;
those who didn't make it, Sun, Yahoo, etc.

Although Palo Alto Networks is not Microsoft or Google, the future, especially in
tech, is unpredictable. Arora has joined the ranks of top Indian CEOs with his new
status as a billionaire. As CEO of Palo Alto Networks, a Fortune 500 company worth
$100 billion, he is still young enough and ambitious enough to take it to the next
level. Goetz said the board was very pleased with his performance "Nikesh is one
of the best tech CEOs in the Bay area and the globe. I hope he's at Palo Alto a decade
from now, but I won't be surprised if one of the trillion-dollar tech companies come
knocking and make him an offer that he just can't refuse, but he's not leaving us—
unless he's taking the CEO role somewhere else. He's not going to be number two."
For now, Arora seems happy where he is and is focused on establishing Palo Alto
Networks as the undisputed leader and evergreen cyber security company. He sees
no reason why its market share cannot double to 10 or 15 percent.

Microsoft, Google, Adobe and Palo Alto Networks all started out as technology
startups that were "disrupters." Today they are the establishment. Microsoft with a
market cap of $3 trillion is the most valuable company today[46]. The challenge that
Nadella, Pichai and others like them face, is do they have the vision and capability
to remain ahead of the technology and future disrupters?

At its height, Bell Labs invented the transistor, laser technology, solar cells,
computer circuitry, and the Unix operating system. It counted nine Nobel laureates
and four Turing prize winners among its scientists. IBM, launched artificial
intelligence and taught machines to play chess in the fifties and worked with NASA
on space exploration in the sixties and dominated the computer industry through
the eighties.

Some of Americas biggest tech companies—Kodak, Blackberry, Dell,
Netscape, CompuServe and Blockbuster, all leaders in their area have faded into

the past tense. Even the disrupters—companies like Intel which groomed many Indian engineers—have not recovered the luster they had when Andy Grove and Gordon Moore were there and are struggling.

The future is constantly being rewritten in Silicon Valley. Who will dominate and who the winners will be is up for grabs. Artificial intelligence certainly seems to be the new frontier, and its constellation of stars is only just emerging—in the same way that, in the world of computers, Steve Jobs and Bill Gates rose in the seventies and we saw the fortunes of established leaders of the tech world like Xerox and IBM decline, giving way to disruptors like Apple and Microsoft. For now, Nadella seems to be navigating Microsoft with an innovator's mindset and has shown the vision and nimbleness to avoid the pitfalls of both the innovator's dilemma or what I call the founder transfer gap—where often the inspiration that drives a company and its ability to innovate dissipates once the original founder is gone, and the company just lives off the old ideas or products and limps along until it becomes irrelevant or extinguishes itself.

Narayen of Adobe and Arora of Palo Alto both are craning their necks around the corner to make sure they stay on top of AI and expanding their acquisitions of innovative start-ups. Not every move works out—such as in the case of the Figma deal for Adobe which was stymied by European regulators. Adobe is incorporating AI into all its systems, but as we have seen in the case of Google and its rocky launch of Gemini, the path is not always smooth.

The tech world is obsessed—for now—with large language models and the greater world of AI, but there are many things that could throw off what seems like the super-charged tech companies' seemingly inexorable rise. AT&T, for example, seemed invincible until the government forced its divestiture in 1982. Although it still exists, it is hardly considered a major corporation. We still know the Rockefeller name, but Standard Oil is no longer the dominant oil company in America. Nadella, Pichai, and Narayen are in charge of some of the most significant companies of our generation. With cyber security threats looming large, Arora's ambitions for Palo Alto could be important, and the reason I felt he should be part of the group. Will their names be mentioned in the same awe with which people refer to Bill Gates, Sergei Brin, or Mark Zuckerberg? Their companies have hit their highest peak under their leadership. That skill set is genius enough, but making sure they don't preside over their decline will be the ultimate test of their gifts.

CHAPTER 9

The Genius of Chandrika Tandon

When you don't look at boundaries, everything seems connected.
Everything seems possible.

CHANDRIKA TANDON

I first met Chandrika Tandon in 1996 in a hospital waiting room. We had both come to visit a mutual friend—Tino Puri, a senior partner at McKinsey who was recovering from cardiac surgery. Tino had helped recruit Chandrika to McKinsey years before, and he and his wife Rajika, a dancer trained in the Indian classical tradition, were family friends I had known a long time. Having moved to New York early on, their home had become a gathering place for Indians who were newly arrived. Always welcoming, Tino had mentored many young professionals trying to make their mark in the corporate world.

Hospital waiting rooms seem to absorb the anxiety and trepidations of its occupants. They are gloomy places to spend time in, but Chandrika radiated energy and warmth, bubbling with enthusiasm about her work. I was taken by her positive attitude and her description of her career and decided to visit her in her office a few months later. On the wall hung interviews and profiles of her from *Investors Daily*, *American Banker*, *Forbes*, and *Business Week*.

What makes Chandrika exceptional is her ability to rise to the top of her profession regardless of the goal she is pursuing. At Citibank, she won accolades for coming up with a whole new system that increased their profits. This brought her to the attention of McKinsey, who took a chance on recruiting her. Her outstanding performance there catapulted her into a partnership. When she left to become an entrepreneur and start her company Tandon Capital, she had no underwriters or partners to help her succeed. She not only succeeded but became very wealthy in the process. At the pinnacle of her success, when she was on a first name basis with all the key bankers in New York, she gave it up to focus on her first love—music. According to her, when she first came to the United States for six weeks with Citibank, she had decided to get a PhD in business and minor in music, which was never far from her heart. Although she did not go back to school then and opted to join McKinsey, she had made enough money by 2000 to revive her musical abilities. Her first record "Soul Call" was nominated for a Grammy in 2011. It takes a special kind of genius to hit the peak of every profession you take on. Tandon also turned to philanthropy, serving on several boards and, together with her husband, donating $100 million to NYU in 2015 to establish the Tandon School of Engineering. The spectrum of Chandrika's achievements is breathtaking. In an interview with her, I have tried to discover what inspired her to succeed and the many constraints, cultural and other, that she had to overcome.

Chandrika's story cannot be told without describing the spectacular success achieved by her younger sister Indra Nooyi, who rose through the ranks to become CEO of Pepsi in 2006. She was the first Indian American woman to head a Fortune 500 company. Indra would grab headlines for breaking barriers in the corporate world. In 2015 and 2017, *Fortune* magazine ranked her as the second most powerful woman in America, outranked only by Mary Barra, the CEO of General Motors. What distinguished Chandrika was her creativity, combined with an appetite for risk. Her genius lay in reaching the top no matter which area she decided to wade into—consulting, banking, or music.

The sisters arrived in the United States for the first time in 1978 with the last name Krishnamurthy. Within a short time, Indra was married and changed her name to Indra Nooyi. Some years later, Chandrika would do the same and became Chandrika Tandon. While both sisters achieved extraordinary success, I have deliberately chosen to focus on Chandrika whose genius dazzles.

For the sake of avoiding confusion, I have referred to them by their first names throughout.

✻ ✻ ✻

The Two Sisters from Chennai

Chandrika Krishnamurthy's first visit to New York in the fall of 1978 was brief. She had come on a work assignment for Citibank. She returned to New York during the blizzard of 1979 for a job interview with McKinsey & Company. She managed to survive the storm and landed the job despite being pathetically ill-equipped for the weather, wearing a borrowed coat two sizes too big for her, open sandals, and a sari. Five years later, she made partner, becoming the first Indian American woman to do so. Most would have felt this was enough of an accomplishment, but Chandrika was driven.

In 1992, now married with a baby, Chandrika ventured into what seemed like a void at the time and started her own company. As she sat alone in the empty office on the 32nd floor, she wondered if she had made a mistake trying to make it on her own, a woman and an immigrant without the trappings of an established company, but her fears were short-lived. At McKinsey, she developed a stellar reputation as the go-to person when it came to restructuring failing banks. Garry Scheuring, the CEO of Midlantic Bank (PNC), came knocking, and she soon counted Chase Manhattan, Bank of America, and Uni Banco of Brazil among her clients.

It was not the first time she had plunged into an unfamiliar situation, courted risk, and managed it successfully. Before being recruited by McKinsey, she had worked for Citibank in India right after college. She was 21 years old in 1975 when Citibank sent her to Beirut, just as it erupted in full-scale civil war. Chandrika remembers the constant shelling and the streets in flames every night she was there. She would zone it out by focusing on her work, which she found both absorbing and a learning experience.

CT: We read about civil wars being terrible and buildings burning and streets in flames, but it doesn't mean anything beyond the paper it's written on until you experience it. Citibank had brought 15 to 20 young people to Beirut in 1975, because that's where their Middle East North Africa training center was located, when the civil war broke out. I had gone with a friend to see a film about Vincent Van Gogh called *Lust for Life* at the theatre in Al Hambra, the main street. The man at the ticket booth demanded 400 pounds rather than the posted price of three pounds. He said we were the only ones in the theatre, and it was going to cost that much to run the film for us. Not having the money, we refused and left. Two hours later, the theatre was bombed. We were later confined to our rooms at the Holiday Inn for days, as there was sniper fire everywhere. The situation deteriorated so much that Citibank sent us all home. A few months later, I heard that our hotel had been razed to the ground.

MA: Did your parents object to your going to a war zone?

CT: By the time I went, I was financially independent, and I didn't think I needed their permission. I had fought those battles already.

Chandrika had rejected the norms and restraints that Indian families generally put on their daughters' freedom of movement. It was far beyond the norm for a young, unmarried girl to move about unchaperoned when they were growing up unless it was to specific destinations such as school or work. Going to a war zone was unthinkable, but she had stepped beyond her veil and was on a forward trajectory.

At Citibank, Chandrika quickly outshone her peers by inventing a financial system to evaluate gains and losses that were subject to swings in currencies.

CT: I had invented a whole new methodology to translate gains and losses, which is a big part of the P&L. If your assets are fixed, with different durations and are denominated in rupees and the currency fluctuates, a lot can go wrong. The concept of swaps was not popular at the time, so I came up with my own embryonic way of managing risk by removing the big fluctuations and that took away the uncertainty and we began to make a lot of money. Citibank sent me to New York in October 1978 for six weeks. I was to explain my system for evaluating risk and show them what I had done it in India so they could adapt it. I was very competitive and I was climbing up the ladder and had fantastic mentors, but I decided I wanted to go to the United States to study. When I arrived, it was fall, the weather was perfect, and I decided it would be wonderful to pursue a PhD in the United States.

Chandrika shattered boundaries early. Her family was conventional and a career in finance was the last thing they had in mind for her. Her mother made it clear that once she completed school, they expected her to enter into a marriage, preferably arranged by the family just as her own marriage to their father had been. Her mother had already started collected cooking utensils for her dowry, but Chandrika had other dreams.

CT: One of my earliest memories was of my mother exchanging all her old silk saris to buy stainless steel vessels. The old saris had real gold thread woven into them and even if they were a hundred years old, the man would buy them for the gold and would exchange it for three bowls or two spoons. My mother liked to say, "Like a sparrow I'm building a nest piece by piece." She would say that because she had two girls who she "had to get married," it was her duty. It was what was intended to happen and was the sort of zeitgeist that we grew up with.

Indra Nooyi corroborates her older sister's recollections of growing up in a traditional South Indian Brahmin family in her autobiography. "My parents never hugged or kissed us or said 'I love you'; love was assumed. We never shared fears or hopes and dreams with our elders. They were just not the kind to have these conversations."[47]

When Indra was a teenager, she also became aware that her mother was "stockpiling items for our marriage trousseaus. Whenever she saved a little from the family budget, she'd buy two of the same items and put them away for Chandrika and me. She filled the cupboard with stainless steel pots and pans; silver trays, plates, and cups; and a few items of gold jewelry."[48]

In an interview with David Rubenstein, she said of her mother, "She gave us hopes, but then anchored us firmly on the conservative South Indian values of you have to get married at 18—which didn't happen... but that's what she kept telling us."[49]

MA: You belonged to a very traditional family. What was their attitude toward female children?

CT: My parents had been married a couple of years before I arrived and there was a great deal of excitement about the pregnancy. Everyone wanted a boy to continue the lineage. My mother's labor was difficult as I weighed 10 pounds and I was a forceps delivery. I was told that the doctor's words as soon as I came out was, "After all this effort, it's just a girl." The whole premise was that girls are a burden as they require dowries. This story was repeated to me several times over the years by my mother.

MA: When you decided you wanted to get an education rather than get married, did she feel you were disruptive?

CT: It was much more than that. I wasn't merely disrupting her plans; I was being rebellious and breaking all the rules. There is a Tamil expression which is, "The way the head shakes, the rest of the body will shake." I had to think a lot about my head shake, because that is how I was conditioned. At a recent high school reunion, my friends told me that at 14, my mother told my classmates they would be coming over when we turned 17 because I would get engaged and she would have me married at 18. I was the first born, so the implication was I needed to follow the path so my younger sister Indra would not be adversely impacted.

Indra admits that the pressure to conform was on Chandrika, who was the eldest. "I know that Chandrika, the elder daughter, beautiful with curly hair and a great smile, felt the pressure. I definitely benefitted from being the second daughter in this case. I could operate below the radar."[50]

A younger brother Nandu arrived some years later. Indra doted on him and, once she was working, would buy him his first bicycle and send him pocket money. Like Chandrika, he was a brilliant student and followed his older sisters to the United States to attend Yale and MIT. Although he never attained the heights of his high-performing sisters, Chandrika points out that within the family he is their mother's favorite child.

Chandrika was academically gifted and excelled in school. Indra admits that her grades were mediocre compared to her sister's, who was an academic star in the family, but Chandrika's determination to reach for the sky put her in constant conflict with her mother, whose carefully laid out plans for her daughter's matrimonial prospects kept getting pushed aside. She felt she paid a high price for pushing past the barriers that surrounded her at home.

CT: I decided I wanted to attend Madras Christian College. It had started the most prestigious accounting and business program (B Com) and Professor Swami, revered within the institution, was taking a very selective group of students. The class was 450 people, but the program was not widely available to women. There were only four women in the class, but I applied and was accepted and was determined to go. I faced two problems. It was co-ed and an hour away. I had to go on hunger strike to overcome the families' objections. My mother used to say that when you put fire and cotton together it's combustible. The implication was that nothing good would come of a co-ed education. It was all about preserving family honor. She had no problem with my going to college as long as it was the local girls' college nearby. The nuns from my school who, as far as I knew, had never left the convent walls walked to my house to get my mother to relent. My mother had put her foot down, but their arrival at my house created such a sensation on my street that she backed down. I was on day two of my hunger strike and had been crying all day, but the nuns persuaded my family that I was well-behaved and should be allowed to go.

MA: Were your siblings supportive?

CT: They were too young at the time. This was my fight and a solitary one, but I paved the way for Indra. By the time she finished high school, going to Madras Christian College for her was a no-brainer. If the nuns had not made the trip to my house to convince my mother to let me go to the college I wanted, I'm not sure I would have been allowed.

Although Indra acknowledged in her memoir that her sister taking on battles with their family removed the pressure for her, she gave a somewhat disingenuous answer to David Rubenstein when he asked how her parents reacted when she decided to go to Yale. "This is perhaps the biggest mystery of them all, because my conservative mother and my supportive father actually allowed me to come to the United States. It shocked the hell out of me. I would have thought my mother would have fasted for days and thrown a temper tantrum. She didn't... They even bought me an airline ticket. Even today I wonder how they did it. What caused them to do it?"[51] Nooyi was likely basing her fears on her mother's reaction to Chandrika's bid to pursue her education.

Families are complex, and sharing a past does not leave people with similar recollections as the way they experienced situations can be dramatically different. In her memoir *My Life in Full*, Indra's description of growing up in 1960s Madras is both evocative and idyllic. Her descriptions of the cultural constraints, her mother's preoccupations, and the daily symphony of growing up in a multigenerational home built by her grandfather are touchingly sentimental but seem devoid of any conflicts. During my interview with Chandrika, the scars of some of her earlier conflicts with her mother still cause her to flinch.

MA: Where did your determination and belief in yourself come from? Your mother did not support your dreams. Was your father an important figure?

CT: My father was very loving but remote. He had a small job and traveled for work constantly and was away a lot. It was my grandfather who was my rock growing up. I was very close to him, and he was the love of my life. We had a ritual every night at 8 p.m. where we would sit together and chat or read. He had an old-fashioned selection of books including the works of Shakespeare and introduced me to literature. By the time I was 13, I could recite about 200 poems and verses from Shakespeare. My grandfather indulged me despite our modest financial circumstances. I once fell in love with a purple sari. It wasn't expensive, but given our family's circumstances, my mother said we could not afford it. We were really quite poor. We lived in a beautiful house that my grandfather had built, but he lived on a pension. I pleaded with my grandfather, who thought about it and then told my mother to purchase it for me. I still own it. His love for me was unconditional, and as he got older, I would go to his room several times a night to put my head on his chest to make sure he was alive. I was so afraid he might die and when he did, just before I left for Beirut, I was devastated.

After excelling at Madras Christian College, Chandrika decided to apply for admission to the prestigious Indian Institute of Management, India's equivalent of the Harvard Business School. Her family did not think she would get in. Her uncle told her it was like winning a Nobel. Every year, of the approximately 230,000 who apply, only 0.1 percent are accepted. She was one of them.

CT: My natural path after I finished my BA would have been to study law at Madras Law College. It was my best subject, and my grades were off the charts. Both my grandfathers had practiced law. One was a judge and the other a lawyer, but I had set my sights on going to IIM in Ahmedabad. My determination to go there was sealed when an uncle asked me what my future plans were after I graduated from my undergraduate college. I had done extremely well, and I told him that one of my professors had suggested I go to IIM. He scoffed at the idea and told me I would never get in and admission to IIM was like winning the Nobel prize. We were in a restaurant, and I was so incensed by his dismissiveness I wanted to dump the Rassam in his lap! I decided then that I would prove him wrong. Getting admission was a daunting process. They interview 500 finalists for 100 places. I was relatively young and inexperienced compared to the other applicants, many who had already acquired some work experience. What got me in was music. I had performed on All India Radio and my repertoire included French and English songs, a fact that I had included on my bio. They grilled me for over an hour during my interview on topics like contract law, but a professor who had spent time teaching at the Sorbonne and was very suave and sophisticated asked me with some disbelief if I could really sing in French. I had never left India or Chennai or been on a plane, for that matter, so I could see why he was skeptical. The professor asked me to sing a song in French. I did. The room fell silent. I got in. Later, the professor congratulated me on my accent.

MA: Was it hard to leave home and your sheltered existence to go to another city for college?

CT: The hardest thing was leaving my grandfather. By the time I left for IIM, I needed a mental break from the constraints of living at home with the strict rules that were supposed to govern my behavior and keep me eligible for marriage. I wasn't allowed to go out for fun during college. My friends, including the boys, would come to my house. My mother was very sweet to them and would give them coffee, but I was only allowed to go out with the girls and had to observe strict curfews. I once broke a curfew unintentionally. My friends came with me to apologize to my mother, but I was punished. The motto was, "Spare the rod and spoil the child." I got a lot of rods from her. I rebelled when I went away for graduate school and stopped communicating and writing letters home. Once I began working at Citibank, I was financially independent and didn't feel I needed anyone's permission to do what I wanted.

MA: How did your family respond?

CT: My mother is indomitable. Nothing stops her. She took it upon herself to write to one of my professors to let him know they had lost contact with me because I had not written to them. Professor Bhattacharya, who became my mentor, called me to his office and scolded me. He was almost seven feet tall and towered over me and told me to call my mother to let her know I was okay. He was so taken by my mother's actions he visited her when he went to Chennai. I was furious with my mother, but I recognized she would stop at nothing to look out for her children and was a force of nature.

MA: Did you excel at IIM?

CT: Not initially. The institution was dominated by men. We were just eight women in a class of 100, and many of the students were from the famous Indian Institutes of Technology and had studied physics or engineering. Several were gold medalists, others were "toppers" and they had five years of college compared to my three, which was standard for my major. I had very little math and got a D in my first math class, but the students helped me catch up. They were so wonderful. The subject I did well at was accounting, taught by Professor Bhattacharya. I had studied it as an undergrad and I love numbers. When you put a spreadsheet with financials in front of me, I see all sorts of relationships. I never forget numbers. I rocked that class.

MA: How did you make the move to America?

CT: In 1978, Citibank sent me to New York for six weeks to explain my methodology for evaluating assets to see if it could be applied to other branches. It was my first time in the United States and my goal was to apply for a PhD program in the United States I looked up the name of professors at NYU who taught accounting and identified Joshua Cohen from the phonebook and went to see him. I had no transcripts or GMAT scores, but after he grilled me for an hour, he agreed to take me on as a student and told me to get my paperwork in order. Thanks to serendipity, my career took a different turn. Professor Bhattacharya, my mentor from IIM and probably the person who had the most profound academic influence on my life, connected me to his friend Frances Hershkowitz from McKinsey my last day in New York. After a long lunch that extended to over four hours, she insisted I should join McKinsey. She took me to the McKinsey office and introduced me to Linda Levinson, the first woman to make partner. A few months later, when I was back in India, I got a call from Tino Puri, a McKinsey partner, requesting an interview. I remember it was New Year's Day and I was partying. We met in Delhi the next day and our one-hour interview slot lasted several hours—we shut down the restaurant! The following morning at 8 a.m. he proposed I fly to New York for formal interviews. He had been on the phone with his colleagues after our meeting and arranged for me to have over a dozen interviews over two days. At the time, I was juggling my options between an offer from Citibank to go to Columbia or pursue my PhD. McKinsey offered me a job which I accepted, and the rest is history.

MA: The interview process sounds brutal. What was your experience like working in the United States for the first time?

CT: Not everyone at McKinsey wanted to hire me. They only recruited the top 5 percent from places like Harvard and Stanford. I did not have an American degree and I was younger than their average applicant and had just one prior job experience. The Indians who worked at McKinsey had degrees from Harvard, Oxford, and Berkeley. Puri, who recruited me, was an Oxford graduate. Tino suggested to some of his colleagues that had expressed reservations about hiring me due to my lack of work experience that they recruit me as a top graduate student. This was 1979. McKinsey was barely 1,000 people and they were not looking at Indians thinking he could be the next tech billionaire. They saw a woman with a sari and a red dot. During the interviews I was asked about my clothes and if I would be willing to shed my Indian outfits for Western attire. The implication was clear—I did not look professional. For the next several years, determined to succeed, I worked all the time and never saw daylight. I traveled constantly. If I came home on a Friday night I'd be back on a plane on Sunday. I worked weekends staying up all hours of the night writing documents. I had no personal life.

MA: Were you trying to prove yourself?

CT: I knew the kinds of fees we were charging clients and felt if I took a coffee break, I was wasting their money. Coming from India, spending $4 on a shirt felt like a lot of money, so I was very conscious about doing the right thing for the clients. In 1986, I was made a partner.

MA: How did you find time to get married or have a child? The hours seem exacting for a woman.

CT: I got married in 1986, the same year I made partner. By then I was a very strong partner in the financial services division. I had worked at McKinsey for seven years and was a high revenue earner. Clients would specifically ask for me to work on their projects.

MA: Making partner was quite an accomplishment. You were the first Indian American woman partner at McKinsey. What do you think they saw in you?

CT: The two things I think people would say about me was first, I was a singular problem solver. When presented with a puzzle with lots of pieces, I can see the pattern that others don't. I can see it before anyone else—it's just how my mind works. I also saw cost curves in a different way. There was a big securities firm who was a client. They were operating in the main market with the very big corporates, but they were not big in the middle market or on the small side. After I had examined the institution for a week, I concluded they were never going to succeed in the market they were in, regardless of their dream of making a mark there, but if they could shift their dream to the mid-size market they would do well. Their path to success was crystal clear to me but I got beaten up by the board. The partner I was working with disagreed with me, as he felt I was taking them away from their strength, but he agreed to present my ideas. A year later, the institution followed my strategy, and it was a spectacular success. They applied the wisdom they had gained from the big markets to the new target and benefitted from the first mover advantage. My clients loved me, but it took a while to make it as I had to overcome my ethnic accent and lack of clothes sense. A client from Boston took pity on me and educated me on how to dress.

MA: I heard you took to wearing bow ties and garters. What was that about?

CT: Clothes weren't important to me. I just found the cheapest clothes I could get away with. Looking back, I realize my clothes were truly horrible. I was coming home from work at midnight and leaving for work at dawn. I owned two pairs of Ferragamo shoes—navy and black. I occasionally left home with mismatched shoes. I then read a book called Dress for Success by John Molloy. I went from saris to suits and bow ties.

MA: That was a leap, but why the androgenous look?

CT: I wasn't used to showing my legs because of our culture, so I wore pantsuits. American boardrooms were full of people dressed in black, navy, and gray. I wore thick brown suits that I had bought on sale, and then one of my friends said she couldn't bear to see me dressed the way I was and took me shopping. Until then,

I had spent $800 on clothes over the first three years and wore the same three suits over and over. I saw a video of myself that we used to prep for interviews and cried to see how terrible I looked. My friend Wendy took me shopping and got rid of a lot of things in my closet. It was the first time I spent $2,000 in one go on new clothes.

MA: What about the bow ties?

CT: I had a few shirts made in Hong Kong, but they were open necked. The bow ties solved the problem. The book *Dress for Success* showed women wearing bow ties. I had a client who wore bow ties, and he would straighten my bow ties for me, and it became a joke between us. Maybe I was trying to conform to my environment and fit in. People who come here for college have time to acclimatize, but I had no ramp-up period. I was thrown into work as soon as I arrived.

The two sisters had arrived in America at almost the same time. Indra would become the poster child for Indian American success and women's empowerment in corporate America. At the height of her career as the first female CEO of PepsiCo, she was talked about as one of the most influential women in business and profiled in newspapers and magazine articles. She was not a risk-taker in the way her sister was, but while she followed a more conventional career path working her way up the corporate ladder, she was spectacularly successful by the end. Her public persona exploded when she became CEO. The corporate world was dominated by white men, and that presented different challenges to both of them.

MA: Did you encounter any gender discrimination or racism on your way to the top?

CT: I've been asked this question a lot being one of the first women to break barriers, but the short answer is, I've never walked into a room thinking I'm a woman of color. I've always walked into the room thinking I'm the best professional that there is, and I know my subject and what I am doing. If I didn't know a subject, I invested all my time on it. A lot of times, I didn't see the light of day. I wasn't doing it out of any consciousness that I was a woman who had to prove herself, I just wanted to be the best I could be. When I am asked to give a speech, I feel I'm there because I have something to say, not because I was a token-something. I'd often be surrounded by men who played golf, discussed wine and baseball. I had nothing to contribute when I first started 43 years ago, as schmoozing in business was all alien to me. Sometimes they would turn to me and ask if I knew an Indian in Hong Kong who had cheated their company of a million dollars. Now there were over a billion Indians, why would I know some random person just because we were both Indian? I could have taken it two ways—that I was being racially profiled, but I was careful not to fall for the bait and instead turned it around saying lots of people cheat banks, but I don't know this individual. But I did learn about sports and came to enjoy it. This was before the "Me Too" movement and microaggressions.

Indra had started her career as an intern for Johnson & Johnson in India while she was studying business at IIM Calcutta. When she graduated, she worked for a textile company and rejoined Johnson & Johnson to market sanitary towels—a sensitive assignment in a country like India, where topics like feminine hygiene were taboo. It was 1977, and she observed that many of her college friends had gone overseas to pursue post-graduate programs, mostly in America. She decided she would expand her horizons and determined that a move to the United States would be the best avenue. Not everyone was going to be lucky enough to get recruited like her sister, who had something special to offer that made her stand out. Indra decided her best bet was to apply to Yale, where a new business school was being established focusing on public and private management. Indra was accepted and received financial aid which made her attendance possible.

Not having traveled overseas before, Indra also had to find her way, from opening a bank account to finding vegetarian food. At Yale, she was befriended by other immigrant or foreign students who helped her settle in. She loved school, which was a radically different experience from her education in India. She admired her professors and found the curriculum stimulating, but she felt like an outsider among the largely preppy student body who kept within their Ivy League and elite boarding school cliques. "I was considered smart and hardworking, and people liked me fine, I think. But I was also largely invisible and conscious how international students, especially from developing countries, were grouped in people's minds. Diligent but no style, funny accents, socially inept. There was no explicit rejection of us but no deep welcoming."[52]

Like her sister, Indra had her own challenges with clothes, having brought ill-fitting copies of Western attire from India. Her insufficient shopping skills and lack of style were on full display during her interviews for a summer internship. A kind female advisor suggested she wear a sari to her next interview. She did and got an offer from Booz Allen Hamilton that would put her on a path both professional and personal that helped shine her way forward. Much later, with the help of a professional, she would define a style for herself with expensive well-cut suits, pearls, a short haircut, and a flowing scarf.

During the summer after her first year, Indra was introduced to a young Indian man called Raj Nooyi when she moved to Chicago for her summer internship. He was an engineer who became her constant companion, and by the end of the summer they were engaged. He checked all the boxes: caste, religion, and background. Their respective families met in India and immediately took to each other, and their engagement was officially celebrated 10,000 miles away by their relatives without the bride and groom in attendance. Indra refers to her husband often as her lifeboat and greatest support.

Indra joined the Boston Consulting Group after Yale and spent over six years learning about the consulting business. For a while, the two sisters lived parallel lives working for prestigious consulting companies, but they remained in their own orbits, only meeting occasionally for family get-togethers. They were both managing an unrelenting travel schedule with grueling hours. Indra calls it a phase in her life that was an intellectual high and physical low. Her shoulders were misaligned from lugging heavy briefcases and garment bags every week.

In May 1986, Indra crashed her car and woke up in a hospital. She had crushed several bones in her hips, was bleeding internally, had a concussion, and was covered in cuts. The whole family rallied around in support. Chandrika flew to Chicago and their younger brother Nandu came from New Haven where he was a student at Yale. Her mother had also moved to the United States after their father's death and was looking after Indra's daughter Preetha. It took time to recover from the injuries. Indra reassessed her priorities and decided to move on from consulting. "The time away from work made me reassess my priorities," she said. "I had a daughter now, and the endless travel and long hours no longer felt exciting. I wanted to be close to home." She decided to leave Boston Consulting and accepted a job with Motorola.

Chandrika had made partner at McKinsey the same year that Indra chose to quit consulting. After working for another six years, she decided to start her own company.

MA: Was it hard to leave McKinsey?

CT: Yes and no. It's hard to leave when you have an established reputation in a place. I was one of the highest billing partners with a great stable of clients. I wanted to standardize what I had been doing so I did not reinvent the wheel each time. A company is an aggregation of multiple functions. We were in a regulated industry, and I saw a lot of waste and many inefficiencies but also an opportunity. I knew that if I could create a model that worked and play for multiple value by investing in the companies, I would succeed. I moved from consulting to becoming an investor and entrepreneur. I was trying to buy a bank, but I failed. I'm a great believer in the long arm of karma. I was on my last month's savings in 1992 when Garry Scheuring of Mid-Atlantic walked in the door. Scheuring did not know me, but he was meeting with Bruce Wheeler who had been a client years ago that I had helped. He told Garry that if he planned a major restructuring, I was the one person he should have on his team. He made the connection and Tandon Capital took off.

At Motorola, Indra would forge a deep and lasting friendship with her boss, Gerhard Schulmeyer, a German businessman. In 1989 he moved to Asea Brown Boveri (ABB) and insisted Indra join him in Connecticut. They had worked together for close to eight years. Schulmeyer quit the following year, but this time Indra did not follow him. Indra had a talent for developing enduring relationships with her bosses and stayed in touch with them. Her dedication to the personal side of business would later help her define a new type of management that was people-driven and made her a very successful leader.

When Indra and her husband first moved to Connecticut, she tried to take over a rental in New Canaan from her German boss but was turned down by the landlord who did not want to rent it to Indians. She was told by several people that she would not fit in with the lily-white people in New Canaan or Darien. They ultimately moved to Greenwich, where another daughter, Tara, was born in 1992. Two years later, she interviewed for the position of senior vice president of corporate strategy and planning at PepsiCo. The decision that both sisters made would put them on a trajectory to becoming the most consequential women in the corporate world.

Indra, unlike her sister, was not a risk-taker. Her jobs had all been conventional choices for an MBA graduate: Boston Consulting, Motorola, and finally Pepsi in 1994—although the glass ceiling she shot through when she was made CEO of Pepsi in 2006 was anything but conventional. She was the first woman to head Pepsi and would be the 11th female CEO in the Fortune 500 club along with Meg Whitman of Ebay, Anne Mulcahy of Xerox, and Patricia Russo of Lucent Technologies. More importantly, she was the first Indian American CEO of any gender to head a Fortune 500 company. She said a friend at an investment bank called her to say "that he and other Indian Americans in United States business were holding their heads a little higher and feeling they may be taken more seriously as potential leaders in their own firms because, for the first time, an Indian American was finally heading up a quintessential American consumer company."[53]

The corporate world was still a white male club. Indra had steadily worked her way up through the ranks at Pepsi. Her boss, Roger Enrico, had made her an essential part of his team, although when he flew his senior executives to one of his vacation homes on the private plane, she was never included. It was always an all-male event. Indra had felt disrespect and hostility from male colleagues when she was asked to make presentations on strategy that evaluated their various departments. In 1996 she threatened to resign due to a lack of support from management. Things quickly changed for the better after that and the CEO persuaded her to stay, making her CFO in early 2000. She would help Pepsi buy Quaker Oats and Tropicana, but the inequities she had put up with were only addressed by the next CEO Steve Reinemund. He appointed Indra president of PepsiCo in November, and in 2001 she was named to Pepsi's board of directors. Reinemund, an ex-Marine who had grown up with a single mother in Queens, noticed Indra had never been given a raise after being made CFO despite all her added responsibilities, nor had she received stock options that other male executives had been offered as part of their compensation. Indra was now properly compensated with a substantial pay raise and stake in the company. When she became the fifth CEO in 2006, she would push the HR department to close the gap between men and women's compensation, but discovered the bias was deeply ingrained.

Indra felt that the corporate world made few concessions for women. "Female leaders have this much tougher than male leaders because the world of power is designed for men," she said. "Women are always breaking ground as they navigate the upper reaches of business, government, or finance. We have to demonstrate our gravitas in a world where authority and brilliance, to many people still look like an older gentleman... I had heard of and seen male CEOs throw things and use four letter words with great gusto, apparently a sign of their passion and commitment. But I was well aware that showing any of these emotions myself would set me back."[54]

Looking back, both sisters acknowledge the toll their work took on their personal life. As Indra noted, "I wonder why I am wired this way where my inner compass always tells me to keep pushing on with my job responsibilities, whatever the circumstances... I love my family dearly, but this inner drive... has taken a lot of time away from them—much to their dismay."[55]

Incapable of moderating her dedication to work, Indra was back putting in long hours and was away from home at critical moments for her children. "From 1994 to 1999, I worked and worked and worked. I'd go home at night, take a shower, put on my flannel nightgown to show the girls I wasn't leaving, put them to bed, and sit up reading mail and reviewing documents until 1 or 2 a.m. I was almost never around for dinner... Preetha missed me a lot in these years. She was an adolescent, and much of what she saw was a busy, stressed-out mother." Indra recognized that juggling home and work put intense pressure on women, but she also knew she was driven and couldn't change.

Chandrika was also racked by guilt at the amount of time she spent away from home when her daughter was young. She said she spent an insane amount of time on planes when she was working on the bank in Brazil and Sun Corp in Australia—commuting to New York, sometimes flying 22 hours from Brisbane for a 48-hour stay to attend a parent-teacher meeting or be there for a recital. She was constantly fielding childcare coverage, meals, and making sure her daughter's doctors and dentist appointments and playdates were kept while half a world away. By the time Indra Nooyi became president of Pepsi and a few years before she would become CEO, her older sister was reevaluating her life. From her days at Citibank and her partnership at McKinsey, she was the creative talent, an inventor, and the ideas person. Over the next decade she singlehandedly built a company that restructured many of the most well-known banks, but by 1999, Chandrika felt she had made enough money in her lifetime and decided to stop working full-time to pursue her first love—music.

MA: At one point you decided you had made more money than you knew what to do with. When did you pivot to a career in music?

CT: By 1999, I felt financially secure. My company was well set—no one was doing what I was doing—but I was ready for another challenge. I had just been offered a project in Europe that was worth millions of dollars, but I walked away from it. We had been close to signing the deal and it was already with the SEC when I had second thoughts. Restructuring is an all-consuming project. It meant once again being on another continent, far from my family. It was not as bad as doing a project in Brazil or Australia, but I asked myself, what if I died now? Do I want to do one more deal? I went through a spiritual crisis and began questioning my life. I didn't go back to music right away, but just thinking about music made me happy. I knew then I had to pursue it. I burnt a lot of bridges and walked away from money, fame, and being on a constant treadmill. I had to fire a lot of people and had to let people down, so initially I slowed down and took smaller deals to keep things going. Eventually I wound things down to focus on music. I had to find teachers and study again. I have always been a perfectionist and like to immerse myself. I kept a foot in the business world—I joined boards and got involved with New York University's Stern School of Business.

Women are often held to a different standard in the workplace. In the case of the two sisters, they were discovering that their success in the boardroom had to be downplayed with the people they cared about most—their family, who resented sharing their mother with their work.

"You realize you can't have it all as a woman," Chandrika told me. "We beat ourselves up because you try to be the best in every sphere, and it becomes a vicious spiral emotionally."

Indra had largely avoided the long spell of conflict with her mother that had defined Chandrika's relationship, but she remains a towering person in their life. Her mother had been an enormous help to her. Indra was grateful that she moved in when her first child was born. Determined to return to work quickly, she relied on her mother to help with childcare, which created its own tensions as her mother had her own way of doing things. Always abstemious with her praise, Indra has mentioned her mother's exacting standards. While she does not go so far as to call her a "tiger mom," Indra tells the story of her mother cutting her down to size to make sure she knew her place at home when she come back after a long day at work to share the exciting news of her promotion to president of Pepsi. "I was just informed about 9:30 at night by a phone call that I was going to be the president of PepsiCo. I went home to tell my family... and mum opens the door... I said, 'Mum, I have got news for you,' and she said, 'Before the news, go get some milk.' I said 'It's 10 o'clock in the night. Why should I get milk?' I noticed that my husband's car was in the garage. I said, 'Why didn't you tell him to get the milk?' She said, 'Well, he came home at eight and he was very tired, so I let him be. Now, you go get the milk.'" Indra was upset, but she went and got the milk and banged it on the countertop and said, "I had big news for you, I have just been appointed president of Pepsi and all you care about is the milk." Her mom looked at Indra and coldly replied, "What are you talking about? When you walk in that door, just leave that crown in the garage, because you are the wife, the daughter, the daughter-in-law, and the mother of the kids, and that is all I want to talk about. Anything else, just leave it in the garage. Don't even try this with me anymore."

Indra always seems to be able to turn around a difficult family interaction and derive a lesson from it. On a visit to India, her mother insisted she get dressed by 7 a.m. to receive visitors. Indra noticed that although the visitors greeted her, they turned to her mother to compliment her on Indra's success. They congratulated her mother, not her, for her achievements. Indra says it was an awakening, and she realized that her parents deserved the credit for the person she had become. When she returned to Pepsi, she began writing letters to the parents of her employees, describing the work their child was doing and thanking them for the gift of their child. She claimed that rather than being seen as intrusive, everyone, parents and employees alike, were delighted.

MA: Your mother was a dominant person in both your lives. Did her way of raising you hinder you?

CT: My mother is one of the most brilliant people I have ever met, and she was also gifted musically but never did anything with it as she had to look after everyone in the family and take care of the house. She was an incredibly unfulfilled person, and it's a great sadness. Like many women of her time in India, her life was spent looking after others. We had a tough relationship because my mother had very high standards for me. It ranged from how I would sing to the work I did in the house. It felt critical even if it was coming from a good place. Her playing field was so small. She had lots of implied boundaries. Hers was the only parenting style I knew. I feel I absorbed those lessons and sadly repeated it with my daughter—I wanted so much for her to do well. One day, when she was 12, she sat me down and told me she was a good child and was as determined as I was about doing things well. She asked me to trust her. It was one of the most profound conversations I have ever had. They say child is the father of man; that was true for us. Our Hindu philosophy tells us to treat our children like they are a guest, to honor and love them so they can flourish. I wish I had understood it. It's easy for me to look backwards and see what I had been through with my mother, but to lack the understanding and repeat the mistakes—that was on me.

MA: Is the young Chandrika different from the person you are today?

CT: When I was young, I wanted to have an impact, be perfect at everything. Being perfect at everything was a badge of honor. My drive was internal. I felt others could do more, my clients, my daughter, but I also felt I could do more. I was always falling short of my own expectations. I didn't enjoy the moment because being perfect was an obsession. I had three miscarriages and felt I had failed. I am older and I think wiser now. I found meditation and redefined myself to accept myself and music has helped me find the way. I still want to have an impact.

MA: Do you have any regrets?

CT: Regret is a wasted emotion. Today, I want to give back and spend some time in service. I found New York University's Stern School of Business and became a distinguished executive in residence. I got involved in the school and taught and mentored students. I did that for a decade before I got on the board and made significant contributions to NYU. The donation to the engineering school happened when I was a member of their executive committee and I saw an opportunity to transform what was a mediocre polytechnic school into a world-class school under the aegis of NYU that would serve many Pell grant kids, many who are low-income or first-generation immigrants who comprised the majority of the student body. I am chairman of the board of the school and love spending time with the students, who are all doing brilliant things with AI and technology and experimenting for the future. I have a front row seat to an amazing transformation in an academic institution. People tell me I've done a lot for NYU, but I feel I've enriched myself by being there. I am the one who has gained. I am working towards my twin goals of economic empowerment through education and emotional empowerment through music. I want to live a life of intention. I run a community choir with senior citizens in Manhattan and I am working on connecting communities through music.

Talent seems to flow in their veins. After Chandrika's first recording "Soul Call" was nominated for a Grammy in 2011, she would go on to produce three more albums. She performed at Lincoln Center in New York and the Kennedy Center in Washington, D.C. She was invited to sing at the National Mall in 2023 in front of millions of people for the World Cultural Conference with luminaries such as Jaishankar, India's foreign minister; several ambassadors; and members of the White House.

Indra retired from PepsiCo in 2018. Total shareholder return during her 12 years as CEO was 149 percent. The company had returned more than $79 billion in cash to its shareholders, and dividends were growing at 10 percent a year. Net revenue jumped 80 percent to $64 billion in 2018 and market capitalization rose by $57 billion.[56] But Indra was proudest of the influence in making Pepsi a more green company, instituting changes under her direction to adopt planet-friendly production and reduce the sugar and salt contents of their products to make them less harmful to the consumer.

Both sisters are still young enough to have an impact. Chandrika has a clear path through her music and philanthropy.

Indra is still defining hers, but empowering women in business seems on the top of her list.

The Healers

CHAPTER 10

The Medicine Men

Give me your doctors, your scientists, ready to work hard...

In July 1965, President Lyndon B. Johnson signed the Medicare bill, which would have a lasting impact on the health care system in the United States. Millions of Americans over 65, including people with disabilities and end-stage renal failure, now had a right to medical care. When Medicaid became federal law the same year as part of Title XIX of the Social Security Act, coverage was extended to people who fell below a certain income level. Johnson used the power of the presidency to enroll 20 million Americans, which conformed to his vision of building a just and equitable country—he called it the "Great Society." Making health care for the elderly and the poor a national program was a monumental task given that most hospitals and medical facilities in the South were still segregated. By the end of 1966, only 12 hospitals and nursing homes remained segregated.[57]

Ironically, in 1963, contradicting the sudden rise in demand for medical care across the country, the American Medical Association's Council on Medical Education and Hospitals had recommended that medical schools reduce their enrollment by 10 percent. Hospitals suddenly swamped with patients faced a future that had "doctor shortage" blinking in red lights. Caught between the immediate increase in patient load and staring at a looming crisis, they began looking overseas for doctors to fill the gap.

When Deepak Chopra, who today is internationally recognized as one of the leaders of the integrative approach to medicine, arrived in New Jersey in 1970 fresh out of medical school in India, he got a firsthand introduction to the situation. "When I walked into the ER for my first shift," he recalled, "the doctors who showed me my locker and gave me a tour of the acute facilities were not

Americans. There was one German, but the rest had Asian faces like mine, from India, Pakistan, the Philippines, and Korea... What had brought so many foreign doctors together was the Vietnam War. A severe doctor shortage had arisen as the army drained away medical graduates while other young men, who might have wanted to become doctors, were drafted to fight."[58]

War had added an additional layer of stress on the health care system. During the Vietnam War, the shortage of men in the labor force had become a cause for concern. More than 9 million Americans—mostly men—served on active duty between 1961 and 1975. Medical personnel were needed in the war effort, adding to the shortage of available doctors for civilians. Thanks to advances in medical care on the frontlines, many more soldiers were surviving their injuries. Seventy-five thousand severely disabled veterans returned to the United States, many of whom would need years of continuing care, increasing the pressure on an already overwhelmed health care system.[59]

Europe no longer supplied qualified doctors looking for overseas opportunities; they had plenty of jobs at home. In the forties and fifties, Indians still considered the U.K. as the place to go for higher education, but by the sixties it had lost ground to America. There was a class of research-oriented doctors in India that had reached the limit of the resources that Indian institutions had to offer. They had no choice but to come to the West if they wished to pursue their studies. As Dr. Bibhuthi Mishra, an Indian physician recalled, "I left India after doing a specialization in internal medicine. I wanted to do work in molecular biology in DNA and immunology and although there were a few labs in India, only one was doing advanced work of an international standard and they didn't take students. The money being spent on biological research in India in 1981 was pitiful. Many of my friends in the field who were gifted were leaving. The first place I went to was London, but there was no comparison to the United States where substantial investments in medicine and biological research were being made ever since Nixon began the Cancer Institute. The U.K. funding was limited unless you were at the top institutions. I was working on a research paper, but a group in the United States overtook me. The lab in the United States was like a palace compared to

India. I wanted to pursue the work I was trained to do, so I moved to the United States Today, India has caught up, but in the eighties, there was no choice really."[60]

The United States had become the number-one destination for Indian graduates in STEM fields, but there were other reasons why America was such an attractive destination. It was a country of immigrants and a more welcoming environment for immigrants from India. Sanjiv Chopra, who rose to become a professor of medicine at Harvard Medical School, followed his older brother, Deepak to Boston in the seventies. He observed, "Our father's generation had gone to England to complete their training, but they had encountered a British ceiling. Indian doctors in England were allowed to rise to only a certain level, and when they returned to India they were behind their classmates in seniority and only rarely caught up... When people asked us what our plans were when we finished medical school, America was the obvious answer."[61] Initially, some Indian-trained doctors had gone to the U.K., but the attraction of opportunities in the United States convinced many of them to move.

The most pressing need for doctors in the United States was among its most run-down or underserved populations, who resided primarily in cities or in rural areas like Appalachia. The 1960s saw a precipitous decline in urban areas of its wealthier, white population who were leaving en masse for the suburbs. This left urban areas with a lower tax base and far fewer resources as businesses followed suit and urban decay set in.[62]

The shift to the suburbs had been facilitated by the massive highway-building program undertaken by the government after World War II, which had the ancillary benefit of making it easier for people to commute. The GI bill had created opportunities for its white beneficiaries,[63] and the relocation of businesses outside of urban centers had extended communities outwards. The migration of African American Southerners to the North that increased during this period combined with desegregation and the race riots in the sixties, contributed to what was called "white flight"—the white population moving out of cities in droves.

Wealthy, well-resourced hospitals moved with their clients to the suburbs, the preferred place for many doctors to practice. It was not easy for a hospital in downtown Newark or Detroit, still burning from the race riots, to attract a well-to-do white graduate of Harvard Medical School to practice there.

India's Brain Drain

When the United States began issuing medical visas after the sixties, many Indian doctors applied to go, frustrated with the working conditions at home. India's medical infrastructure was woefully inadequate and underfunded. Government-supported hospitals and health centers suffered chronic shortages of medical staff, medicines, diagnostic equipment, and even electricity during the fifties, sixties, and seventies.

Abraham Verghese remembers several friends who, like himself, had lined up at the United States Consulate to get a visa. His was a routine stamp as he had a visa, but he recalls a morning when six hopeful doctors were refused. A friend of his, one of the lucky ones granted entry, won the visa case officers' empathy with his directness. "Sir, craving your indulgence, I want to train in a decent, 10-story hospital where the lifts are actually working. I want to pass board-certification exams by my own merit and not through pull or bribes. I want to become a wonderful doctor, practice real medicine, pay taxes, make a good living, drive a big car on decent roads, and eventually live in the Ansel Adams section of New Mexico and never come back to this wretched town, where doctors are as numerous as fleas and practice is cutthroat, and the air outside is not even fit to breathe."[64]

Hospitals in major urban areas in India lacked everything from x-ray machines to labs. Some doctors who came to the United States said they were good at what they did because in India they had been forced to be creative working with such few resources.

For an Indian doctor, under-resourced hospitals were a fact of life. Learning to make do was par for the course. The poverty in places like Appalachia or South Central Los Angeles was no worse than in rural India or the slums of Mumbai. Doctors arriving to work in America were already primed for its underserved areas.

This was a huge setback for the country, as Prime Minister Jawaharlal Nehru had invested in setting up medical colleges to train doctors to provide health care for Indians. The All India Institute of Medical Science (AIIMS) in New Delhi was a symbol of the excellence he was aiming for. Like the IIT engineering colleges that he had established, this was to be a world-class medical college along with its affiliated research institute, the Indian Council of Medical Research (ICMR). AIIMS has an acceptance rate of 13 percent and has produced many of India's most well-known doctors, including Deepak Chopra. Unlike the IITs which were constitutionally meritocratic and have remained remarkably impervious to influence, the medical schools and other universities were subject to constant pressure, not unlike influence peddling in the United States by legacies and donors.

Attempting to prevent the "brain drain," India made it difficult for doctors who wanted to leave. In order to get a job in the United States, Indian doctors had to take the ECFMG, a qualifying exam to practice medicine in the United States India did not allow the test to be taken within its borders, hoping to prevent Indians from leaving. Those who had the means went to a neighboring country to do so.

On a visit to India in the eighties, I went to see my cousin at a well-known public hospital in New Delhi where she worked as an OB-GYN surgeon. She had graduated from the prestigious AIIMS medical school, her older brother was an internist at a nearby hospital, and my uncle, a family physician who had instilled a sense of public service in his children, ran a clinic for the underserved community in central Delhi. We had grown up together as members of a large extended family and were more like sisters than cousins. I was used to sitting at the dining table and hearing them discuss diseases and treatment options for various patients, but seeing firsthand the conditions under which she worked made me feel inadequate. It also instilled in me a great sense of admiration and gratitude for not just for her but for all her colleagues who accepted these working conditions as part of everyday life.

I was shocked to see three women taking turns sharing a hospital bed, squabbling for space and sharing their food with family members mixed in with the patients. It was summer and there was no air conditioning, and although the staff was constantly swabbing the floors with disinfectant, the stench was nauseating. "Don't faint on me," my cousin sternly warned me as an attendant carried open bowls of ether into the operating theatre. Her biggest worry today was a shortage of blood. The blood banks were always low on supplies, and the Indian women she saw were chronically anemic. She dreaded having to do surgery without making sure she had an adequate supply of blood, but a combination of illiteracy, a culture where families refused to let a man donate blood in case it weakened him, and limited funds made this difficult. These were problems a doctor in the West would not have to think about. "I don't hold it against my friends and colleagues who left to go overseas in the eighties," she said. "Conditions here can get to you; it's the little everyday things that make providing care difficult." She told me that on the weekend, she would take me around Delhi and show me some of the luxurious offices set up by her friends who had gone into private practice, assuring me that you no longer had to leave the country to do well in India. I asked her if she had considered private practice as she got older. "No," she replied sharply. "Look at the needs. In a country like ours, it's mindboggling. Besides, the cases are complicated and challenging. You'd never get this experience at a private clinic. My friends who go to the United States say it's a breeze after India."[65]

Being a doctor in India is highly respected, but India also respects healers that follow other traditions. Homeopathy came to India in 1881 when a specialized college was established there. In 1973, the Indian government of India recognized homeopathy as a legitimate form of medical treatment, and today there are 200,000 registered homeopaths in India; it is the third most popular form of medical treatment after traditional Ayurvedic medicine. It is not unreasonable when someone tells you they are a doctor in India to ask if they are an allopath or homeopath. Indians tend to be more open to integrative medicine and alternative healing, although in my family, doctors trained in Western medicine were mostly dismissive of anything that wasn't rooted in science.

According to data from the American Association of Physicians of Indian Origin (AAPI), 9 percent of the doctors in the United States are of Indian origin, despite being just 1 percent of the population. There are approximately 80,000 Indian American physicians practicing in the United States and about 40,000 Indian medical students and residents. It is a profession that appeals to Indians.

A quarter of the doctors in the United States have degrees from foreign countries and many, including Indians, play a critical role in serving rural communities and lower-income, disadvantaged urban communities. African Americans and Hispanics are more likely to live in "health care deserts"—areas with no primary care physicians—while foreign-trained doctors have often been on the frontlines of providing care to many of these communities across the United States[66]

Abraham Verghese attributes his recruitment to filling the needs of the underserved areas. "We only turn out X number of medical students, but we have X plus N slots funded by the government for residency training programs, which is the cheapest way to take care of the masses in public hospitals. I came because of that. You take an exam. I got here because there is a need. You're not going to Harvard, but you go to one of these mills in New York, LA, Chicago, Philadelphia, Highland Hospital in Oakland, and others like it. In El Paso, Texas, where I taught for 11 years, all my residents were foreign graduates."

In his book *My Own Country*, Verghese, who in the late seventies arrived in the United States as a newly minted doctor from India, describes the once-grand county hospitals that descended into critical states due to understaffing and underfunding. The hospitals were teeming with patients whose problems revolved around drug addiction and trauma. It was commonplace to see foreign physicians who bore little resemblance to the patients they served.

"At hospitals that took foreign physicians the work was grueling, the conditions appalling—but only by American standards—and the supervision and teaching often minimal because of the sheer volume of work," he observes. "This was particularly true in hospitals that were not university affiliated. The scut work... was endless and brutal... I was amazed by the number and variety of foreign interns and residents... Some hospitals were largely Indian, some Pilipino, others Latin or East European."[67]

Countries like India and the Philippines were an attractive pool to recruit from as they had the additional advantage of having been being trained in English. Although that has now expanded to other countries, Indians remain dominant in the medical field. Dr. Nitish Jain, a pulmonologist practicing in rural Minnesota who was interviewed during the COVID-19 crisis, said that the Indian health care professionals' contribution to the United States has always been exemplary but noted that though there were thousands like him working on the front lines, immigration laws have become more stringent, and many Indian doctors are stuck in a green card backlog. "Back in the seventies when India physicians started coming to the United States, the hospitals used to send cars to pick them up from airports. ... This is how badly America needed medical professionals. ... Now, due to the stiff competition, it is only the best and most diligent professionals who make the cut."[68]

The Chopra brothers came in the early seventies when it was relatively easy to obtain a medical visa, the process being enabled by the shortage of doctors. There were also American foundations that matched doctors with community hospitals who needed medical staff. Both brothers had attended elite medical colleges in India but received graduate training and their specialization in the United States.

But in the 1970s prejudices lingered and foreign doctors sometimes had to prove themselves. When Deepak Chopra clashed with his medical examiner about the cause of death of one of his patients, his judgement was overruled despite his correct diagnosis. Chopra had graduated from AIIMS, the highest-ranked medical college in India. His father was an eminent cardiologist who had treated the British viceroy Lord Mountbatten, but in the United States he was just another foreign-trained doctor. "Our attending physicians were all Americans. They typically didn't consider anyone trained in Asia to be a real doctor. Even the single American intern on staff, who had gone to Bologna, Italy was suspect. The more tactful attendings tried to conceal their prejudices, but the implication was never far away."[69]

Progressive social movements in the seventies and eighties began to change people's attitudes. Fortunately, those biases are long past, with a quarter of doctors now holding degrees from foreign countries. Today, the surgeon general, Vivek Murthy, is of Indian descent, though he went to medical school in the United States.

During the recent coronavirus pandemic, it was impossible to turn on the television without an Indian doctor explaining the situation or being consulted on the disease. Dr. Ashish Jha became a leading spokesperson for the government, while Dr. Sanjay Gupta of CNN was the first person each day to bring us the latest medical information during lockdown and reassure us that everything would be all right before we went to bed each night. Many of the medical specialists that appeared on talk shows were of Indian descent as well. Indian doctors were once again part of the nation's critical health care resources, with many working round the clock on the COVID-19 crisis, but what has truly distinguished Indian American doctors has been their ability to communicate with the public.

Of the many immigrant physicians who moved to the United States from Iran, Pakistan, the Philippines, and several other countries, the Indian medical community distinguished itself by producing gifted writers. Siddhartha Mukherjee won a Pulitzer prize for his book on cancer, *The Emperor of All Maladies*. Abraham Verghese attended the Iowa Writers Workshop and has written several bestselling books. Deepak Chopra writes a book a year, sometimes two. They along with Vivek Murthy, and Atul Gawande are all competent physicians, but their genius lies in the books they've written, the talks they've given, and the empathy with which they engage the public. Except for Dr. Gawande, who was born in the United States to Indian immigrants, the others were all born overseas, yet their impact has been monumental.

CHAPTER 11

Deepak Chopra

Prayer is you speaking to God,
meditation is allowing the spirit speak to you.

: : :

Instead of thinking outside the box, get rid of the box.

DEEPAK CHOPRA

In the 1950s, India was a remote country that floated somewhere on the periphery of America's consciousness. Images of snake charmers and poverty intermingled in an exotic tapestry of tales fed by British writers like Rudyard Kipling and a fickle press who for a while was besotted with Jawaharlal Nehru, India's modern prime minister. Jackie Kennedy's visit to India in March 1962 added another colorful dimension to America's exposure to India. *Life* ran a spread of her trip among palaces and elephants while dressed in glamourous outfits, making it chic to visit India and bringing the maharajas into temporary focus. When the Beatles discovered Maharishi Mahesh Yogi and the wonders of meditation, it was dismissed as a passing fad by most people.

The sixties were a time of flower children, pot-smoking hippies, and anti-war protests in America and it was in this milieu that the first wave of strait-laced, buttoned-up Indian immigrants, who had been raised to revere their parents and respect their elders, were just landing on America's shores.

I had heard about Indian "gurus" coming to America and strange stories of cults that gave Hinduism a bad name, so I was deeply suspicious of anyone who came to the United States who did not have real legitimacy in India. People in India were surprised by the gullibility of people in the United States. During the height of the hippie movement, Indians would joke that if they were desperate for money, all they needed to do was come to the United States, call themselves a guru and pontificate, and they'd have a following.

I have witnessed firsthand the growing popularity of yoga and meditation in America. It has moved from the hippie domain to mainstream culture. Today, everyone's grandmother is doing yoga, and it is being taught in schools. Meditation programs have been introduced in prisons and are used to treat PTSD. Chopra credits Maharishi Mahesh Yogi with bringing Transcendental Meditation (TM) to the West. He feels that the Maharishi made a genuine contribution by exposing its benefits to a Western audience, but that his role was compromised by a skeptical press, controversial stories about his relationship with the Beatles, and his general "exoticness."

If there is one person who deserves credit for the transformation in attitudes toward Eastern concepts of healing in mainstream American culture by providing them legitimacy, it is Dr. Deepak Chopra. As a medical doctor, a member of the American Association of Clinical Endocrinologists, and a fellow of the American College of Physicians, he possessed a legitimacy that gurus like Maharishi Mahesh Yogi lacked. Chopra was critical to not only the acceptance of the integrated approach to medicine in the United States medical community, but its eventual public embrace. He has written 93 books, using his expertise in science and medicine to bridge the gap between Western medicine and Eastern philosophy to help people achieve a mind-body balance.

Time has called Deepak Chopra one of the top 100 heroes and icons of the twentieth century. He is famous for revolutionizing modern medicine by advocating for holistic approaches to health.[70] As he has written, "In the eighties, alternative medicine implied a rejection of mainstream medicine, largely as a reaction to the American Medical Association's overt hostility to anything not taught in medical school. ... By the beginning of the nineties the editorial page of the *New England Journal of Medicine* had to confront a fact that deeply distressed the medical establishment: More Americans were going to alternative practitioners than to MDs."[71]

Chopra's early life was that of any driven immigrant doctor in the United

States. Newly married, he and his wife Rita had left New Delhi with the standard eight-dollar government allowance. Luckily, a generous uncle who was an admiral in the Indian Navy had given them a gift of a hundred dollars saved from a stint during an overseas assignment.

Chopra was assigned to an ER ward in a New Jersey hospital almost immediately, where on his first day he had to deal with gunshot wounds. Practically no one had guns in India, so civilian patients with gunshot wounds were nonexistent. He learned quickly on the job.

His long shifts at the hospital while working to secure his next residency or fellowship left little time to absorb the cultural changes swirling around him. Much of what Indians knew about American culture had been acquired from reading comics books and watching the few films that had come to India, mostly starring John Wayne and Elvis Presley, but Chopra was consumed with work. He was leading the predictable path of every successful Indian immigrant doctor—out before dawn, home after dark in a day spent between private patients, hospital rounds, and office appointments. The arrival of children was followed by more hard work, a house, a mortgage, and a residency in endocrinology. After several years of the same grind, he felt that something was missing from his life: "The stress of 18-hour days couldn't be shrugged off anymore. He relieved his stress the usual way that hard driving professionals in the seventies and eighties did— smoking excessively and drinking. He wondered whether the answer might lie in meditation. ...The sixties were long past. ...TM was already so established it had become passe."[72]

Abraham Verghese was a fellow in infectious disease in Boston at the hospital where Chopra was a practicing endocrinologist. He remembers Chopra well: "I don't think Deepak would remember me as I was quite junior, and basically our paths just crossed after my night shift when I handed over my patients in the morning, but we had a mutual friend, Irv, who was Native American. They had similar philosophical interests in meditation, Tai chi, and Native American techniques. Irv has great respect for Deepak. Deepak was not a celebrity then; he was just a medical doctor."

Chopra met the Maharishi in 1985 and was instantly drawn to him. He and his wife had begun to study meditation a few years earlier with his wife and found it a healthy antidote to the stressful life he was leading of a driven, ambitious immigrant doctor. On an impulse, he left his lucrative medical practice to join forces with the Maharishi and pursue alternative healing. "Meditation was something I instantly loved," he recalled. "...I felt no insecurity that India was reclaiming me. If I was going into the light, it was hardly a brilliant flash. What lay ahead was unbelievable however. Maharishi's ambition to change the world hadn't died as his reputation faded. He needed a younger surrogate to make his dreams come true and, unwittingly, I was about to step into that role."[73]

Chopra eventually outgrew his master teacher. One of his admirers, Laurance Rockefeller, whose mother was a believer in Buddhist teachings, encouraged him to branch out on his own to pursue his mission. By 1992, Chopra was ready, and the following year, luck intervened at just the right time—Oprah Winfrey invited him to be on her show. His book *Ageless Body, Timeless Mind* instantly became a *New York Times* bestseller and made him into a household name.

The idea behind the book was that positive lifestyle choices including diet, meditation, and exercise can cause profound biological changes down to our genes. By capturing your consciousness, you could essentially determine your destiny.

Oprah and Chopra went on to produce an online meditation course which Chopra claims has taught six million people.

Chopra has made some complicated statements that have incurred the wrath of the scientific community. Some physicists objected to his use of the word "quantum" in his book *Quantum Healing*, and in 1998 he was awarded the satiric Ig Nobel prize for "his unique interpretation of quantum physics as it applies to life, liberty, and the pursuit of economic happiness."

A 2019 *New Yorker* profile observes that "Chopra's work evinces a consistent skepticism towards the scientific consensus—he has called into question whether evolution is merely a process of the mind—and a firm belief that mental health can determine physical reality."[74] In the late nineties, HMOs and some insurance companies in California began to express a willingness to provide coverage for alternative medicine, though according to Chopra it has taken a long time for the medical establishment to come to terms with alternative medicine.

Verghese thinks there is a lot of jealousy when you achieve the sort of superstardom that Chopra has. He was thoughtful about why the medical community that they both belong to reacted to Chopra negatively. "Deepak was breaking the traditional medical mold, or, they are too bothered by his celebrity to be engaged by what he is saying. Most of the people who judged him, I would guess, have not read his books. I find what he writes quite compelling, regardless of whether I agree with everything. It's interesting that he's been almost shunned by academic medicine and the medical profession, but he doesn't need them because he's so above them. Now, of course, he's so sought after, even at medical institutions."

One of the criticisms leveled at Chopra and other nontraditional practitioners like Dr. Andrew Weil is that their focus is largely on the individual rather than on society and its institutions. One critic observes, "In emphasizing individual responsibility for health, wellness and spirituality, Weil and Chopra provide an alternative form of medical hegemony. ... It is doubtful whether their advice on health and well-being has much meaning for many working-class people and other people of modest means around the globe."[75]

One of the reasons I was moved to profile Dr. Chopra was precisely because his appeal crosses lines of class and ethnicity. That is his genius. Here is a story that a *Washington Post* reporter told me about Chopra: "The moment I realized that Deepak Chopra had really crossed into the mainstream and was not just someone whose teachings on mindfulness or alternative medicine were impactful on coastal elites was in the mid-nineties when I was traveling with a federal agent in rural southwestern Virginia to track down illegal alcohol smugglers. The illegal moonshine was being produced in stills in the hills of southwestern Virginia and it was the agent's job to go and bust up the stills and apprehend the distillers. We were driving through rural country roads and the agent pops into his cassette recorder a Deepak Chopra tape and proceeds to tell me how much Chopra has influenced his life, his struggling marriage, and his very stressful job. He said as a law enforcement officer it calmed and centered him."

I had not read any of Deepak Chopra's books earlier. I had of course heard of him, but I was a natural skeptic when it came to what I called "mind-body stuff." I started reading in preparation for my meeting and discovered I was learning a lot. Random people shared that they too read his books, including a server at a coffee shop who saw me reading one.

Is there any philosophical question about life that Chopra has not answered in one of his 93 books? I have not read them all, but I am amazed at the breadth of questions he covers. You may or may not agree with his concept of consciousness or the idea that everyone is part of the same mass of energy, but like Dr. Verghese, I found them compelling. Listening to his talks and interviews, I was also impressed by how comfortable he is with science. Some of the people who interviewed him clearly admired his work while others were aggressive and wanted to question him on the science, but he never got rattled and was up to date on the latest information. Chopra has co-authored books with Dr. Rudolph E. Tanzi of Harvard Medical School and physicist Menas Kafatos and has discussed the use of controversial topics such as psychedelics and artificial intelligence. When we arranged to meet, he said he had no interest in discussing himself as he was now caught up in the mystery of life.

Chopra was slim and smaller than I had imagined. He has the quality of air. There was a lightness to him as well as a kindness. He wore a rather distinctive pair of red shoes and his trademark black-rimmed glasses with the etched silver markings on the side, which added a bit of flash to his otherwise unremarkable attire. He has curly, slightly unruly hair, and his appearance was more reminiscent of an artist than a doctor.

I was a little intimidated initially, but his casual, easy manner put me at ease. Our interview is not about how he became a success or reached celebrity status, but more about his reflections on life and his philosophy.

MA: You have been such an important figure in changing America's approach to medicine and healing. You started out as a medical doctor, yet your books explore and address such a vast number of philosophical and life questions. How did you get that way?

DC: I have no explanation for it. There is no explanation for existence, so if there is no explanation for existence, we don't have an explanation for anything that is in existence. Where I am or where I got to is the same thing. Accident? Randomness? Unpredictability, creativity, they all come from situational circumstances that allow you to evolve to a place that are not distracted by the hypnosis of the collective mind. We think we are individuals and are unique, with a mind, with opinions, but we are products of the cultural collective mind which has been recycling ideas for 40,000 years—ever since the cognitive revolution. Every generation repeats and recycles the previous generations' ideas, aspirations, memories, and longings and reflects the ecosystem that you grew up in and the influences that you experienced in your early life. My mother was a great storyteller, particularly in Indian mythology in the oral tradition and was a great influence on me. My father was trained in the Western scientific tradition with a secular view of the world, and I myself trained as a doctor. That, combined with the rigor of training in America, made me see things through different lenses. I got into the habit of not accepting any dogma or philosophy or science without questioning it, whether it was a cosmologist, a quantum physicist, or a Nobel laureate. I would ask, "Is it true? How do we know it's true? What if it wasn't true? What is true?"

MA: Isn't that the way a scientist would approach an inquiry?

DC: Even science is dogma.

MA: Can you give me an example of what you mean?

DC: Even the history of genetics, take Watson and Crick—just because they became a genius in one area doesn't mean they are correct about everything. Crick was a neuroscientist and famous as the co-discoverer of the double helix. He was a physicist and biologist, but then he decided he was an expert on consciousness and wrote about it in an essay called "The Astonishing Hypothesis," which says the brain produces consciousness, and everyone quotes him and he's so astonishingly wrong and no one questions him.

MA: What is he wrong about?

DC: That the brain produces consciousness. This is something I've been obsessed with for the last 40 years.

Chopra said he is used to being challenged on his views. During a debate at Caltech with the Skeptic Society, a journalist from ABC told Chopra that there was a physicist in the audience who had worked with Stephen Hawking and who said that his theories were spurious.

DC: He got up in the middle of the debate actually and grilled me on consciousness and tried to ridicule me, and it became a huge story in the press. After the debate, the allegations became very public, so I wrote to him and said, "You know everything about physics, but you don't understand consciousness," and I invited him to walk with me in Central Park in New York so he could teach me physics and I could teach him about consciousness. He came and we didn't agree on much, but we did become good friends and he suggested we write a book together and it briefly became a *New York Times* bestseller. He received a call from Stephen Hawking's daughter who said she had been told by an Oxford geneticist that her father's co-author was working with a fraud, and so Hawking was disinviting him from his seventieth birthday party. Well, he stood his ground and told the daughter that although he didn't agree with me on everything, I was no fraud, and if Stephen wanted to disinvite him, he should also know they would no longer be producing a book together. Hawking apologized and invited me to the party as well.

Somehow, one wouldn't have expected that level of pettiness from Stephen Hawking. Chopra was not surprised. "Nobel laureates are just like anybody else," he said. "I have now met every single prominent Nobel laureate. They can be emotional, or maybe they are just confined by their knowledge. Sometimes too much knowledge interferes with your ability to explore reality."

Chopra went on to describe a remarkable 67-year-old woman he met on a flight whom he described as a genuine genius. He was struggling with a Sanskrit translation, and she looked over and translated the entire passage for him. She had never been to India or formally studied the language, but she told him that she could read any language. Born to a poor mining family in Michigan, she was a talented dancer and had gone to ballet school in New York but was told that she was too short to be a professional dancer. She also attended Yale Medical School, where she got in with the wrong crowd, dropped out, and started using drugs, including heroin. After a period of addiction and psychotic breakdowns, she found a psychiatrist who helped her. This psychiatrist introduced her to a Nepalese girl who worked in her house and suggested she help her translate her letters from home as a project to keep her busy. She reduced her medications and discovered she could understand any language. She picked up German, French, Russian, and Hebrew instantly.

DC: She said she tutors college students. I asked her what subject, and she replied any subject—math, biology, chemistry, languages. I told her, "You're a genius." I asked her what she attributed this to, and she said she had multiple personalities, and realized she had no personality. She was totally egoless with zero personal identity and was able to assume all identities. She had total freedom to choose. It was, in a way, very Vedantic. I told her I wanted to know more about her and asked if she would write down her theories and life story. This woman personified genius. To have no identity is genius. This woman was more interesting than any Nobel laureate I've met.

MA: It's a great story, but where does her ability come from, the knowledge base?

DC: It's like being a great Shakespearean actress and being able to assume any role. The knowledge isn't consciousness. To have no identity is genius—she can play any role. There is something called data, something called information, something called wisdom, and something called transcendence of all of the above. That is the ultimate, which is what Vedanta or the original Buddhist thinkers talked about. There is no reality except a formless field of conscious knowledge in chapter 13 of the Bhagavad Gita.

MA: What about the genius of Einstein?

DC: Einstein is a good example as he was always struggling with existential conundrums, and he was never sure which side to be on. He had a wonderful conversation with the poet and Nobel Laureate Rabindranath Tagore, which was pivotal. It shows the greatness of Einstein. He was humble enough to admit to Tagore that science was his religion. I am fascinated by cognitive scientists. I learn from them, people like Don Hoffman who broke away from the dogmatic view of the world. I also like to befriend sages, psychotics, and geniuses—you can learn a lot from them too.

MA: In your book *Metahuman*, you propose a theory of creation and the universe that contradicts and challenges the dominant Judeo-Christian view of creation and God. Does that put you at odds with the religious right in the United States and the Christian Church?

DC: Well, it's not just the Christian right but all traditional religions including Hinduism, although the sages of the Upanishads articulated the same things I've said. During the Reagan era, I gather there was a directive in the United States government to get rid of Eastern influences. I went through a lawyer to find out if I'd been mentioned, as Pat Robertson was a huge critic of mine and had called me dangerous and the devil. Jerry Falwell was not a fan either. They wanted to get rid of Eastern gurus. I think the actual teachings of Christ are quite liberal. I've also been to the Vatican and had some very good conversations with Pope Francis. The cardinal from Argentina wanted me to speak to his mother and asked me to conduct a meditation in the Sistine Chapel. I asked if the Pope had agreed, and he said we could go ahead. None of the East Europeans came but all the Latinos attended. It was like a boy's club. Very political.

MA: In a conversation with Marianne Williamson, you both talked about the world being insane and you pointed out that we are a speck in the cosmos. So, what's the point of anything?

DC: There is no point. It's entertainment. But in terms of the whole world being insane? It is.

MA: You said we are sleepwalking towards extinction. Are we?

DC: Yes, 100 percent. Just look around. Climate change, nuclear weapons, cyber warfare, chronic disease pandemics, socio-economic injustice. It's a perfect recipe for extinction. The last extinction was 65 million years ago. Dinosaurs were wiped out in less than a week, then we emerged, so maybe we are another experiment in evolution that did not work.

CHAPTER 12

Abraham Verghese

I think we learn from medicine everywhere, that it is, at its heart,
a human endeavor, requiring good science but also a limitless curiosity and interest
in your fellow human being, and that the physician-patient relationship is key;
all else follows from it.

ABRAHAM VERGHESE

Abraham Verghese might have never become a doctor had it not been for the fortuitous intervention of a book, a helpful aunt, his own grit and determination, and a certain amount of serendipity. Verghese was enrolled in medical school in Ethiopia in 1974 when civil war broke out. A Marxist-Leninist rebel faction overthrew the emperor Haile Selassie in a coup d'état, interrupting his studies and plunging the country into a cycle of chaos and violence that would last for years.

Verghese's parents, who met in Ethiopia, were schoolteachers and part of an expatriate community from India that had been recruited by the emperor to help modernize the country. Their sons, George and Abraham, were born in Africa just 22 months apart. A third brother, Philip, would follow 13 years later. The two older siblings grew up together and would remain close throughout their lives. Verghese often refers to his older brother as his rock. George, who had a gift for mathematics, left to study in India at the prestigious Indian Institute of Technology in Madras when he was just 15, around the time Philip was born.

George describes himself as the conventional older son, with Abraham being more rebellious: "Abraham didn't do anything wild, but he did things I wouldn't step into doing. He did what he felt he wanted to do. I remember I was often the intermediary between Abraham and my parents. I felt protective, in both directions. My mom once had him face the wall for something he did, and when my dad came home, Abraham pointed to the other corner and told my dad there was a corner for him. Everyone found that rather amusing. I would come home with 'A's on my report card, but Abraham's grades were more mixed, and although I don't remember our parents ever saying anything or comparing us, Abraham used me as a benchmark."

Abraham Verghese was a voracious reader, and it was a book that led him to medicine. When he was young, he devoured the children's book author Enid Blyton, E.M. Forster, and Shakespeare. By the time he was entering puberty, he had come across *Lady Chatterley's Lover* and was riveted. He picked up Somerset Maugham's book *Of Human Bondage*, expecting a bodice ripper; instead, it inspired him to become a physician. The protagonist, Philip Carey, is an orphan and has a club foot. He goes to Paris to become an artist, and in a moment of truth confronts the reality that he is unlikely to find success and decides to study medicine—but it is when he begins working in the wards with patients that he truly finds his calling. Verghese was inspired by the words, "Philip saw humanity in the rough, the artist's canvas, and he said to himself, this is something I can be good at."

George Verghese remembers when his brother fell in love with the idea of becoming a doctor and feeling concerned about some of the challenges he might face. "Abraham followed me to India to do pre-university. He had decided he wanted to do medicine. He wrote some entrance exams but didn't get into the medical schools he wanted in India as it was very competitive and returned to Ethiopia. He didn't have the path laid out for him in the way I did. For me it happened quickly, but he was waiting for it all to connect, so it was a relief when he got accepted to medical school in Ethiopia. Once he connected, he was quite independent, but Ethiopia was becoming politically unstable, and our parents had decided to emigrate to the United States. My parents left after his second year. He was doing well until the political upheaval."

Verghese's path to becoming a doctor did not follow a straight line. It would take grit, determination, and, in the end, a great deal of perseverance. He was in his fourth year of studying medicine when schools in Ethiopia were shut down due to the political situation and he was forced to leave the country. "When I left

Ethiopia, I was happy to get out," he said. "It was a very violent time. Out of the 35 classmates, some defected and joined the Eritrean Liberation Front, fighting the military government. Others joined the Royalists, trying to reinstate the emperor. Some were tortured and killed. One individual who had been below me had been fighting for 22 years and ultimately became prime minister. Tina Brown asked me to interview him, which I did for *Talk* magazine. My mood when I got to the United States was sheer relief at getting out—we had all been brought up on images of America, and here I was. My relief quickly turned to anxiety as I recognized it would be hard to get back to medical school, as the two systems were completely different and there you don't do an undergraduate degree as you go straight to medical school from high school."

Verghese's first job in the United States was in a nursing home in New Jersey as an orderly. He recalled cleaning bedpans and making beds and has often said it was a profoundly humbling experience: "I had been a medical student dealing with disease until I came to the United States. It was here that I had my first exposure to the warehousing of elderly people in nursing homes. There was an army of people like me, mostly people of color, being bused in by van from Newark to Westfield, New Jersey to care for mostly white people in a nursing home. Later, I got a job at a hospital and my colleagues were mostly nurses and nursing assistants and I developed a real appreciation for who was really caring for the patients for 23 hours and 55 minutes of the day. The doctor might be there for a few minutes, but the nurses really provide the 24/7 care. I still feel a great kinship with the nurses. It was also my first exposure to blue-collar work. It was backbreaking, intense, and poorly paid."

It was a difficult two-year period for Verghese. "When I started at the nursing home," he recalled, "I didn't know what was going to happen. It was such an uncertain time. Once I got the nursing home job and was assigned the night shift, I joined the blue-collar work force. I took my parents' car, worked the night shift, and fell in with the blue-collar crowd and lost the medical school thread. I kind of lost any vision of getting back to medical school."

His brother George, in the meantime, had graduated from IIT and was now in graduate school in New York pursuing a career in engineering, but he continued to worry about his brother. "I'd go home on weekends and see Abraham, who was living at home, kind of depressed, wondering if medicine was worth pursuing. He was working as an orderly, but it wasn't something he was thrilled about."

It was a book that helped Verghese find his footing again. Books have always been fundamental to his life. They have been his source of inspiration, his guide, and also his celebrity. Like guardian angels, specific books guided his decisions. *Of Human Bondage* had led him to his vocation, and now another would help him find his way back. Without its fortuitous appearance in his life at this critical juncture, Verghese might not have become the iconic physician that we have all come to admire. Following his stint at the nursing home, Verghese had found a job working as a nurse's aide in a hospital that was affiliated with a medical school.

"Medical students used to come through regularly," he recalled, "and one day a medical student left a textbook on the counter. It was Harrison's *Principles of Internal Medicine*, which I had known and loved and memorized in medical school. I saw it and had an epiphany. I realized I had gone through too much to just let medicine go. All those years studying, dissecting bodies, the high stress exams—I realized I couldn't just walk away from it, and I knew then, as I held the book in my hands, that I had to finish. In the meantime, my aunt in New Delhi, India had been working behind the scenes to get permission to have my studies accredited in India.

Verghese got on a plane, returning to the land of his ancestors, a country he did not know well except for holidays spent at his grandparents' home. Despite being born in Africa, Verghese was an Indian citizen like his parents. But unlike the rest of his family who were cocooned within an expat environment while they lived in Ethiopia, he had actually lived with Ethiopians at university once his parents left and felt like part of the local community. India was remote, an existential identity. Although he could relate to the food, language, and certain cultural markers, he had no idea how to navigate the opaque Indian system on which his future now depended.

The Indian bureaucracy was nicknamed "the license Raj" for its infamous reputation of requiring tedious paperwork for the smallest, most insignificant endeavor. Connections were essential and graft rampant. Even for a student, negotiating the system if you were unfamiliar with it and lacked an advocate would have been impossible, but his aunt helped him and his persistence paid off. "I spent a year in India petitioning the various entities and cutting through the bureaucratic red tape to gain admission to a medical school that would give me partial credit for my prior studies," Verghese recalled. "I finally got admission into the third year of medical school. My life was taking off again. My career was back on track, I had a girlfriend, and I was able to afford a little car."

Verghese had been through civil war, displacement, and a loss of identity, and now that he had found his way back to his calling, he was driven. Becoming a physician was no longer just a romantic inspiration; it consumed his being. "When I went to medical school the first time, I was young and took a lot of things for granted," he said. "When I went to America, I was still young. But the second time around, once I got into medical school in India, I was highly motivated to succeed. I had been through a lot, I was older than my classmates, I had worked at blue-collar jobs that they wouldn't dream about soiling their hands with, and so now I had a certain resilience and determination. I was a different kind of student than what I had been in Ethiopia. I was focused and studied really hard. I had become a different person."

Verghese had lost two years of medical school, but he was internalizing the experiences he was accumulating. They would find their way into his writing, his humanity, and his approach to patients, making him into one of the most profoundly influential and admired physicians of our time. For some people, geography determines identity; for Verghese, it was his vocation that defined him.

Verghese is an infectious disease doctor, a professor at Stanford, an acclaimed writer whose books have appeared on the *New York Times* bestseller list four times, a humanitarian, and a recipient of the National Humanities Medal. One of his most important contributions has been to embody the ideal physician, inspiring a generation of future physicians at a time when many are experiencing burnout and leaving the field. I caught up with him in early May 2023, the week that his new book *Covenant of Water* had been picked by Oprah. He had just returned from speaking at two different venues in Los Angeles, but still looked dapper in a lavender shirt and dark jacket that complimented his olive complexion. His perfectly matched handkerchief added an old-fashioned touch to his otherwise sleek, trendy outfit. He spoke in a soft, attentive manner and was thoughtful about some of the interactions he had been having with his audiences.

AV: Yesterday there were about 40 young physicians in the audience. These are typical of the physicians that have been reading my work since they were in medical school. They project on me this pied piper quality, representing that aspect of medicine that they had hoped to practice. I didn't invent this. It's the ideal that we teach but the reality is so far divorced from what they experience that they are burnt out. They talked about this last night. People are leaving medicine in droves. It's a known phenomenon. I've become a voice for the humanistic aspect of medicine. Not by design. My TED Talk has been hugely influential to medical students in particular and has a million-plus views.

In a world that has become increasingly reliant on technology, including in medicine, Verghese has been a vocal advocate for prioritizing a strong patient-doctor relationship. He worries that today doctors neglect the importance of the physical exam and prefer to rely on lab tests. In his TED Talk, he provides powerful examples of diseases that were initially missed because a patient was not examined thoroughly with "hands on body." I personally saw him get a standing ovation, with many in the audience having tears in their eyes, after a talk he gave in 2009 about the need to maintain a human connection to one's patient as a critical component to the diagnostic and healing processes. He has spoken about the ritual of handwashing before entering a patient's room as fulfilling the function of a pause button before crossing the threshold of a sacred space.

AV: That first moment when a physician enters a room and meets a patient is critical. If they form a good bond, everything else follows: compliance with medications, follow up visits, etc. If they don't, everything is off. So much is predicated on that moment of initial contact. Milan Kundera writes about how it's the same with a man and a woman, and how the first moment between them determines what's going to transpire as their love story unfolds. The whole method of medicine is to emulate the great clinicians you trained with and model yourself on them. It's become harder to find those models for medical students because all of us are caught up in this big industrial machine. At Stanford we have come up with a checklist called Presence Five based on a large study. We interviewed all kinds of providers who needed to make a connection, from policemen to therapists to suicide prevention, including observational studies of many clinicians.

In 1980, Verghese returned to the United States as a newly minted doctor, and the Indian physician network in America helped him find his feet. People he knew from medical school in India who had come before him had fanned out across the country, so with a few phone calls he was able to connect with friends and contacts and work out which hospital to apply to in just about any city in the United States Through the network, he got useful tips on which hospitals accepted foreign graduates their first year, which ones never promoted them, and where someone, even a stranger, would inevitably offer you a place to stay.

Verghese decided to accept a residency at East Tennessee State University. He had arrived with a family to support and began to moonlight near the Appalachia border on weekends, pulling 60-hour shifts.

AV: When I moved to Tennessee, I was struck by the sheer number of foreign physicians in small towns around Johnson City. I used to moonlight in some of these towns and they had tiny hospitals and ERs. Some had just 40 or 50 beds. There may be one white family physician, the rest—the cardiologist, OB-GYN, etc.—were all foreigners. People in the towns had private medical insurance thanks to the coal mines, so the practice was reasonably lucrative, but doctors who were trained in big cities faced a dilemma once their children got to high school. The parents worried that the education in the small town wasn't good enough and felt they either had to send their children to boarding school or move.

It was difficult to entice young American medical school graduates to practice in these isolated and often depressed rural areas where reimbursement depended heavily on the health of coal mines and doctors being willing to have a large proportion of Medicaid patients in their practice. Inevitably, foreign doctors, many of them Indian, filled the need. In his book, Verghese describes a comical situation involving the Indian doctors who served this population: "I had once tried to reach Dr. Patel, a cardiologist, to see a tough old lady in the ER whose heart failure was not yielding to my diuretics and cardiotonics. I called his house, and his wife told me he was at 'urology Patel's' house, and when I called there, I learned he and 'pulmonary Patel' had gone to 'gastroenterology Patel's' house."

The former national editor of the *Washington Post*, Rajiv Chandrasekaran told me that for him, Verghese personified the impact that Indian immigrant physicians have had across the country in small, rural, poor communities: "There is so much attention focused on the superstar Indian doctors," he said. "Those who are on television or are making major research breakthroughs or are academics, but the impact that Indian physicians have had in small communities in Appalachia, in the Midwest, and the Deep South has been utterly transformational in the lives of ordinary Americans and Abraham embodies that and his book provides a window into that. What legions of Indian physicians have done to keep rural health care clinics open to provide essential services to people in what would otherwise be health care deserts is an enormous contribution to the health and well-being of the American people. Without them, millions of Americans would have much poorer health care options."

I pushed back, suggesting that Indian physicians went to these areas because it was a visa requirement or where they found a job rather than out of any altruistic motivation, but he pointed out, "If you ask the people who are alive today because of the work those physicians have done, I think it's been transformational for them. Maybe they went there because they had few choices, but they showed up, did what they did, faced their own forms of discrimination, but they continued to serve, persevered, built new lives. I think when you take that at scale, there's been a profound impact."

Dr. Vivek Murthy, the United States surgeon general, found Verghese's book *My Own Country*, "incredibly powerful because Abraham spoke of his immigrant experience as a physician coming to America, not necessarily being fully understood by the people he was seeking to serve and gradually gaining acceptance, respect, and honor through the work he did for a community. I saw my own father's story in his. My father also came here as an immigrant physician, set up a medical practice among people who didn't fully understand them, and yet they were fiercely committed to people and to service."

A lot changed after 1980. Indian physicians no longer had to rely on their friends and began to organize. In 1982, they set up the American Association of Physicians of Indian Origin (AAPI) which currently represents 80,000 Indian American physicians and 40,000 Indian American medical students, helping members with information and placements and holding seminars and conferences. A new physician arriving today can call them and get connected to a chapter and assigned to a mentor in his or her state.

Tennessee became an important inflection point in Verghese's career. It was where he met Steven Berk, an infectious disease specialist who became his mentor and directed him to his field. Berk helped arrange a fellowship for Verghese at Boston City Hospital in 1983, which housed the country's premier infectious disease training program. This is where he was first exposed to patients with AIDS. When Verghese finished his training in Boston, Berk persuaded him to return to Tennessee.

By 1985, the AIDS crisis had begun to spread to rural communities. Young people who had migrated to cities to live uninhibited lives, including gay men, had contracted HIV and were now returning home sick. Verghese got to know them— not just the patients, but their families, because that is what it was like to practice medicine in rural communities. He integrated himself into the community. He discovered that sometimes being a foreigner worked in his favor: "More than once I had the sense that a patient was opening up to me ... because of my foreignness. The preacher with penile, rectal and pharyngeal gonorrhea was a perfect example. He didn't think I would pass judgment on him—perhaps he felt I had no right to pass judgment on him. And so he came to see me regularly for new venereal

Kanwal Rekhi and Suhas Patil with Silicon Valley entrepreneurs, and Indian Prime Minister Atal Bihari Vajpayee

Kanwal Rekhi at a TiE conference

Indra Nooyi and Chandrika Tandon with their brother and grandfather

Chandrika Tandon

Satya Nadella addresses shareholders during Microsoft Shareholders Meeting

Shantanu Narayen, CEO of Adobe

Atul Gawande

Fareed Zakaria in his study with Brody

Abraham Verghese presented
with the National Humanities
Medal by President Barack
Obama

Nikesh Arora, CEO of Palo Alto Networks,
in conversation with Eric Schmidt, former
chairman and CEO of Google

Siddharta Mukherjee being honored by the Vellore
medical foundation

Deepak Chopra

Shannon Finney/Getty Images

Congressman Ro Khanna addressing constituents on Capitol Hill

Vivek Murthy, United States Surgeon General

TASOS KATOPODIS/AFP via Getty Images

Mr. Neal Katyal

Neal Katyal takes part in the hearing of Neil Gorsuch (2nd L) during the Senate Judiciary Committee confirmation hearing

Photographs, unless specified, courtesy of the participants

problems that indicated to me he was not practicing safe sex. ... Would he have been as comfortable ... with the internists who were local boys?"[76]

Verghese differed from other physicians and Indian American doctors in that he was indifferent to the accumulation of capital and investments and the trappings of suburban life. He spent time among the shadows where his patients lived, made house calls, and befriended many members of the community. He rode motorcycles and absorbed the world around him. He was moved by the mounting crisis and wrote a scientific paper hoping to push for more funding for AIDS research, but worried it failed to convey the scale of human suffering caused by the virus. In 1990, he took a sabbatical to write about it.

Verghese was married during his years in Tennessee and had two sons while he was there. He admits that his deep involvement with his patients took a toll on his marriage. His wife, Rajani and he had begun to drift apart by 1990, pulled by different gravitational forces each pushing them towards a different destiny. The more absorbed he got into the world of his patients the less he had in common with his wife and the warp and weft of life and its familial obligations. The marriage would not survive the next phase of his life as he embarked on his writing career in Iowa. Later, at an AIDS clinic in EL Paso, Texas, he would meet his second wife and father another son, Tristan. That marriage would also end in divorce.

Verghese was admitted to the Iowa Writers' Workshop, a prestigious program for gifted writers. His nonfiction book *My Own Country*, which was a result of his time there, was a *New York Times* bestseller and a finalist for the National Book Critics Circle Award. To a vast number of Americans, his was the voice of compassion in writing about his experiences working in rural Virginia and elsewhere in Appalachia where he was introduced to the ravages of the AIDS epidemic in the eighties. A reporter explained to me why he thought *My Own Country* was so important for its time. "I think in *My Own Country*, he, in a breakthrough way, helped ordinary Americans understand the human side of the AIDS crisis in a transformational way just like the musical *Rent* was transformational."[77]

It was through this book that Verghese was able to convey the depth of the suffering endured by his patients. Vivek Murthy said it was one of the very first books he read about medicine, and it affected him in a deep and profound way. He had been thinking of going into medicine at the time and hoped to serve in the way Verghese had served his patients. Dr. Atul Gawande, a renowned neurosurgeon and writer himself, read *My Own Country* as a medical student and said it was formative for him.

Verghese was exploding as a talent. Not only had he become the physician's ideal as well as a symbol of the contributions of the immigrant doctor, but now he was communicating his medical philosophy through his writing and reaching a larger audience.

I caught up with Verghese at a writer's conference in Idaho in July 2023 where he was being honored with the Writer in the World Award. His recent book, *The Covenant of Water*, took him 10 years to write. Oprah Winfrey called his new novel one of the three most important books on her shelf. She was effusive about the book during an interview with him the week it was published in May 2023, making it into a six-part podcast and possibly a film. The magic of the "Oprah effect" immediately catapulted it to number one, making it Amazon's bestselling book. In this, he was following in the footsteps of another Indian American doctor and beneficiary of the "Oprah effect," Deepak Chopra whose book *Ageless Body, Timeless Mind* had a similar trajectory when it came out in 1993.

Ever since the book's release, Verghese has been under constant pressure to speak and give interviews. He was very gracious and dodged his various well-wishers and admirers—who tend to mob him at these events—by meeting me at 8 a.m. so I could ask him a few more questions about his meteoric success, the risks he took on his journey, and how it affected him.

MA: When you went to Iowa to pursue your love of writing, did you worry about the risk of reentering medicine? Earlier, your medical career was interrupted not by choice but due to political circumstances, and you had to struggle to complete your medical education and become a doctor. Yet you took a risk?

AV: I took a risk, but I also knew I wasn't doing it forever. It was a finite period. One of the lessons I had learnt from my HIV patients is that you don't postpone your dreams. These guys were younger than me and they were dying. Some had accomplished so much. I admired the way gay men had traveled and done a lot in their life. By comparison, my life had been fairly narrow. I learnt that if there is something you want to do that is important, don't wait till someday when you might have time.

MA: But what about the other part of your life? You had worked so hard to become a doctor, were you taking a career risk?

AV: I never really worried, because what was the worst that could happen? Any physician with a license can moonlight in emergency rooms or urgent care. I was able to cover for someone at an HIV clinic in Iowa. I was moonlighting. The medical faculty were very supportive. They knew what the Iowa workshop was and so they understood. They were the only faculty in the whole country that got it and didn't think I was insane to do this. When I finished, they even offered me a job. The place I took a risk was in academic medicine. I had papers and a certain standing in my area, but I wasn't wedded to money in the same way as other physicians might be. It's not that I didn't value it, but I didn't want to keep working in a small town, surrounded by Asian physicians where everyone knows you. It had begun to feel like a prison. I saw this as a break—I knew I wanted to write about my experience, and I also knew I would return to medicine. Ninety-nine percent of the people who come to Iowa don't continue with their writing, so I wasn't sure how it would all work out.

Verghese was curious and a risk-taker, key characteristics of most geniuses, but he put in the hard work—Gladwell's 10,000-hour rule. If the measure of success is the number of books sold, Verghese's time in Iowa was wildly successful. He would henceforth wear the dual hats of writer and physician.

MA: In your podcast with Oprah, you said that the immigrant is given voice when they come to America and that geography is destiny. Could you tell us how you found your voice here?

AV: A place like Iowa doesn't really exist anywhere else, in India or Ethiopia where in some ways at this moment in time the culture is heading backwards. Every kind of experience was invited to thrive and flourish here and to have their voice. I'm not sure if I had remained in India or Ethiopia that I would have had this thought to write a book, so part of the culture here is allowing me to feel I can express myself in these ways. I have really embraced being an American as it has allowed me to just be a hybrid Indian American who was born in Ethiopia.

MA: You finally admitted on Oprah's podcast recently that you are a "writer," yet you have said that your core identity is that of a physician.

AV: It really is. How could it not be after all these years? That how you interact with the world and look at the world. Even if I were to give up medicine, your lens is still clinical. You look at people and you're not only reading their body, but you also read their psyche, their wound that make them present a certain way. You don't judge as much as you try to understand.

Verghese seamlessly wove medicine into his writing. His second book, *The Tennis Partner*, was also a work of nonfiction that dealt with doctors who struggled with addiction. Verghese published his first novel, *Cutting for Stone*—an epic story encompassing generations and continents, in 2009. It reflected some of Verghese's own experiences of political turbulence, exile, and migration from Ethiopia to America.

The book's protagonists were physicians, and among its 658 pages were detailed medical procedures including liver transplants and fistulas. The book sold more than 1.5 million copies and was on the *New York Times*' bestseller list for two years. His most recent book, *Covenant of Water*, is set in Kerala, his ancestral home in India. It also has a significant medical aspect, dealing with leprosy and providing expansive details of procedures and disease pathways.

MA: When you worked in rural Tennessee, there was a great deal of stigma associated with AIDS. You have written about another stigmatized disease in *Covenant of Water*—leprosy. Can you talk about the stigmatization of disease?

AV: Since I specialize in infectious disease, things like leprosy and HIV is part of what I do, but all illness carries a metaphor. The metaphor of tuberculosis was that it was a romantic disease that happened to people like Keats and Shelley and people like that, whereas cancer was seen as a metaphor for losers like Hubert Humphrey. This is not my metaphor—it was historically the public perception. Diseases like leprosy became synonymous with revulsion; to be treated like a leper became a metaphor. When HIV came along, it was accompanied by shame, secrecy, rejection and developed its own metaphor of revulsion. Susan Sontag wrote a book about AIDS and its metaphors. The metaphor became more potent than the disease. I had patients who committed suicide because they had HIV. HIV didn't kill them. The metaphor killed them. I had trained in infectious disease, but when this disease landed in our lap, a lot of us who were trained in infectious disease were ambivalent about it. Not about treating the patients, but how our specialty had become overwhelmed by this one disease. I then read *And the Band Played On* by Randy Shilts and I was so moved by the book, I suddenly realized this was my calling. The book depicted heroic people stepping forward at the CDC and elsewhere, including gay activists, and it shifted my own thinking and I embraced it wholeheartedly instead of worrying about moving away from pneumonia, etc.

MA: You said in one of your interviews that life is a terminal condition and that we are sometimes in denial of our own mortality. As a doctor, you must be reminded of this on a daily basis. Have you observed differences between Americans' and Indians' attitudes towards mortality?

AV: John Irving said that life is a terminal condition. I think that in general people all over the world are in denial of their own mortality, but perhaps more so in America. The culture seems unprepared and family members get agitated and can be almost combative at the moment of death. What they're really dealing with is angst. Not having been with their parents, they now want to do something and demonstrate their filial love by advocating, sometimes in destructive ways, to put people on ventilators who shouldn't be, or keep them in ICU. I used to think it was different in India, but nowadays medicine for the affluent in both countries doesn't look very different.

MA: You have talked about a group of powerful men who have formed a support group that have included you. You have spoken movingly about how they are your go-to friendship clan and were very supportive during your divorce.

AV: Men are coy about their deepest friendships and are stressed in different ways. My group does what the kitchen table succeeds in doing for many women. But now one sees book groups or prayer groups—which mine is—which had a use beyond its stated function. Although my group begins and ends with prayer, it is much more of a support group. A lot of powerful men become pretty isolated. You may wish to be friends with other colleagues, but there are conflicts of interest that prevent you from exposing your vulnerabilities.

I asked Verghese if a camaraderie existed among the extraordinarily gifted and successful literary physicians of Indian origin: Deepak Chopra, Siddhartha Mukherjee, Atul Gawande, and himself. Did they ever get together or call each other to consult over patients or projects or just the emotional toll of success? I was disappointed to learn that there was not much beyond a formal relationship. There are, of course, significant age differences among them and most live in different cities, but the threads of their compassion spring from the same cultural DNA.

Vivek Murthy, who first encountered Verghese through his books, said, "Abraham reminds us that long before modern medications and technology, there was a very powerful tool that we had as healers. It was our ability to show up in people's lives, to listen with empathy, and to express our compassion and provide support. He reminds many of us in the medical profession that we can't lose sight of that as one of the most important tools we have as healers." The surgeon general's own concern with loneliness and meditation aligns with Deepak Chopra's philosophy and much of Atul Gawande's book *Being Mortal*—it's all part of the same collective cultural tissue. All of them, while keeping their day jobs, have become bestselling authors whose ideas have influenced a generation.

CHAPTER 13

Siddhartha Mukherjee

Science is among the most profoundly human of our activities.
Far from being subsumed by the dehumanizing effects of technology,
science, in fact, remains our last stand against it.

SIDDHARTHA MUKHERJEE

The most striking aspect of Dr. Siddhartha Mukherjee's appearance when you first meet him is his hair. His unruly curls, stylish clothes in mostly charcoal and black tones, and melancholy looks remind me of James Dean, a Hollywood icon who tragically died in a car crash at age 24. Mukherjee, a Rhodes Scholar and winner of the 2011 Pulitzer Prize for his first book, *The Emperor of All Maladies: A Biography of Cancer*, is on a quest to find a cure for certain types of cancer. Mukherjee's wife, the renowned artist Sarah Sze, was a 2003 winner of the MacArthur Fellowship, also known as the "genius grant." She represented the United States at the Venice Biennale in 2013, and her work has been collected and shown in many of the major museums, including the Guggenheim and the Museum of Modern Art. Crowned by no less than *Vogue* magazine in 2016 as "The Most Brilliant Couple in Town," they are among the most glamorous and sought-after couples in New York, their inboxes regularly flooded with invitations to every gala, opening, and major social event.

Mukherjee is an associate professor of medicine at Columbia University's Medical Center, where he is also a practicing oncologist and heads a research lab at Columbia that studies blood cancers. His team is developing innovative new treatment options using T-cells, which have been a paradigm shift in cancer pathology. Mukherjee has been at the forefront of adapting AI-based algorithms to discover human medicines that are currently in clinical trials across the globe, spanning novel therapies for ovarian, breast, and endometrial cancers as well as leukemias and lymphomas.

He has written four bestselling books, and is a regular contributor to the *New Yorker, The New York Times, Nature, The New England Journal of Medicine,* and other journals and is constantly on the interview and lecture circuit. Mukherjee is also an entrepreneur and founder of several bio-tech start-ups. Each of these commitments is the equivalent of a full-time job. To describe him as driven is an understatement.

Mukherjee admits that the demands on their time can sometimes be overwhelming. He and his wife are raising two daughters. With their combined commitments, it is understandable that Mukherjee says he often responds to invitations with a two-word response: "Apologies, unable."

In addition to all his scientific accomplishments, Mukherjee is a gifted musician trained in Indian classical music. He is a member of a jazz band and has performed publicly, including at Lincoln Center in 2023.

I met with Mukherjee on a grey day at the end of March 2024, with winter still clinging to a recalcitrant spring in New York. Mukherjee's penthouse apartment had the virtue of being full of light even on such a cloudy day. It was tastefully decorated with an eclectic mix of Buddhist and Chinese antiquities and modern art, including several of Sarah's paintings. Mukherjee was enthusiastic about the artwork and seemed to have a genuine appreciation for their beauty, particularly the ancient Buddhist pieces. The apartment had a comfortable, lived-in look, and Mukherjee made cups of hot milky tea for us in between answering calls from patients and answering my questions, which ran over several hours.

I had spent a considerable amount of time thinking about Mukherjee's path to success and what it took to reach the heights that he has. Many of the people described in this book have had interesting and often challenging paths to success which have not always followed a straight line. Those individuals are an inspiration for many who study their trajectory and learn valuable lessons on "how to succeed." But I believe there are some exceptional cases in which people are just born gifted, and Mukherjee is one of those individuals. Unlike Satya Nadella and

Shantanu Narayen, he was an academic star from the start; he did not have to find himself. He did not encounter the obstacles experienced by the older generation of discrimination or a lack of support. The timing and circumstances of one's birth can be a hidden benefit. For someone trying to examine his career to discover how he won a Rhodes scholarship or a Pulitzer or got into every prestigious school, examining his career may not provide the obvious lessons for success.

Were Mukherjee to win a Nobel Prize for his innovations in cancer treatments, it will complete his circle of achievements. But Mukherjee is not without his demons. He has had to navigate his enormous and early success as it layered additional pressures on him. He has been open about his struggle with depression, which has at times been debilitating. Mukherjee always found his inner strength and was able to overcome these bouts, but it required medication and treatment.

What follows is a conversation in which he opens up about his youth, what drove him to study science, and his reflections on work, politics, ethics, and the future of medicine. His reflections on the path he took and the ecosystem that nurtured him illuminate some of the necessary ingredients to achieve success.

MA: There is an evident lack of trust that has developed between scientists and the medical community and the public, and politicians like Trump and Robert Kennedy have compounded the problem. Does this become a global trend and how has it affected your work and the medical community?

SM: One of the pillars in this nation is innovation, so it's very disheartening to see people attacking the very idea of innovation in every form, social, medical and technological. What I find surprising is the general antagonism to science, not just specifically directed at something like the COVID vaccine, because this general suspicion has consequences. It affects talent and the next generation of thinkers, innovators, and scientists. Personally, I've managed to insulate myself from these kinds of attacks mentally and spiritually, but I worry about the larger impact on society. The impact on science funding in not inconsequential. The budget for NIH has not kept up with inflation, and technology is being manipulated to spread disinformation. People see technology as spreading disinformation even though it is being used to heal people, and that negative perception is something that is new. It's a very dispiriting moment for scientists.

MA: What were you like when you were young? Were you studious? When did you become interested in science as a subject to focus on?

SM: I was always very academically inclined. Even when I first started school. When I was in high school, my interests were wide ranging—literature, writing, science. I was an information hound, so I began to gravitate towards science. People mistake science as being a rigorous subject and assume it's methodical and just about facts, but scientific thinking actually allows you to be very playful with ideas. A lot of people say they like the process of discovery, but what I loved and still do is the process of thinking and embracing the paradox of being skeptical but open at the same time. The best scientists are playful people because they have a mischievous relationship with the discovery of ideas. Many of the great stories of science begin with people doodling. There is a reason people say that something was a "napkin idea" because often it was written on the back of a napkin.

MA: At one point you had become rebellious, and your dad was worried about you. Did it last long?

SM: I was hyperactive. My dad dragged me to a shrink who reassured him I was just bored. Some of the smarter teachers in my school directed my energy academically. By late high school I had channeled some of that manic energy. I was very, very driven and decided I wanted to apply to go to college in the United States This was before the internet and computer, so it was a tedious process writing by mail to each college for information and sending in handwritten applications by mail. I did it by myself; my parents were uninvolved. I then announced I was going to Stanford once I was accepted.

MA: Why Stanford?

SM: I had been accepted at Harvard and Stanford. Harvard had sent a package with picture of Harvard Yard covered in snow. I took one look and thought I would freeze to death and picked Stanford! Stanford in 1987 was not the preeminent university it is today. It was on the rise, but there was something about its newness that attracted me. For me, it mirrored America and in some subconscious way my desires. Harvard represented the traditional and Stanford the future. I wanted to be carried along with the wind of progressiveness behind my back.

MA: Did the atmosphere of Silicon Valley or the start-up culture have any impact on you and your later life as an entrepreneur?

SM: The start-up world did not exist in the same way then. There was something in the air, and Stanford had a famous computer science department, but I was in a different field. Stanford was where science got very exciting for me. It wasn't about science being a technology tool but something that could have human impact. I met Paul Berg, who was doing incredible work in genetics and would become one of my mentors and a great friend. By my second year, I understood that recombinant DNA was about to change the entire universe of medicine, biotechnology, and genetic engineering. I believed medicines would come flying out of the discoveries being made right here on campus. I cold-called Paul, who had never taken on an undergraduate in his laboratory, and told him I wanted to work with him as his lab was involved in some very important fundamental discoveries. Paul looked at me and asked what I knew about the subject, and I remember I rattled off everything I could think of at the time and why I was excited about it. I must have persuaded him as he agreed to take me on and we became lifelong friends.

The number of people who are able to make the leap from scientific discovery to human medicine are extraordinarily few. It requires you to be fluent in two completely separate languages. He was one of the first people to realize that his discoveries had deep implications for human beings. This transitional leap was taking place at Stanford. Paul, a transformational thinker, won the Nobel Prize in Chemistry in 1980.

MA: What made you choose to go to a traditional place like Oxford University on a Rhodes Scholarship if Stanford was where innovation was taking place?

SM: I wanted to work on immunology and continue some of the work I'd done on genetics and the Epstein-Barr virus. Oxford was at the forefront of this research and, in particular, I wanted to work with Alain Townsend. Alain was a physician and can look at a paper and at once recognize not just its scientific implications but its medical significance. He made an incredibly important discovery widely celebrated in my book about the way T-cells work, which is the basis for our understanding of how vaccines work and so much else. Once I was at Oxford, I realized I needed a medical degree in order to be able to get to the next step, which was curing people. So, after completing my DPhil, I applied to Harvard Medical School. I really believe it's the best medical school, and as a training ground, it was extraordinary.

MA: You already had a doctorate from Oxford. What was driving you to get the additional medical degree? Were you trying to prove something?

SM: It was not the degree but the end goal of acquiring a certain skill set I felt I needed in order to be a transitional researcher, which is a rare species. In order for me to actualize my goals, I needed the disciplinary education to walk through to answer the questions I was asking. There are not that many doctors who have invented medicines. I wanted to be that transformational researcher.

MA: You were deeply affected by members of your father's family who suffered from mental illness, yet you chose to study cancer rather than neurology or psychiatry. Can you talk about your academic decision?

SM: I thought very deeply about psychiatry, but the area we call molecular psychiatry was in a relatively infant phase. We know more now, but we still don't understand fundamental things about the brain. We have an anatomical map, but how complex phenomena like consciousness, sentience, and self-awareness connect to each other at the molecular level is still not well understood. In 1989, we knew even less. Cancer was a more tractable problem, and we knew more about the genetic origins of cancer. Technologies were being developed for new medicines and in the 1980s and 90s it was still "the big problem." It was one of the great mysteries to solve. I was consumed by the Epstein Barr virus, which is heavily linked to cancer in certain parts of the world. I started trying to understand it in Paul's lab at Stanford and continued to work at understanding it at Oxford.

Mukherjee was working on one of the deadliest forms of cancer—myeloid leukemia. While he was on vacation in Mexico with his daughters with no internet, the idea of a radical approach that inverted the conventional way of treating cancer came to him. He devised a way of making cancer cells "visible," which made them easier to target.

MA: You have every conceivable scientific degree and, in addition to being a medical doctor specializing in cancer, you now head up your own lab at Columbia University where you are doing groundbreaking work on cancer therapies that some say may put you in the running for a Nobel Prize if it is successful. Can you describe the unique innovation that you have come up with?

SM: The normal approach to treating cancer has been to kill cancer cells and try to minimize the collateral damage to normal cells and target the therapy as much as possible during chemotherapy. But there is always collateral damage to the normal cells. I have tried to reverse this normal paradigm of cancer therapy on its head. Our innovation is to first protect the normal cells. The key body of our work is to figure out a system to protect the normal cells upfront by changing their genetic makeup and then attacking the cancer cells. It is an inversion in the thinking process. I'm saying let's forget the cancer cells for a minute and focus on protecting the normal cells and the field it occupies. Once the field is protected, the cancer cells are exposed. No one has attempted this approach. I call it "the emperor's new clothes" to carry the theme from my first book. The emperor only becomes naked once everyone else (normal cells) is shielded with protective clothing. This as an idea had been percolating in my head for a while, but the technology wasn't there until CRISPR. Sometimes you have a solution to a puzzle, but you are ahead of the science. You have to wait for the technology to develop to solve your problem. Paul, who knew about my idea, had just emerged from a seminar at Stanford where he heard Jennifer Doudna describe her work and he told me that someone had just solved the technology that would enable me to pursue my idea. Initially, I did not believe him, because I was unaware of her work as it had not yet been published, but once he described the technology, I realized it was what I had been waiting for. Jennifer and her partner would win the Nobel for their work on CRISPR. We have now transplanted 10 patients with this technology. They are CRISPR-modified humans and all 10 have survived. They have all been done here.

MA: Are you developing this technology in your lab or your start-ups?

SM: My basic work is done in my lab, but it costs close to half a million dollars. It's done on mice, tissue culture, and cells, but in a dish. What my biotech companies allow me to do is to both scale and convert the knowledge into human medicines. I have about nine different companies operating in different countries that conduct human trials for a much lower cost. I have to keep a distance from the commercial aspects of it because of conflict of interest issues. I am involved in the scientific phase, not the commercial aspects.

MA: Who runs these trials?

SM: I can't run the human trials, but we have professionals who do it. The one in India is being run by a team of doctors. We work on CAR T-cell technology there. The goal is to democratize treatment. The hope is to make the T-cells at a fraction of the cost in India and offer them to patients who need it. We have treated 25 patients successfully there. You need highly trained people in a facility that is very tightly controlled because you are handling cancer and viruses. We finally have a facility that meets the standards. There are monthly audits and random inspections.

MA: Where else are you working?

SM: There are currently six pivotal trials being run in different places, which are all registered. They are completely new molecular entities and, if they are successful, will enter the human pharmacopeia. There is a regulatory process and each of them is at a different phase of getting FDA approvals. Once they are approved, they will hopefully become medicines if they prove to be successful. So far, they have all shown to be successful and met their endpoints and are moving forward to the next phase of FDA approvals. To give you an example, we are working on using a technique where you change the metabolism in patients with breast and endometrial cancer. It turns out cancer cells are uniquely dependent on certain nutrients, and if you starve the cancer cells without starving the rest of the body you can impact the cancer. No one has tried this before as the standard treatment till now has been chemotherapy. It is in a phase two trial. We are working on leukemia and that start-up is a Boston-based company and it is in phase two-B, which means it is on an accelerated track for approval as the FDA thinks it's promising. Myeloid, which also came out of my lab, is a company in Australia working on breast cancer in phase one.

MA: Is there an evolutionary rationale or purpose for cancer? What is your view on the Peto paradox on why certain large mammals like elephants or whales are resistant to cancer?

SM: Biology has very few unifying theories. Evolution is one of them. Cell theory is another and the universality of the genetic code is a third. But unlike physics, which has multiple equations and laws, there are relatively few in biology. Generally speaking, pathophysiology arises as the obverse of physiology. As we age, we become aberrant. The same mechanisms that have an evolutionary benefit early in life can take on an aberrant form later and become pathophysiological. We start off with one cell and become trillions of cells. Under normal circumstances, a cell knows when to grow and multiply and when to stop. I use the example of when you cut your hand, your wound heals itself because your cells divide and close the wound. But why don't you grow a new hand? It's an absurd yet profound question. It's because our cells, under normal circumstances, know when to stop growing. It is essential to our survival, but when the process goes wrong and cells don't shut off, they grow at the wrong time and in the wrong place and that becomes cancer. The evolutionary answer for some animals is that they evolved specifically to avoid extinction. They are multicellular and they evolved mechanisms to avoid cancer. In the elephant, for instance, we know there are specific genes that suppress the development of cancer. The fascinating question to me is what is the cost? Peto's paradox must come at a cost. There is always a flip side to the question.

I realized that Mukherjee's mind was far too evolved as a scientist for me to elicit any meaningful nuggets by going down this road with my limited knowledge of both science and medicine. Having read his books and watched his interviews, it was clear to me that he was on a mission to find a cure. I spoke to some researchers in the field who all held him and his work in high regard, so I am following a game he played with his mentor Paul Berg in guessing who gets the next Nobel. I am rooting for Mukherjee, although it may be years before his contributions are recognized.

One fact that became abundantly clear from reading his trilogy was how interdependent inventors, scientists, and Nobel laureates are on the discoveries of those who came before them. Scientific genius is incremental, and you stand on the shoulders of those that come before you. Mukherjee was undoubtedly born gifted, but even he needed CRISPR to be able to progress just as others in the scientific community have based their discoveries on the theories of others. Given the communal aspects of genius in the scientific community, I thought I would probe to see what Mukherjee thought made for "genius."

MA: How would you define genius? Are you born with it and, like Einstein, wake up with the theory of relativity a revelation from God or is it acquired?

SM: Einstein was an exceptionally gifted mathematician. Geniuses think outside the box. But in retrospect, Einstein asked profoundly simple questions that no one had asked before, like what would it be like to ride a beam of life? But, as the saying goes, a fool can ask more questions than a wise man can answer, so I believe you also have to have the disciplinary quality, the analytical ability, and the 10,000 hours. Asking questions on its own is not enough. The urban mythology is that an Einstein was born with brilliant ideas, but he spent hours devoted to working on his subject.

Mukherjee believed that a curious mind was essential, as was analytical ability, but there was no shortcut to the hours you needed to dedicate to your subject to be exceptional.

Mukherjee felt the urge to write about cancer as he began his advance training as an oncologist at the Dana Faber Cancer Institute in Boston. Initially, he planned to write a journal, but it quickly grew into a much larger project as he began to explore the disease's history. "As I emerged from the strange desolation of those two fellowship years, the questions about the larger story of cancer emerged with urgency; How old is cancer? What are our roots of our battle against this disease? Or as patients often asked me: Where are we on this "war" on cancer/ How did we get here? Is there an end? Can this war ever be won?...I used the past to explain the present."[78] Although the book is 570 pages, his first draft was 1,800 pages. Some scientists complained about things that had not been included, but when you have to reduce a book by more than half, a lot ends up on the cutting room floor! On average, it has taken Mukherjee five years to write each of the books in the trilogy.

I asked Mukherjee about how he found the time to write given his day job and which one of his books was the hardest to write. He said he wrote on weekends and at night, and his preferred place to write was in bed.

SM: The book on cancer in some ways was the hardest because it was the first, but *The Song of the Cell* was the most challenging because of the structure. I spend a lot of time thinking about my books and their form before I start the process of writing. In *The Song of the Cell*, I decided to write it according to cells rather than chronology, so it wasn't linear in the way chronology guides you. And once you abandon chronology, I had to knit it together. You find you are walking alone, so that was a difficult song to sing. I spend a lot of time on writing as words matter, you need to have a sense of the music of words.

MA: *The Gene*, in many ways, is your most political book. You not only take us through the history of gene discovery but point out how science has been manipulated through history, such as in the case of eugenics. One of the people you dedicate the book to is Carrie Buck. Were you trying to warn us?

SM: *The Gene* was a difficult book to write because I wanted it to be simultaneously a very personal book but also a very scientific book and a political book. The three very different tangents had to be pulled together around the idea of genetics, and the political aspect is important as the conversation about eugenics is being revisited. The use of genetic and ethnic cleansing of individuals and populations is not only part of our history but has been revived. The conversations around euthanasia have been raised in different parts of the world. So yes, I believe it's not a moment too soon to revisit this conversation.

In *The Gene*, Mukherjee points out a gruesome fact: "Readers from India and China might note, with some shame and sobriety, that the largest 'negative eugenics' project in human history was not the systemic extermination of Jews in Nazi Germany or Austria in the 1930s. That ghastly distinction falls on India and China, where more than 10 million female children are missing from adulthood because of infanticide, abortion, and neglect of female children. Depraved dictators and predatory states are not an absolute requirement for eugenics. In the case of India, perfectly 'free' citizens, left to their own devices, are capable of enacting grotesque eugenic programs—against females, in this case—without any state mandate."[79]

MA: You have written about India and China undertaking the biggest unauthorized experiment in genetic selection by its preference for male children, which has resulted in a lopsided population.

SM: Yes, there are many unlicensed clinics that do gender selection and unfortunately sometimes it is through female infanticide, selective abortion, or neglect. You can draw a line above Gujarat through the Hindi speaking belt where the correlation of various economic indices such as female literacy correlate with the skewed gender ratio. I had planned to write about this and what policy mechanisms can be deployed to prevent this. I have spoken with people in the field, but I need to put all the research together.

MA: You made a decision to stand behind your principles and made a political statement when you announced you were getting off Twitter and Instagram. Many progressive leaders and high-profile people, including some who are profiled in this book, have not done that. Can you talk about that? Was it a difficult decision?

SM: During COVID, I was one of the most active users of Twitter to gather information and to give advice. I had come across a very useful poster on COVID and together with my daughters we decided to use the poster and translate its instructions and information on COVID into several Indian languages. We typed it into Google Translate and with the help of Photoshop and posted it on Twitter, and it went viral. I was very active on Twitter. In that case, social media was used to disseminate good information that helped people. Technology is a tool. It's not the tool, it's how you use it. Post-COVID, I began to realize that Twitter was becoming an instrument of disinformation and even moral decay, and I took the decision to leave it. It was a difficult decision but one I felt I had to make, because both these platforms had become corrupted and were causing more malaise than social good. It was hard not to be able to reach hundreds and thousands of people, and maybe one day I'll return to some version of it.

Finding a cure for cancer may not in itself seem controversial, but the field of genetics has become fraught with ethical issues. As gene editing has become a possible mechanism to control for debilitating illnesses to avoid suffering, so has gene enhancement become possible, which has raised ethical concerns among many in the scientific community. The geneticist J.B.S. Haldane, quoted in Mukherjee's book *The Gene*, expressed his concerns as early as 1923, saying that once the power to control genes had been harnessed, "no beliefs, no values, no institutions are safe."

Paul Berg organized the first conference in 1973 and a more formal one in 1975 called the Asilomar Conference in Pacific Grove, California, to discuss the ethical concerns raised by the advances in genetic engineering. It was an attempt by the scientific community to police itself and called for a moratorium on the use of gene editing until the ethical, political, social, and legal implications could be better understood. The overriding concern, Mukherjee writes, is "not genetic emancipation (freedom from the bounds of hereditary illnesses), but genetic enhancement (freedom from the current boundaries of form and fate encoded by the human genome). The distinction between the two is the fragile pivot on which the future of genome editing swirls."[80] But he also points out that not all countries are on the same page or share the same values. It is possible that in a country like China, scientists will not feel bound by the same concerns. In other countries such as India with an active civil society and a government sensitive to having their population experimented on, safeguards have been instituted.

MA: Many third world countries now insist on an ethicist being part of a board when trials are conducted. What's your view on that? Should this be part of trials in the United States?

SM: When a trial is conducted there is what is called an institutional review board (IRB). It consists of people from different fields, and they always have someone that is trained to make sure one doesn't run afoul of ethical barriers. The IRB also insists on patient consent and various universal principles.

MA: Do you think AI is a good thing for medicine and science, or are you worried? Vinod Khosla believes that doctors will be replaced. There is already distance between doctors and patients. What is your view?

SM: Doctors are better at some things, and machines or AI are better at others. Machines are terrible at providing compassion or telling a patient they have cancer. Try to engage ChatGPT in a conversation about your health, caregiving, and the decisions you should make regarding your health and life, and all the vaulted ideas about machines replacing doctors fade away. I agree with Vinod that machines are better at some things. For example, machines are good at reading a radiology report, but they are not good at listening to the patient's concerns. It's an important medical skill to hear the patient and to know when to be quiet for communication and for trust to be established between a doctor and the patient. You often need both verbal and nonverbal communication. For an oncologist, silence and humility can carry as much weight as words. When people are dying, they often have a set of questions or goals. I talk to them about it. I try to create a psychological space where they can begin to accept the inevitability of dying. Telling people they have four months to live is not the way. Emily Dickinson has a poem in which she writes, "Tell all the truth but tell it slant." It's a mechanism to allow for a certain space for someone to apprehend mortality. To tell it slant is to discuss their goals rather than how long they have to live. One method I use is to ask them to think of doing four things. The first is to tell someone they haven't told before that they want to tell that they love them. The second is to be told by someone they want to hear it from that they are loved. The third is to tell someone they have forgiven them and the last is to be forgiven by someone. This is not something a machine can do. Where AI can help is in drug discovery. I'm using AI to make new medicines, so I'm not the person who is going to tell you that machines are bad, but I'm also not going to tell you that they are going to replace doctors.

MA: What scientific question intrigues you the most?

SM: My brain is wired for cancer research, so when I read a scientific paper I think in technical terms and ask, "What we are missing?" Is there something fundamental we might have overlooked in detecting and treating cancer and trying to look for the blind spots.

MA: What keeps you up at night? What is your biggest concern about technology?

SM: I'm very excited about the work that's been done in the AI arena as well as data science. People talk about the existential threat of AI, and I feel that it means nothing unless you qualify its typology. The first thing that comes to mind is the use of AI in defense and warfare, which is an existential threat. The second is the use of AI in penetrating cybersecurity and security in general and identity theft. The third is the use of AI to manipulate political information and, last but not least, is the use of AI in the creation of new forms of matter that may change the way we think of the material world from biological materials to other forms. Those are some of the frightening threats as I see them.

MA: What would you like to accomplish in the next decade?

SM: I think it would be incredible to cure acute leukemias. I think I can see a path to doing this. Last week I stumbled upon some new ideas which we are testing in the lab. It would be amazing if we could find a way to cure myeloma, and I do believe we could potentially cure some forms of breast cancer that are considered incurable. I'd also like to write more books.

CHAPTER 14

Atul Gawande

Better is possible. It does not take genius. It takes diligence. It takes moral clarity.
It takes ingenuity. And above all, it takes a willingness to try.

ATUL GAWANDE

In 2006, the MacArthur Foundation honored Atul Gawande by giving him the "genius grant" in recognition of his insight and compassion in medicine. The award crowned his already glittering resume—Stanford University, Harvard University, Oxford University, Rhodes Scholar, *The New Yorker* writer, and author of highly acclaimed books. Gawande was just 41 years old.

The foundation recognized his contributions as both a surgeon and an author who "applies a critical eye to modern surgical practice, articulating its realities, complexities, and challenges." It lauded his book *Complications*, published in 2002, which was a finalist for the National Book Award, for illuminating the concerns and problems faced by the surgeon in training with insight and compassion.

The journalist Jacob Weisberg, who competed for the Rhodes Scholarship with Gawande and became a close friend, told me that of all his friends, "Atul is the most likely to win a Nobel Prize. What he has done to change surgical practice around the world has surely saved hundreds of thousands of lives and far more over time. It also has to do with the diffusion of ideas that he has articulated and expressed so well."

Weisberg took a liking to Gawande when they first met but remembers him as a simple kid from the Midwest, far from the sophisticated intellectual who is constantly flying between world capitals, advising governments, and appearing on television. "I met Atul because we were both applicants for the Rhodes Scholarship from the Midwest and we hung out in a room in this rather high stress environment all day. Atul was wearing a brand-new suit for the interview that still had the label on the sleeve. I was trying to figure out how to prevent him from committing a faux pas and tell him it needed to be cut off without knocking him off balance." The two were both selected and went to study at Oxford. They traveled across Europe together and became close friends. Although Gawande studied medicine after Oxford and Weisberg was a writer, they stayed in touch. Weisberg was the person who initially encouraged Gawande to write and provided him with his first opportunity to publish while Gawande was still a medical student.

Gawande also became friends with Malcolm Gladwell. According to Gawande, the two would often have long arguments about esoteric things. Gawande had cut his teeth writing for *Slate*, the magazine where his friend Weisberg worked. He discovered he enjoyed writing and was ready to take it to the next level, crediting Gladwell as the reason he ended up becoming a staff writer for *The New Yorker*. In an interview he gave to Emily Kumler Kaplan, an award-winning journalist who covered health at *Boston* magazine, he said, "Malcolm persuaded me to send in a proposal to *The New Yorker*, which they then accepted, and I was off to the races."

Gawande is one of those individuals that fits both the 10,000-hour rule that Gladwell claims it takes to get to genius level, as well as David Epstein, whose book *Range*, posits that successful people are curious and often explore different disciplines before zeroing on the profession that they excel at. Gawande perfected his surgical skills the old-fashioned way—he put in long hours, working 12-hour days and often performing more than 250 surgeries a year. In addition, he taught at Harvard Medical School and the Harvard T.H. Chan School of Public Health. He also found time to conduct research and became the executive director of Ariadne Labs, a joint center for health systems innovation.

Gawande was born in Brooklyn to Indian immigrant parents. His parents were both physicians, among the first wave of Indian doctors in the sixties to take advantage of the new immigration policies under President Johnson that encouraged medical professionals to emigrate to America. Gawande's father, Atmaram, lost his mother to malaria when he was a young child and she was barely 30 years old. It inspired him to pursue medicine, attending medical school in India and then moving to New York to train in surgery and become a urologist. He later married Gawande's mother, Sushila, a pediatrician who had also moved to the United States to work. The young family moved to Appalachia and settled in a small community in Athens, Ohio, where Gawande and his younger sister grew up.

Gawande initially pushed back against the Indian expectation of following in his father's footsteps and studying medicine. "This idea that a bright Indian kid is supposed to be a doctor—I resisted that. I wanted to be a rock star. I played guitar and wrote songs and even had a couple of club shows. I was just terrible."[81] Although he abandoned a musical career, his interest in music is well known. His admits that his guilty pleasure is going to rock concerts. People who operate with him in the O.R. can expect to hear music ranging from David Bowie, The Killers, and Regina Spektor to Modest Mouse, Dido, and M.I.A. He adjusts the music in deference to the age of the members of his team. He likes to joke that he now lives vicariously through his daughter, who not only inherited his love of music but is seriously talented. She attends the prestigious Berklee College of Music and will likely have a career in music.

As an undergraduate at Stanford, Gawande studied political science along with biology. When he went to Oxford University as a Rhodes Scholar, he studied politics and philosophy, but claims he wasn't particularly good at asking the right philosophical questions. Having satiated his desire to explore other interests, he decided that he enjoyed medicine and that, like his father, he particularly enjoyed surgery and was attracted to the blood and guts. He recalls that the first time he made an incision he found it oddly addictive. It is this ability to be candid about his reactions that make his writing so compelling and convincing to read. The descriptions in his books of cutting through skin, its texture and sponginess and thickness, are vivid. His reactions to making split-second life-or-death decisions and admitting to making near-fatal errors, or a description of how he had to grab a patient's heart and pump it to keep him alive, keep the reader riveted and horrified in equal measure.

Gawande is unique in that he has managed simultaneously to excel at more than one profession. He is a surgeon of repute but has equally made a name for himself as a writer. He has won the Lewis Thomas Prize for writing about science as well as two national magazine awards. He has written four *New York Times* bestsellers. Although his first book, *Complications*, was a finalist for the National Book Award, the book that made him famous was *The Checklist Manifesto*, published in 2009.

The concept of creating a checklist for hospitals was not Gawande's original idea. It was started by the critical care specialist Peter Pronovost at Johns Hopkins University to prevent central line infections. In *The Checklist Manifesto*, Gawande describes his journey. Pronovost observed that it was simple things like making sure that doctors washed their hands with soap and that patients' skin was cleaned with antiseptic that made a big difference, so he created a checklist. The results were dramatic. Central line infections at the hospital went from 11 percent to zero. In one hospital that had adopted the checklist, 43 infections and eight deaths were prevented, saving two million dollars in costs.

In a 2017 interview with the economist Tyler Cowen, Gawande discussed the rather odd but dangerous occurrence of surgeons leaving sponges or other instruments behind in patients' bodies. It happened often enough that he published a case study in *The New England Journal of Medicine* in which 60 patients who had been subjected to such a situation were studied. "That was an interesting problem to me because the rate of sponges being left inside people had been steady for 30 years. We had not made it go down at all. It was right around 1 in 1,000 to 1 in 3,000 or so operations. A sponge would be left inside, and it would be a disaster. You would have to go back. About two thirds of the time, people had become infected. One of the 60 was a patient who died because a small sponge had been left in their brain. The usual way we track these things is by consistently counting everything at the beginning and at the end, so it wasn't a broken system. It was a fallible system."

What Gawande realized was that they needed to come up with a technological solution and barcoded all the sponges. It ended up eliminating the problem. The sponges were now scanned in and scanned out. The additional cost of barcoded sponges was easily mitigated by the savings to the hospital and reduced infections in patients.

The Hopkins checklist had a powerful impact, inspiring Gawande to extend the concept to help bring down infection rates in surgical interventions across America and eventually globally through his work with the World Health Organization (WHO). His impact was transformative.

In 2006, WHO approached Gawande to see if he could help the organization improve the safety of surgical procedures worldwide. There had been an alarming rise in infection and mortality rates as the volume of surgeries had grown in its 193 member countries—230 million procedures were being performed annually with complications ranging from 3 to 17 percent.[82] That translated to an annual mortality rate of one million, with seven million patients left disabled. Gawande balked at the undertaking initially. He was still trying to work out how to reduce the errors within his own hospital, let alone taking on the world, but he agreed to help.

He traveled to different countries to observe surgical procedures, met with medical teams, and came to understand the way different cultures and hospitals operated. Gawande took the checklist that had originally been conceived at Johns Hopkins to a whole new level by adapting it to surgery and the operating theatre. Soon it was being adopted by ICUs and hospitals across the country, but it took several years to develop the right checklist and get people to accept it.

He began to research how checklists are created and found ones ranging from Kaiser's in California to Daniel Boorman's from the Boeing Company in Seattle, who developed checklists for flight deck controls for Boeing aircraft. Gawande went to visit Boeing and was given a primer on the importance of checklists for the safety of the passengers.

Good checklists need to be precise. Gawande created a 19-item, two-minute checklist for surgical teams and implemented it in eight hospitals around the world, from rural Tanzania to the United States. Once it was adopted, complications dropped by 35 percent and death rates fell by 47 percent. It was hard to get people to change their behavior and adopt the checklists initially because, as Gawande explains, it involved forcing people to change their culture and values and needed to be done over time, but many were persuaded as they saw the results.

Gawande and his research team began to experiment with different checklists to see what works. Gawande has looked for inspiration in unusual places to come up with the right checklist, having realized that what worked for central line procedures would be different for a cardiac or lung surgery. How did you go from a system where the surgeon is king to working as a team? He went to Joe Salvia, the structural engineer in charge of building the new hospital wing where he worked. The company had been involved in many of Boston's largest commercial construction projects. Gawande tried to understand how these enormous structures came together to become walls, floors, and offices that stood the test of time and how the hundreds of subcontractors worked in tandem to erect a fully functioning building that was also safe. Underpinning the process was "submittal schedule"– code for a checklist–designating everyone's jobs, how they were organized, and the process through which they should communicate. They had checklists that coordinated what everyone did–the essential steps for teamwork.

When I first met Gawande, I was seated next to him at a New America Foundation dinner in 2011. We started to talk about the complications that arise during surgery and the process he went through to create his checklists. He was candid about the resistance he had faced from physicians in embracing the checklists. He explained that it requires humility, a trademark not common to surgeons. Gawande was mulling over a book idea he was working on for surgeons that would be based on direct observation, which could help identify small but consequential things such as the angle they held their arm, or following a similar checklist to the one Johns Hopkins has developed for central lines but adapting one for surgery. By making small simple adjustments, they would become more skillful, make fewer mistakes, and improve outcomes, but he recognized that it could be a hard sell.

In 2014 he published one of the most influential books on how to manage the end of life–*Being Mortal*. It had a profound impact on the medical community and sparked a thoughtful debate across the country about the most humane way to help people through the last stage of their lives.

Gawande is convinced that medicine is so advanced now that it exceeds the capability of any one individual to manage the volume of information and treatment options. Medicine, in his opinion, can no longer be practiced as an individual art form wholly dependent on the skill of one person. It is all teamwork. His perspective may be distorted by his own specialty—surgery—which does require teamwork, but some would argue that there is still room for skilled family physicians, especially those in rural areas treating underserved populations where the skill of an individual is critical.

In an interview with NPR's Guy Raz in 2017, Gawande explains that in the old days, hospitals were a place to convalesce, where a few basic procedures were conducted. "That changed and evolved as knowledge exploded. We suddenly came into a world where we had ... more than 60,000 different ways our human body can fail. But we had generated thousands of drugs. And then we designed 4,000 medical and surgical procedures ... and none of us can grasp the entirety of it. Forty percent of our coronary artery disease patients receive incomplete or inappropriate care. Sixty percent of our asthma, stroke patients receive incomplete or inappropriate care. Two million people come into hospitals and pick up an infection they didn't have because someone failed to follow the basic practices of hygiene." The health care system was under stress, and he was looking for ways to improve it.

Given that medicine is so complex now and has become increasingly dependent on technology, even surgery is often done by robots. The assumption is that machines make fewer mistakes and don't get "tired" the way human physicians do, as Gawande himself has admitted he's felt on occasion. Does this mean that Gawande thinks people's fear regarding AI is justified? Will AI replace doctors? During the interview he addressed some of these questions.

Gawande agrees that technology has helped a great deal in reducing errors and helping treatments and diagnostic capability, but it has its limitations. He points out a critical problem in medicine that can't be bridged right now by AI: Machines are only as good as the data they receive. Trash in, trash out. So, if you plug in accurate bloodwork, heart rates, x-rays, etc., you can get an accurate diagnosis. But often a patient comes in with non-specific pain or is not clear about his other ailments. The doctor is critical in these scenarios, needing to build a diagnosis by touching and feeling afflicted areas and looking for other telltale signs. The doctor also needs to ask the right questions. It is what Abraham Verghese advocates for as a "hands-on doctor-patient" relationship. Often, getting to a diagnosis requires part intuition, part historical information about the patient and visual inferences—critical information that is currently beyond the capability of AI. Gawande suggests that there is a program called "Isabel" where clinicians can plug in data once they've collected the data from a patient and it provides one with several optional diagnoses. But we are not at the stage Vinod Khosla has suggested we are headed, where doctors will be replaced by AI or robots. There is a vast amount of information available on Google which is often now everyone's first medical query or serves as the public's virtual doctor, but for actual treatment one still needs a physician.

By the time I met Gawande, he had been juggling four different jobs: surgeon, professor, researcher, and writer. Any one of these was a full-time job in itself, but he was going full speed at all of them. Jacob Weisberg once told him he was doing too much and asked if he was under stress, to which Gawande replied, "It may look like I'm relaxed and not under stress but inside I'm a seething cauldron of anxiety." Weisberg said that although Gawande had responded with humor to his question, he believes he was being honest. He's not just a machine, but rather makes time for his friends, his music, and his writing.

Gawande's work on creating surgical checklists, expanding them, and amplifying the message through his writing has had a major impact. On its own *The Checklist Manifesto* would have been a remarkable achievement, but *Being Mortal* created just as deep an impression. Dying is an unavoidable stage of life, yet, as Gawande points out, physicians get very little training on how to advise terminally ill patients on the most optimal way to die outside of invasive medical interventions. His book explores a more humane way to end one's days, surrounded by loved ones rather than tubes and hospital staff. His thesis, which highlights trying to understand what is important to the patient and helping them end their lives peacefully, is illustrated by several poignant examples, including his own father's terminal diagnosis. He admits the need to rein in the doctor's instinct—

including his own—to persist with yet another treatment, hoping your scalpel might deliver a miracle despite knowing the likelihood is close to zero, something he had to work on. The book goes a long way in getting the medical profession to shift its focus from the disease to the patient's perspective and needs.

Some writers use their writing as a way to clarify their thinking on a subject. Gawande has used his writing in columns and his novels to amplify his message.

In 2007, he told the *New York Times* that he identifies as a writer first: "I now feel like writing is the most important thing I do. In some ways it's harder than surgery. But I do think I've found a theme in trying to understand failure and what it means in the world we live in, and how we can improve at what we do."

Ten years later, he gave a very different response to Emily Kumler Kaplan: "I'm first and foremost a doctor, surgeon, and I am also a writer. I'm trying to get to a place where my writing can feel like it stands on its own. I love the fact that Oliver Sacks is not Dr. Oliver Sacks, he's just Oliver Sacks. He was first and foremost a doctor, but he had an incredible influence in ideas and in just understanding the world as a writer. So, in some way, that's the thing I aspire toward."

Some of what Gawande writes can be critical of the medical profession. His 2009 *New Yorker* article "The Cost Conundrum" got President Barack Obama's attention and was one of the most discussed articles on health care that year. The late Charlie Munger, Warren Buffett's partner, was so impressed by it that he sent him a donation, which Gawande first returned. Munger then doubled the amount and Gawande donated it to the hospital where he worked.

Gawande was still a resident when he published his first book, *Complications: A Surgeon's Notes on an Imperfect Science*. He was about to go into an operation that would last most of the day when he found out he was a finalist for the National Book Award. Until then, he felt he had been dabbling in writing as a side gig. This was the first time he began to think of himself as a writer with ideas to communicate. He wanted to know, like every first-time author, "Can I do it again? Do I have a second book in me?" Gawande did not grow up around books and literature. His childhood home was full of scientific journals; it is only when he went to college that he was exposed to the world of literature. When he first tried his hand at writing, one of his professors suggested he try something else. His wife, Kathleen Hobson, a former comparative literature major who once worked in publishing, said he's come a long way. She revealed that his first *New Yorker* article took nine months to perfect and went through 22 revisions. Now, he rarely rewrites an article twice.[83] His numerous articles, on everything from the cost of medical care to access to treatment, have informed the public and added to the national debate. Gawande claims that it was only when he started working and had something to say that his writing took root.

As if his writing questioning the fallibility of the medical system, raising the public's trust by challenging his colleagues to improve their skill, and practicing what he preaches isn't enough, Gawande has felt compelled to serve his country and has joined the Biden administration as the assistant administrator for global health at the United States Agency for International Development (USAID). He has had to take a hiatus from *The New Yorker* and his medical practice in order to serve in government. It is not the first time that Gawande has worked for the government, however. Earlier in his career, he was an advisor to Bill Clinton on health care during the 1992 presidential campaign and became a senior advisor in the Department of Health and Human Services during the Clinton administration. He also directed a task force on national health care reform but found the process frustrating due to negative reactions in the public arena.

He currently hopes to narrow the discrepancies between life expectancies across countries, turn COVID into a manageable illness, and improve the quality of primary care in the developing world. His everyday responsibilities and concerns have shifted from a clinical setting with direct responsibility for patients to public health concerns. These concerns reflect those put forward by the World Bank, WHO, and other international organizations. All of these agencies need committed individuals to help humanity, but large bureaucracies have a way of swallowing up talented individuals.

So far, Gawande's work and writing has had a substantial impact. Bringing down infection rates in operating theatres has been transformational. But much of his motivation has come from the immersion in his daily life of his craft as a surgeon. Much of what he covers in his writing, from the cost of health care to mistakes in the treatment of patients, is a result of his experience as a physician. His book *Being Mortal* was inspired in part by the awkward interactions he was experiencing with his own patients. The government places restrictions on employees' ability to freelance on other projects, so we may have to wait for Gawande to fulfill his desire to serve in government before he can come up with the next idea to change the way we approach medicine. Still in his fifties, he still has plenty of time to continue to shape our thinking.

CHAPTER 15

Vivek Murthy

*Giving and receiving kindness are easy ways to feel good
and to help others feel good too. People, organizations, and societies
thrive when they are grounded in a culture of kindness.*

VIVEK MURTHY

Vivek Murthy was just 36 years old when he was nominated to be surgeon general of the United States by President Barack Obama in 2013. It was a controversial appointment as most of his predecessors had been older, gray-haired white physicians with decades of experience behind them.

Murthy had graduated from the Yale School of Medicine 10 years earlier, and several senators had questioned his youth and experience. Others expressed reservations about his neutrality due to his advocacy of the president's health care policies through Doctors for America, a nonprofit he founded in 2009 that sought to improve health care policies in the United States.[84] But these concerns paled in comparison to the objections raised by his main opponent—the powerful gun lobby known as the National Rifle Association, which called him a serious threat to gun owners.

In order to promote its agenda and prevent the implementation of what many would consider rational gun control policies, the NRA not only channels millions of dollars into supporting members of Congress who support gun rights, it spends an equal amount of money opposing politicians who promote gun control. The NRA delayed Murthy's nomination for a year by launching a powerful campaign to stop his confirmation, all because of a tweet he sent in 2012 which read, "Tired of politicians playing politics w/guns, putting lives at risk b/c they're scared of NRA. Guns are a health care issue." Murthy's concerns were not misplaced. According to the CDC, 48,830 people died from guns in 2021, of which half were suicides.

After the Sandy Hook Elementary School shooting in Newtown, Connecticut, in December 2012, Murthy co-authored a letter to members of Congress advocating for gun-safety measures. He was hardly alone in his concerns; the majority of Americans supported his views. According to a recent Pew survey, 58 percent of Americans favor stricter gun laws, 29 percent think they are fine the way they are, and only 15 percent feel they are too restrictive. A whopping 88 percent of the country is in favor of preventing the sale of guns to the mentally ill, and 79 percent want to increase the age of eligibility for gun purchases to 21.

Once Murthy's nomination was announced in November 2013, the NRA led a relentless campaign against him, but he did not shy away from standing up to powerful interest groups. The gun lobby has a reputation for being ruthless, and I remember both fearing for him and watching in admiration in 2013 as he went through a grueling confirmation.

MA: When you were critical of the nation's gun policy, you must have known you were tampering with fire.

VM: When I made my public comments about gun violence it was in the aftermath of the Sandy Hook tragedy in Newtown, where 20 children who were just six and seven years old had died just trying to go to school. I couldn't help but think, what does it say about us as a society if we're not willing to stand up for our kids and do everything we can to protect them? I was also looking at it from a doctor's perspective, as part of a community of doctors who had cared for the people who have been the victims of gun violence over the years and seen the toll that it took. It was not just the trauma following its immediate aftermath, but the recurring echoes that lasted for years afterwards on survivors and families. Its long-term impact was extraordinary. At the time when I spoke up, I was a private citizen and had no plans to serve in government. Later, when I was going through my confirmation process, someone asked me if I regretted what I had said, and if I could go back in time, would I have not said it. To me, it is very clear. I would not have changed what I said because it was the truth. I knew there was some chance that because of those comments I would not become surgeon general, but the choice between taking that risk or backing down from something I believed to be true was an easy choice. In my mind, it was important to do what my parents had taught me and what I had learned in medical school. I need to be able to get up and look at myself in the mirror in the morning. You can lose a lot of things, but when you lose your integrity and your dignity, then you've lost everything.

Murthy speaks softly and with genuine empathy. He has two young children the same ages as the children who were victims of the shooting, and you could tell he was putting himself in the shoes of the parents who lost their children. Murthy exudes a quiet compassion that is disarmingly sincere and seems to come from a deep place.

The NRA had underestimated Murthy's support and his impeccable reputation. More than 100 medical and public health organizations around the country supported his nomination,[85] including former surgeon general David Satcher.

Howard Forman, the director of the MD/MBA program at Yale, was confident Murthy would make it. He said, "He is a thoughtful, nonpartisan, very deliberate physician who sees the role of the surgeon general as an amazing opportunity to be the nation's leading spokesperson on health and public health issues." The Senate eventually confirmed him 51 to 43.

Murthy wears his uniform on official business. The look, particularly with his hat on, is somewhat jarring as though he was playing dress up, as if this gentle physician ought to be in his doctor's white coat, not a stiff army uniform more associated with war. He listens carefully when asked a question, the way you would want your doctor to listen to you when you discuss your most personal problems.

I was a bit surprised to see that he had taken an uber to meet me and had not traveled in an official car with a driver—the perks of senior bureaucrats in government. He explained that he only used a government car when he is on official business.

Murthy is one of those stars that some say was destined for greatness early on. He was the valedictorian of his high school class and, during a stint at Harvard summer school, had fallen in love with the university and decided to apply for his undergraduate studies there. He was accepted and graduated magna cum laude, completing a degree in biochemical science in three years. He was tempted to study economics and literature, but a serendipitous intervention by his father, who he reveres, inspired him and his sister to start a nonprofit called Visions Worldwide while they were still undergraduates. It focused on HIV education in India just as the AIDS crisis was spreading there. The success of their project ignited their commitment to pursue medicine.

Murthy was a high achiever from the beginning and says he was internally driven. He grew up in a home where Indian cultural traditions and religion were venerated, and he was raised to value community. He was named after Swami Vivekananda, a nineteenth-century Hindu scholar, author, social reformer, and one of India's most influential philosophers. His father helped establish a Hindu temple, and his mother wanted him to aspire to the same spiritual qualities as his namesake and recognize that service is a form of spirituality.

What follows is a remarkably candid interview that took a few unexpected turns. Success stories are easier to narrate when you have the highlights worked out and have told the story a few times. But Murthy is instinctively reflective and never sugarcoats his answers, always reaching for the truth even if it's sometimes painful.

MA: Giving back to community was stressed in your family. Did that lead to a desire to serve in government?

VM: I had never been someone who aspired to work in government. I always thought the government was too slow and incremental a path to create change in this world. I was more interested in direct service and entrepreneurship, and how to bring innovation at scale to benefit people's lives. At the end of 2012 or early 2013, I was approached by individuals close to the administration to ask if I wanted to serve in some capacity and I said no, as I couldn't think of a role that would be a good fit for me. But on July 10, 2013—I remember the exact date because it was my birthday—I was picking up my dry cleaning after getting off a red-eye flight, and I got a call from a 202 number I didn't recognize in Washington DC. I decided to answer, and it was the White House calling, asking me if I would be interested in being considered for the job of surgeon general. When I hung up, I had a very strong intuition that this was something I should do. Half of life is distinguishing intuition from the noise.

Murthy was not unknown to President Obama. He had promoted the president's health care agenda during the campaign through his nonprofit Doctors for America. In 2011, the president had appointed Murthy to serve on his advisory council on prevention, health promotion, and integrative and public health within the United States Department of Health and Human Services. Murthy's wife, Alice Chen, an internist he had met at medical school, was not surprised when he texted her about the opportunity to be surgeon general.[86] He was relieved of his position in 2017 after Donald Trump became president. The country was about to go through a severe health care crisis that would almost cripple the health care system. By the time President Joe Biden was in office, 600,000 Americans had lost their lives to COVID-19.

VM: In March 2020 when COVID erupted, Biden's team reached out and asked me to begin daily briefings with him on COVID. We got to know each other and shared many of the same concerns about the impact the pandemic would have on the mental health of the country and shared similar concerns. In a biography of Biden published in 2023, the journalist Franklin Foer writes that the president trusted Murthy as he would his own internist and referred to him as "my doc."[87]

Vivek Murthy is the only surgeon general to be appointed to the position twice. He was reappointed by President Biden in 2021, this time with a somewhat wider confirmation margin of 57 to 43.

MA: What leadership or character traits do you have that made not one, but two presidents pick you as surgeon general?

VM: That would be easier for others to evaluate. Your fidelity in this job is to science and the public interest, not to the president, and you can, in essence, set your own agenda, which makes the job very appealing. That is what I did in medicine. I listened to the patient and let that shape my treatment strategy. President Obama and his team were interested in modernizing the Office of the Surgeon General and adapt it to the needs of a changing world, and for good reason. The ability to use data and get direct feedback from people to drive what one does is rare, but it is what we did.

MA: Finishing a Harvard degree in three years and graduating magna cum laude is quite an accomplishment, some would say the mark of a very driven student or a genius—which is it?

VM: People think I finished early because I was really smart, but there was a reason I accelerated my studies. I chose to graduate a year early because our family was going through a difficult time, and I was concerned about our family's finances.

Murthy's parents left India in 1972. They came from farming communities in southern India, and, although they were educated, they faced limited prospects in India during the sixties and seventies like many of their generation. They decided to go overseas, and their first stop was England, where they worked for several years. Murthy was born there in July 1977. A year later the family moved to Newfoundland just as winter extended its grip over the remote Canadian province. Murthy's father had accepted a job as the district medical officer and arrived not knowing a soul. The howling winds and freezing temperatures could not have been further from the warm climate of southern India where they had been raised. It would have been a difficult transition had it not been for their seven years in the U.K. which had helped to acclimatize them to the west. Bundled up in coats and snowshoes, the Murthy family became part of the community. Murthy's father made house calls, delivered babies in hospitals, sutured wounds in the clinic, and took care of the dying. The community, in return, embraced them. The Newfoundlanders would babysit Murthy and his sister, bring pies and fish for the family, and dig them out of the snow.[88]

When Murthy was three years old, the family uprooted itself once again to start a new life in the United States, settling in Miami, Florida where his father had been offered a job as a faculty member at the University of Miami. Later, he set up a flourishing family practice with the help of his wife. Much of Murthy's youth was spent in his dad's medical office, where he and his older sister Rashmi helped out after school greeting patients, cleaning the office, and assisting with paperwork. They were inspired by their parents' dedication to their patients. Murthy recalls seeing patients looking anxious as they walked in and more reassured as they left. They credit their exposure to their father's practice as a key reason behind their choice to become physicians.

Murthy's father had taught his children to give back to the community and dreamed of helping people in India. He was befriended by a Sri Lankan who had gained the trust of members of the community and encouraged their philanthropic aspirations, even suggesting that he would like to support worthy causes. Murthy's father connected him to Rashmi and Vivek. The man agreed to fund their "Visions" project which would train young students in India to educate and spread awareness about AIDS. The first year went as planned—the program had done well, and he agreed to fund the second year. That's when the scam was revealed.

Unbeknownst to the Murthys, the "philanthropist investor" was a con artist: Murthy's father had been taken in by a Ponzi scheme. Murthy and his sister, on the basis of the commitment of the "philanthropist" and the success of the project from the previous year's work, recruited 10 other students across the country to spend the summer working in India with them. They had run a two-week training session before their anticipated departure, but when they went to the airline to pick up their tickets for Bangalore, they were told that they had not been paid for. This would be the moment Murthy not only grew up but grew strong and understood what he was capable of.

VM: When I called the airline to confirm our tickets and was told the tickets hadn't been purchased, I was shocked. We reached out to the sponsor and were unable to reach him. The more we looked into it, the more suspect it all began to seem, and I'm wondering, what's going on here? Well, it turns out that our sponsor is an international con artist. He would live in a community for a few years, gain their trust, then disappear with their money. We now have 10 students who were trained and ready to go on the project and had dedicated their summer to doing this. With five days left to go and no sponsor—it was a defining moment in my life. I had two options. One was to give up and call it quits and try to salvage one's summer, or forge ahead and raise the $15,000 in five days. Life is a series of choice points. All the people were looking to me and my sister to see which path we would take. In my gut, I knew we had to make this happen, and I decided to stick with the plan and find some way to raise the money. We called everyone we knew, we got local papers to run articles, we held fundraisers and plied the friends and family network, and slowly raised $100 here and $200 there, but in the end, we raised the money. It took a week longer, but we did it and took everyone to India. It was a pivotal moment because it showed that even in the face of severe adversity, if we stuck together and were determined, we could find a way forward and prevail. Whenever I faced leadership challenges or managing conflicts, I always looked back to the summer of 1996, and I know I can get through it.

MA: You said you graduated early because you were concerned about your family's finances and that your time at Harvard was stressful.

VM: The con man traveled the world and preyed on South Asian communities, gained their trust, then swindled them. What he had done was become close friends with several families in our Miami community, including my parents. He had come to know my parents and knew my father had philanthropic dreams about what he wanted to do for the world. He convinced my father to pursue his dreams and do charity work for the betterment of humanity, and turn over his life savings to him to manage so he could generate the income my father needed to maintain two kids in college, etc. Well, he disappeared with my parent's life savings, and we were faced with a terrible situation. So, at the time, I not only had the responsibility of those 10 kids who had placed their trust in me and committed to spend a summer in India, whose parents were wondering why they weren't doing a normal summer job, but I was dealing with our family having lost all their savings. I finished Harvard in three years to save on a year's tuition.

Murthy's world had been altered. While the loss of innocence is inevitable as people grow up, he shed his youth, participating in all family discussions going forward, financial and otherwise, and he embraced his ability to lead in a crisis. He used his disappointments to strengthen his character, and what was remarkable about him is that he has done it without the residue of bitterness. He not only succeeded on the most fundamental personal level, but his project "Visions" would continue for eight years. He was building his "genius" capacity.

Murthy participated in a research project at Harvard that involved the development of a vaccine for Staphylococcus, a type of bacteria that hospitals often see in post-operative patients. He had applied to Harvard Medical School and was crushed when he did not get in. Instead, he went to Yale, where he soon stood out. Esther Choo, a fellow medical student who speaks admiringly of Murthy, said one of their faculty preceptors told the students that they were all bright, but that Murthy would make his mark in a very big way. She added that no one took offense because it was so obvious to everyone. He was always the moral center of the group, as well as being unflappable and calm.[89]

Murthy graduated from Yale in 2003 with an MD and an MBA and returned to Boston for his residency at Brigham and Women's Hospital.

MA: By any standards, you should have been a sure acceptance at Harvard Medical School. How did you feel when you did not get in?

VM: I was crushed and felt like I had totally failed because I had built it up so much in my head that this is where I needed to be, etc. I had got into Yale and a bunch of other medical schools, but sometimes you can get so blinded by what you think you need that you forget you have great options. I remember talking to my dad the night I got the rejection letter and telling him how sad I felt. He just listened and then said that it may end up being a good thing even though I felt upset right now. His view was that going to a different institution with a different philosophy and culture could expand my horizons and help me grow. At the time, I was annoyed with him because I felt he didn't understand, but in retrospect he was 1000 percent correct. When I visited Yale, even as an undergraduate, what struck me was how warm the community was, and I thought, "Wow, it feels like people here really take care of each other." At the time, I chose Harvard. I had a couple of close friends at Harvard, but I really felt quite isolated and lonely there, and it ended up being a stressful period in my life, as I mentioned. But when I went to Yale for medical school, it was the first time I really felt a sense of community.

Murthy graduated from Yale's medical school with an MD and an MBA and returned to Harvard for his residency. Despite his positive experience at Yale, deep down he still hankered after Harvard.

In 2007, he diversified his skills and co-founded a tech company called Trial Networks that optimizes the quality and efficiency of clinical trials. The following year he became an activist, founding Doctors for Obama in 2008 as a way of engaging physicians in the political process, all while keeping his day job as an internist, a hospitalist, and a professor. His mentor at Harvard, where he had served his residency, suggested Murthy apply for a promotion to a full professor. The idea appealed to Murthy, but Harvard was not done misjudging Murthy's potential.

Just before President Obama offered Murthy the top medical job in the administration, Harvard rejected Murthy's application for a promotion to become a permanent member of the faculty at its medical school.

MA: Do you think if Harvard had offered you tenure, you would have rejected the offer from the Obama administration to serve in government?

VM: When I was a student at Harvard College applying to the medical school, I really thought I needed to be there, but when I was in residency training there, having gone to Yale Medical School, I knew I could be at potentially different institutions and do well. What hurt a bit was the feeling that the institution I had dedicated so many years to didn't value the contributions I had made or display an interest in having me be part of the community. Had I not been declined a promotion I might have stayed longer, but instead it pushed me to think more broadly about what else I might want to do, where I would like to be, and what perch I would like to do it from. I had done clinical medicine and global public health work and I had started a technology company and built a grassroots advocacy organization. The job of surgeon general was an opportunity to bring together all the seemingly disparate threads in my life and apply the collective experience to advance the health of the country. What in academia may have been criticized as being all over the place, was an asset in government, although at the time when my promotion at Harvard was declined, I didn't realize my value added.

The surgeon general has a unique ability to be able to highlight a particular public health issue using the power of their office. The dangers of tobacco use, the obesity epidemic, comprehensive sex education, and addiction are among the causes that previous surgeon generals have focused on. Murthy identified loneliness and isolation as a national epidemic and sought to address the issue through social connection on an individual level and via national strategy.

Research shows that while loneliness has been linked to insomnia, depression, and anxiety—symptoms that are easy to understand since many of us may have at some point experienced something similar, even temporarily—what is less known is the linkage of loneliness to higher risk of heart disease, strokes, diabetes, addiction, self-harm, and dementia. A 2009 global study conducted by Dr. Julianne Holt-Lundstad, with over 300,000 participants, confirmed that the "impact of lacking social connection on reducing life span is equal to the risk of smoking 15 cigarettes a day, and it's greater than the risk associated with obesity, excess alcohol consumption, and lack of exercise."[90]

Malcom Gladwell said, "Vivek Murthy reminds us that our national conversation about medicine has been too narrowly focused on hospitals, doctors, and drugs—and not enough on human connections that sustain us."[91] Gladwell placed Murthy's book *Together* in the same category as Atul Gawande's *Being Mortal*, both being rooted in humanity.

MA: Where does this deep well of empathy come from? This sensitivity to personal suffering that seems unhurried, an unusual gift in today's world. Is it from personal experience?

VM: From a very young age, I felt things very deeply. That wasn't always a good thing for me because I was deeply affected by people's reactions and events around me, and when I was young, I wasn't able to process and make sense of some of the negativity or people's disapproval. During my childhood I had experienced the pain of rejection and loneliness and put-up facades and so I recognize the flickers of sorrow and suffering in others and try to reach out in the way I saw my parents reach out to their patients, which was my ultimate life lesson. We didn't know many people when we moved to Miami, but my parents' patients were their community, and when my father made house calls or went to the hospital, we sometimes went along and saw the interactions with his patients. My mom is not trained in medicine, but she ran the practice and engaged with the patients on an emotional level. They were so thoughtful and responsive towards their patients. It was a life lesson in how to care for people. Finally, my parents were very spiritual, and my mother gave me a foundation in Hindu philosophy. She told me that the reason Indians greet people with folded hands and say "namaste" is that we acknowledge the spark of God in each human being, and the God in me salutes the God in you.

It is somewhat ironic to learn that someone so accomplished, who came from a supportive family, suffered bouts of loneliness even as a child. As a young immigrant boy, Murthy struggled to fit in. He understood what it was like to feel insecure, subject to peer pressure, and isolated.

It was in grade school in Miami that Murthy first began experiencing severe anxiety. "When my parents dropped me off in front of my school each morning, I'd have this sinking feeling in the pit of my stomach," he recalled. "It was like first-day jitters, except it repeated every day of the school year. I wasn't scared about exams or homework. I was worried about feeling alone. And I was too ashamed to tell my parents that I was lonely. Making that admission would have amounted to much more than saying I didn't have friends. It would feel like admitting I wasn't likable or worthy of being loved."[92] It would only be in high school that Murthy found a group of friends and felt like he belonged.

MA: You describe feeling anxious and lonely at an early age. Looking back, was this a result of being an immigrant, being Indian? How did you get through that period? What tools did you use?

VM: I will share the reason why I felt that pit of fear in my stomach. Part of it had to do with my personality. I was shy and an introvert. Add to that we were immigrants and different. I moved to Miami when I was three and there was no one in my school whose parents were from India. Nobody ate the same food as us, and I was made painfully aware of my "otherness" when I brought Jalebis, an Indian dessert that I loved, to school one day. The other kids looked at it and made fun of it and it made me feel sad and somewhat humiliated. It was the distaste with which people sometimes looked upon the food we ate, the clothes we wore, the bindi my mom adorned herself with—all the cultural things Americans did not understand. Young kids made fun of it, so I felt alienated, and being shy made it harder to reach out and make friends. I would get called names in a pejorative way; one that I remember was "tomahawk boy." Kids in elementary school didn't always distinguish between Native Americans and Indian Americans and trying to get them to understand the difference seemed insurmountable at the time. Did it make me sad that my differences separated me from the group? Yes. But I never ever remember feeling, "Gosh, I wish I wasn't Indian," or wishing my family ate the same food or looked like everyone else, because I had been brought up with a strong sense of identity. I was proud to be American, and at the same time, my parents had inculcated in us a strong sense of pride in our culture and religion. Although I didn't share my loneliness with them, my family was my most important resource and their unconditional love sustained me through this difficult early period.

MA: What type of dad are you? Strict? Easy-going? Worrier, overprotective, or hands-off?

VM: I thought I knew what sort of parent I would be, but I was wrong. You don't know till you become one. I thought I would be strict and hold my kids to account, but it turns out I'm the softy in my family. My wife and I take turns. I am stricter about what they eat and make sure they drink enough water and pray before bedtime, but if my son wasn't feeling well, I'd just let him stay home from school. I feel a deep bond with my kids and have learned a lot from them, particularly about being in the present. They found a rubber toy once and threw it up and it got stuck to the ceiling. They were so thrilled and kept throwing toys at it, trying to get it down. I was trying to do hundreds of work-related things and finally I just put it aside and joined their delight and it was pure joy for those 15 minutes. We had a wonderful time together. I also love doing funny voices, making up stories and being the goofy parent. Of course I want my kids to do well in school, but I don't want them overscheduled in the way American childhoods have become, where you do 10 activities after school and on weekends. The one thing I had as a child which I worry many kids today don't have is unstructured time to explore and play outside. I played football, soccer, or would take my bike and spin around the neighborhood for hours at a time. I also loved to read, and read everything, biographies, fiction, and I got my homework done but not at the expense of exploration. By second grade, children start getting assessed in math and English and begin comparing themselves to other children. How do we interpret this? I want my children to enjoy reading and good at math and proficient in history because it opens up the world to us and teaches us about cultures, but I also don't want their lives to be shaped around getting into a certain college or fellowship for them to see themselves as successful. I know that is a path that as a society we have pushed families and kids down that track, but as much as possible I'd like to find a different path—one with more balance.

A 2018 AARP study found that one in three American adults over 45 were lonely. Other countries have reported similar findings, showing a strong correlation between loneliness and suicide rates. According to the CDC, suicide is a leading cause of death in the United States. More than half the people who choose to end their life are over 65 years old, with men accounting for 80 percent of these deaths. In 2021, 48,183 people died by suicide, 12.3 million American adults seriously considered suicide, 3.5 million planned a suicide, and 1.7 million actually attempted it. It was the second-leading cause of death for children between the ages of 10 and 14 as well as young adults 20 to 34 years old.[93]

Suicide is a global problem, responsible for 800,000 deaths a year. According to the World Health Organization, South Korea, Japan, South Africa, and Eastern Europe have particularly high rates of suicide. Hanging is the most common method, followed by the ingestion of pesticides. It is the leading cause of death among those in the 15 to 39 age range.[94]

In the past decade there has been a great deal of reporting in the Indian press on farmers committing suicide. Suicide rates overall have risen over the last 50 years. In 2021, India had the highest number of suicides in the world—164,033, to be precise. It is now recognized as an emerging public health issue in the country. The suicide rates for women have risen even more sharply than men and is twice the global rate.

MA: Why do so many more men commit suicide?

VM: There is a lot of pain in our society for a lot of reasons. I think loneliness and isolation is a big part of the pain and certainly increases the risk for depression, anxiety, and suicide. But you compound that pain, particularly on men, by imposing on them a culture where it is difficult to talk about their pain without shame. For many men, issues around self-worth are tied to how we define success. If you tell a man that your primary source of self-worth is tied to your income and how much power you have in society and to not needing anyone else and being stoic, that is not healthy for most men and may cause loneliness and isolation. Some men may thrive under those circumstances, but others do not. We tell boys at a young age that to be a real man you should not depend on other people or express your emotions, but it's okay to express anger. It's not a healthy way for men to approach adversity and face challenges and personal difficulties. Often, people medicate the pain, but a lot of that accumulated pain gets transmuted into self-harm. We see people in this country with severe and sustained trauma who have served in uniform and have legal access to lethal means of suicide. The rate of completed suicides is dramatically higher than if pills or other means are used. One of the reasons we see higher rates of suicides among men is their ability to access firearms.

MA: Do people of different ages handle it differently or use different self-destructive methods to medicate?

VM: It's a good question. There are differences, but alcohol and drugs are common across the board, whether they're opioid drugs or illicit drugs used to numb pain. I worry about other practices as well; you see so many. There are a host of addictions to worry about, but the bottom line is we are not getting at the root cause of pain.

The columnist Nicholas Kristof saw some of this pain firsthand and wrote about it for the *New York Times*. "More than one-quarter of the children who rode the No 6 school bus with me in Yamhill, Ore., have died from drugs, alcohol, suicide and so-called deaths of despair. These pathologies are linked to social isolation. I've seen how old friends self-medicated with meth or alcohol in part because they were disconnected from community, and then addiction and criminal records left them even more stigmatized and isolated."[95]

In a recent article in *The Atlantic*, Hillary Clinton echoes Murthy's concerns over loneliness, adding threats to our democracy to the list of negative outcomes. She attributes alienation and loneliness to the rise of demagogues such as Donald Trump and Rush Limbaugh and their ability to sow division.[96]

MA: Could you comment on the Hillary Clinton assertion in the *Atlantic* article that makes several references to your book that the rise in alienation in the United States has allowed populism to thrive?

VM: I think when people feel lonely and alienated, it becomes easier for them to become exploited or manipulated by other people who promise them a sense of belonging, even though it may cause harm to themselves or others. A classic example is gangs. I interviewed gang members and people who've been incarcerated. Many of them told me they joined a gang because they didn't have a place where they belonged. Many didn't have families they could rely on who loved them, and many were moving through what felt like a very unsafe life alone. The gang provided them with a community and gave them a sense of belonging and a false sense of security. I worry that as a country, this will be true with foreign adversaries as well. The more divided we are, the easier it will be for a third country who does not have our best interests at heart to divide us. So, I do think if you are disconnected, it's hard to hate people up close and you are more likely to give them the benefit of the doubt, but when you don't know someone, it's much easier.

Murthy has been joined by officials in other countries who have recognized the seriousness of the problem. Japan now has a minister for loneliness and Sweden's minister for social affairs has been ahead of the issue. Stuart Andrew is the British minister for loneliness and has tried to promote community projects such as hiking and neighborhood clean-up projects, encouraging private and public engagement to build communities and connect people.

Murthy advocates paying close attention to our social connections and relationships as an antidote to loneliness and a sense of alienation. According to researchers, there are three broad circles of relationships: intimate, relational, and collective. The most important and the one that consumes 60 percent of our time and energy is our intimate inner circle. This could be a spouse, partner, family member, or close friend. The second is the relational circle: people we interact with regularly, our close friends, parents of our children's friends, people at work we get on with, etc. We invest 40 percent of our emotional energy on them. The remainder is our community: neighbors, colleagues, distant relatives, and the world at large. According to a now-famous long-term study at Harvard on happiness, the circles are flexible, with people migrating between them due to circumstances that may shift. Beginning in 1938, the study followed the lives of 268 men over several decades and showed that inner circle relationships were better predictors of health and happiness than IQ, wealth, or social class.[97]

At one time, doctors made house calls, knew their patients well, and were part of the community, just like Murthy's father in Newfoundland and Dr. Verghese in Tennessee. There are still some vestiges of the practice in India and Europe, but the transient population in urban areas, high cost of gas, and parking and traffic congestion has made it rarer. In the United States it has ceased to exist. When I lived in London briefly in the eighties, there were designated parking spots in every neighborhood for a physician, and I recall seeing them in France as well. These small conveniences eased the ability of caregiving, but urban pressure has eroded the old, more humane structures of society.

When Dr. Verghese made house calls in rural Tennessee, he learned a lot about his patients. He was able to see if they were cared for, what they ate, if their environment was supportive or depressing—all predictors of the health outcome he might expect of his patient. Those connections are another thread that's being lost from the fabric of life that holds people together.

MA: What are your thoughts about Medicare's 15-minute rule per patient versus the house calls of the old days? Is reform needed?

VM: Prescribing a set amount of time that every clinician should be spending with each patient doesn't make room for the human element in medicine. The relationship between a patient and their doctor is a therapeutic part of medicine that is deeply underappreciated. It allows the doctor to better understand what the root of the problem might be. Time spent with the patient builds trust, and each patient is unique and may require different amounts of time. As technology improves, we can use it to get better data to manage health resources better. We should be looking to marry technology data and personal relations. In a system where there are multiple insurance companies and people lose their doctor when they change their jobs and insurance—and the recent trend towards what feels like a more commoditized version of medicine has been harmful to relationships. Most patients want to know their doctor and want their doctor to know them. The relationship is central to healing, and any move away from a relationship-based medicine ignores the reality of human nature.

MA: Vinod Khosla holds the view that AI will soon replace doctors.

VM: AI can have a very positive impact on medicine if managed closely and correctly and we protect the relationship between patient and physician. We've evolved over thousands of years to be in a relationship with one another—I don't think you can replace human relations and emotions with AI. I think what AI can do, that would be very helpful—is reduce some of the administrative burden; read scans and generate differential diagnosis with potential therapeutic options. These are all places where AI could improve our performance. If AI takes over some of the tasks it could liberate the physicians and provide them with more time for their patients, something that has been severely lacking in the last few years. But we need to continue to invest in the human patient-physician relationship.

MA: There is a big problem in this country with doctor burnout. Many physicians are leaving medicine, and medical students, before they even graduate, are feeling stressed and compromised about the ideals that made them go to medical school in the first place. Are you concerned?

VM: Last year I issued a surgical advisory on health care worker burnout. Twenty-five percent of doctors and 52 percent of nurses say they plan to leave their clinical practice. That portends disaster for the overall population. The nature of their work has become increasingly problematic, involving less time with patients and far too much time filling out forms, dealing with prior authorizations, and sitting in front of computers managing increasing barriers thrown out by insurance carriers. This is on top of the extraordinary educational debt taken on by these professionals, which has become a challenge. Traditionally, we haven't extended mental health care to health care professionals, which is ironic. You can see why people are dropping out of the profession in record numbers.

MA: You recently spoke about the "hustle culture" experienced by students you spoke with in Los Angeles. Can you talk about that?

VM: In December 2021 we issued a surgeon general's advisory on youth mental health crisis in part after speaking to young people who felt they were caught up in a "hustle" culture. They were chasing fancy internships, fancy colleges, fancy jobs, and the pressure to make money and become famous was not leading to happiness. They were struggling with anxiety and depression. We were very concerned by this. Culturally, we have defined success in a way that I do not believe is leading our youth to happiness and fulfillment.

MA: How can you make a difference? Can you transform society?

VM: In government we think of problems as having policy solutions. There are policy prescriptions that can help with the physician burnout crisis and the youth mental health crisis. We can alleviate the administrative burden on health care professionals and reduce debt, but with the youth mental health crisis we have to shift cultural levers. There it's not policy but our beliefs that change culture and reduce pressure. It's about how we define success and what we are asking youth to chase. Pursuing being rich, powerful, and famous may not lead to happiness. This is a conversation I'd like to help shape as surgeon general. Are we choosing to build a people-central life? Social media has taken over our lives as faith organizations and community organizations have declined. We've become more isolated and alone. We need to make people more aware and mobilize people around a strategic plan. But the truth is that unless you change hearts and minds here, policy can't build sustainable solutions. All too often, I've seen a policy win a slim majority; you get it passed finally, then people lose interest, and you realize the policy can easily be reversed. Real sustainable change has to come from the ground up.

Loneliness is a universal problem. The impact of social media on young children, the surgeon general's more recent concern, is something that has resonated with parents across the country. Murthy has publicly called for technology companies to implement safety standards for social media to protect children. Murthy considers excessive usage—more than three hours a day—a risk to brain development, while exacerbating body dissatisfaction, disordered eating behaviors, and low self-esteem, especially among adolescent girls.[98]

MA: After addressing loneliness, you selected the harmful impact of social media on children as a concern to raise from your bully pulpit to try to pressure tech companies to include more safety controls for children. Can you elaborate on this?

VM: Our highest priority should be the safety and well-being of our kids. If we can't protect the mental health and well-being of our children, then nothing else matters. It should be our top priority. For a child struggling with their mental health and well-being, it's harder for them to learn, it's harder for them to build social relationships, and harder for them to succeed and makes it more likely for them to engage in harmful activities such as drugs. It is shameful that we have placed the entire burden for managing social media on parents and children. We've taken this rapidly evolving platform that parents didn't grow up with and is designed by some of the best product engineers in the world to maximize the amount of time that people spend on it. It's just not a fair fight when parents have essentially been pitted against the most talented engineers in the world. To their credit, some social media companies have instituted a few safety measures, but the question is, have they done enough? I think the measures are woefully inadequate. When motor vehicle death rates were high, we didn't throw up our hands and suggest going back to the horse and buggy days, we put in place safety standards and made sure cars had airbags, seatbelts, and standards that were followed. We need something similar. Companies have not been transparent with all the data they have about the impact of their platforms on the mental health of kids, which leaves us operating in the dark. The real harm may be significantly worse than what we know. I have urged parents and schools to create tech-free spaces in children's lives. Young people say they are having a hard time forming friendships and reaching out to others. I have children who have told me they would like to interact with other kids during lunch, but everyone is on their devices. I spent seven years building a technology company, so I'm a user and I believe in technology.[99] I don't think technology is good or bad, it's how it's designed that makes the difference and if it hurts or harms us. My concern is that they have been reluctant to put any kind of constraints on themselves. Nearly half of young people are saying that using social media makes them feel worse about their body image.

MA: In your book, you quote the historian Stephanie Coontz's op-ed where she wrote that it was dangerously antisocial to elevate marital affection and nuclear family ties above commitments to neighbors, extended kin, civic duty, and religion. The United States is a society that prizes the individual. How do you reconcile this?

VM: The big question is how we move from a "me" to a "we" mentality, from the idea that independence does not have room for interdependence. We are all people who have benefitted from others, and that needs to be reflected in our popular culture better. In films, media, books; by artists and academics alike. Sending a message that it's okay to need other people is essential as building bonds of affection and collaboration is an ingredient for success. Shifting society towards a more community-centered way of living will only enhance our lives.

In 1937, 73 percent of Americans belonged to a church. By 1991 this had dropped to 70 percent. A new Gallup poll from 2020 revealed a shocking drop to 47 percent.[100] Jake Meador, in an article for *The Atlantic*, writes that this is bad news for America. "Participation in a religious community generally corelates with better health outcomes and longer life, higher financial generosity and more stable families—all of which are desperately needed in a nation with rising rates of loneliness, mental illness and alcohol and drug dependency."[101] According to a Pew research poll, 17 percent of Americans do not affiliate with any religion, up from 11 percent a decade ago. Many of them are millennials, college-educated, and white. The decline in church communities is mirrored in the fraying of urban communities.

      The isolation and loneliness that Murthy says has become an epidemic is particularly acute in urban areas where people get siloed by inequality, migration, unemployment, and a lack of resources. The people that fall through the cracks are disproportionately poor and non-white.

      I remember taking a bus in Manhattan in the eighties going uptown on the East Side. The bus stopped in front of a hospital and a patient struggled to get on with an oxygen tank. The bus driver lowered the steps to make it easier for him but did not get down to help him. I felt increasingly uncomfortable watching the patient try to maneuver his belongings and the oxygen tank. I got up to help, wondering if I was strong enough or if I would be more of a hindrance, when luckily another passenger, a well-built man who looked like he was in his forties and over six feet tall, got down to help him. I was racked by guilt that I had not been the one to help, and felt depressed for the rest of the day, wondering how he got home and if anyone was waiting for him, or if he lived alone.

This scene would have been unimaginable in India. Entire families would go to the airport just to see a relative go overseas when travel was less common. The number of well-wishers so outnumbered the passenger traveling that the airport authority began to charge for non-ticketed passengers wishing to enter the airport. When that failed to deter family members determined to be with their loved ones until their flight departed, the airport authority restricted entry into the airport to ticketed passengers only. Leaving an ailing member of the family to go to a hospital alone would be unthinkable and considered not just a dereliction of duty, but a disgrace to the reputation of the family.

Murthy's book *Together* points out that there are several ways that people can come together to bridge loneliness. Making kindness towards one another a priority and creating community projects are all ways of rebuilding our society.

On a warm Sunday morning in June, I went for a walk in Central Park with my daughter and 18-month-old grandson. I had just finished reading *Together*, Murthy's book about loneliness and the healing power of human connection. I began to tell my daughter about what a profound impression it had made on me. We didn't have to look far to see the evidence of what Murthy was describing in his book. At 9 a.m. there were people of varying ages scattered across the park, some who were obviously homeless, side-by-side among the many volunteers who come together to work in the park. It is a place of calm in the middle of a bustling metropolis, with quiet shaded pathways and bursts of attractive flowers. Among the strollers, runners, and tourists are individuals who may not be homeless but seemed to be suffering from other problems and look very much alone. In a grassy spot under a dogwood tree, a man pulled out his saxophone and began to play, momentarily turning the park into a communal haven. I saw a homeless man lying on a bench turn his head to listen.

In a fast-changing world that is increasingly dominated by technology, remote work, and artificial intelligence, Murthy urges us to hit the pause button. He often starts talks by getting people to follow him on a brief meditation. It is a tool with its roots in Indian culture that Deepak Chopra has promoted as well, but it is also being applied by educators across America. Found to be effective, meditation has the added benefit of being free.

At 44 years old, Murthy is trying to have a huge impact, and his canvas is all of America. Some leaders see themselves as crusaders—geniuses like Elon Musk and Steve Jobs fall into that category. Murthy views himself as a protector. He wants to protect children from the tech companies and is willing to push them to make social media safer. It is no less daunting than going up against the powerful tobacco companies of yesterday. He is willing to take on the NRA if it means protecting schoolchildren. His ambition to address the problem of loneliness, something he personally experienced as a child, will be more challenging. It is abstract and personal, but by elevating it as a public health concern and putting his weight behind it on a national platform, he has already started a national conversation. It was surprising to see Hillary Clinton respond to his book in an article for *The Atlantic*; it must have touched a chord in her complicated personal life. Murthy was born in the west, but he retains a strong Indian cultural identity that not only influences his values such as family and community over the individual, where duty and obligations are a serious commitment, but leans into his discourses with the public.

MA: You have used meditation publicly. When did you first begin to use it and when did you feel you could promote it in public?

VM: My earliest memory is being taught to meditate by my mother when I was about six, and it became part of my regular routine growing up. I later studied it in medical school in a class called "Healers" for medical students. Meditation is not exclusive to Hinduism. Although it's most closely associated with it, it was practiced by Catholic monks, and the tradition exists in other faiths. I have found that as surgeon general when I put out a series on meditation, particularly around the holidays, a difficult time for some people, the response was overwhelmingly positive. It's a powerful tool to help us deal with stress and to reflect.

MA: Most people your age are barely starting their career. You have already reached what some would consider the pinnacle, what most people achieve at 60. What drives you? And what you do for the rest of your life when you already climbed the mountaintop not once but twice? What would you like to achieve that you have not as yet? Is there any burning desire, professional or personal, that you'd like to do?

VM: I feel in some ways, everything I have done up to now, in some ways, is preparing me for the next stage of my life. The times when I feel most deeply connected to a sense of purpose that gives my life meaning is when I am contributing in some way to someone's life that gives them hope, comfort, or inspiration. It could be as simple as validating concerns they have. I found I was able to do this as a physician, but I would like to do it on a broader scale.

MA: Aren't you already doing this as surgeon general?

VM: There is great suffering in our world, not just in the United States, and across the age spectrum. We are living through a spiritual crisis in our time when people have become disconnected from sources of meaning and purpose, and joy is hard to grasp. Our connection to one another and to God—which gave us meaning and purpose—have become weaker. I know these issues can't be solved by one person or one organization; they require all of us. So, for my next phase I find myself thinking of how to address that deeper spiritual crisis and tell a different story both in the United States and the world about who we can be, what our identity is, and define success differently. I'm not talking about policy or programs but a cultural shift in how we see ourselves and each other and moving away from defining success in a way that's anchored to power, fame, and money towards relationships, contribution, and service. We equip our children with the tools that will get them jobs and the ability to earn money, but that is different from teaching them how to build—recognize what will bring them joy and fulfillment. We want our kids to grow up in a world where people are kind and compassionate. Fear is too dominant a motivator. We want to build a society where love is the motivator.

The Influencers

CHAPTER 16

Leadership in Public Policy

By the 1980s, a new class of immigrants from India began joining the engineers and doctors in America. India's economy had begun to improve, albeit at a glacial pace, and students were now going overseas to study the liberal arts, an area that parents did not previously see as a sure path to economic success. Making money was not the only goal; Indians who came in the eighties and later, wanted to make their mark on the world in other ways. Among them were Fareed Zakaria, who went to Yale and Harvard and would become a public intellectual; Mira Nair, who studied film at Harvard; and Abhijit Banerjee, an economist, who attended Harvard and won a Nobel Prize in 2019.

For the Indians who moved to America in the sixties and seventies, who had no support systems and arrived with no money, achieving economic security was a necessity. Thanks to their hard work, their children grew up in more comfortable circumstances and had the freedom to expand their career choices and branch out beyond engineering and medicine. Some wanted to make a difference in their communities and find ways to give back.

As the new millennium dawned, a new generation of Indian Americans born in the United States came of age, adding their contributions to the evolving coalition of immigrant success in America. Some, like Neal Katyal, Sri Srinivasan, and Preet Bharara, chose to serve the public good via the legal profession, while others entered politics. Nikki Haley, Bobby Jindal, and Ro Khanna were born in the United States and were raised by their immigrant parents to love America. They viewed public service as a legitimate career choice even though it was not an obvious path to wealth creation.

Jindal and Haley, both Republicans, had led the way becoming the governors of Louisiana and South Carolina, respectively, in 2008 and 2011. In 2013 there was only one Indian American elected to the House of Representatives; in 2024 there are five: Ro Khanna, Ami Bera, Pramila Jaypal, Raja Krishnamoorti, and Sri Thanedar. Most of them have been elected from districts where South Asians are not a majority, indicating wide support for them beyond their own community. Indian Americans have also become involved in local politics; close to fifty have been elected to state legislatures in the last decade. In 2020 close to 100 Indian Americans ran for state, local, or national office.

With the exception of the two governors, most of the Indian Americans elected to office tend to be democrats. Seventy percent of Indian Americans vote for the Democratic Party, and Indian Americans officeholders tend to be Democrats. Kamala Harris, whose mother immigrated from India, became the first US senator of Indian descent. She was elected from California in 2016 and four years later, she became vice president of the United States.

IMPACT, a political action committee, has raised millions of dollars for Indian American candidates who want to run for office. It was founded by Raj Goyle, who graduated from Harvard Law School and served two terms in the Kansas legislature.

RG: "I thought I understood politics, but I quickly realized there was no infrastructure for someone like me and I had to learn it all on my own. I was elected at the age of 31 and at that point there were only four state legislators who were Indian American. Mine was a largely Republican district. I'm an infrastructure guy and I felt a support network needed to be built, so I founded IMPACT. I cast around for a funder and found Deepak Raj. He was a generous donor and kicked off the process. Our goal was to help Indian Americans get elected. The most important metric in politics is viability. So now, as political experts, we make sure we support people who are viable."

IMPACT raised close to $15 million during the last election cycle and hopes to raise a similar amount to help Indian American candidates in 2024. The organization primarily helps Democrats.

The accomplishments of Indian Americans in government have enhanced the prestige of public service in the eyes of the Indian diaspora. When Joe Biden picked Kamala Harris to be his running mate in 2020, the Indian American journalist Anand Giridharadas joked that Indian parents were now going to use this as the new standard for their kids. "Please spare a thought for all of us who will now be shamed at Indian family reunions for being neither doctors nor engineers nor even vice-presidential nominees."

Political engagement is a recent phenomenon among Indian Americans, who had stayed away from politics when they first came. Modern India's founding fathers, such as Mahatma Gandhi and Jawaharlal Nehru, were inspiring, ethical, and high-minded figures, but after their passing, Indian politics became riddled with corruption and criminality, leaving Indians with a jaundiced view of politicians. It is no surprise that the Indian Americans who came to the United States for economic or intellectual advancement shied away from politics.

This reticence changed in 2006, when President George W. Bush sought to negotiate an agreement on civil nuclear cooperation with India. Bush needed Congress to amend existing federal law to provide India with a waiver, as India had not signed the Nuclear Non-Proliferation Treaty. Secretary of State Condoleezza Rice and the Indian ambassador called on the Indian-American diaspora for help. They in turn, fanned out and called on their senators and congressmen, holding fundraisers and meetings to persuade the lawmakers to agree to the waiver, which passed in December 2006.

It was the first time that Indian Americans had come together in a politically significant way, and they discovered they had political clout. The passage of the civil nuclear deal would be the turning point in the relationship between the two countries. The Indian community began to support politicians who they felt would advance relations between the India and the United States. Backed by their newfound wealth, they have become a powerful pro-India lobby and been recognized as a growing political force along with USINPAC, which was modeled on the pro-Israel lobbying organization AIPAC.

An explosion of Indian Americans to prominent appointments took place during the Obama administration. Raj Shah was appointed as head of USAID, Vivek Murthy became surgeon general, Aneesh Paul Chopra was named the first technology czar, and Subra Suresh became director of the National Science

Foundation. Sri Srinivasan, a judge on the United States Court of Appeals for the District of Columbia Circuit, is on many Democrats' shortlist as a potential Supreme Court justice. President Obama appointed so many Indians to positions within the government that Diwali, the Hindu festival of lights, was celebrated for the first time in the White House during his presidency.

Both President Trump and President Biden continued the trend. President Trump appointed Nikki Haley as his ambassador to United Nations; Seema Verma headed medicare; and Raj Shah and Kash Patel were some of the prominent Indian Americans to serve in his administration. President Biden reappointed Vivek Murthy as surgeon general and named Vanita Gupta the associate attorney general. But when President Biden under tremendous pressure took the historic decision to step aside from the 2024 presidential race and endorse Kamala Harris as the democratic nominee for president, he broke every barrier. An avalanche of articles on her Indian mother and bi-racial background hit the press. Harris's maternal family are from Chennai and her father, who is Jamaican, is a retired professor of economics who taught at Stanford University. Her parents met when they were students, fell in love, got married but divorced in 1971, when Harris was just seven. Although Harris and her sister Maya were raised by their Indian mother and the Indian community would love to claim the first woman president of the United States as one of their own, she has always identified as black. She attended Howard University, a historically significant Black University, joined black sororities and while she speaks of her maternal family with warmth and respect, she has been unequivocal in affirming her cultural identity as black. It is in deference to her sense of identity that I did not include a profile of her in this section.

This generation of thought leaders and activists has essentially mainstreamed Indian Americans into the tapestry of American life. Today there is a sitting vice president of Indian descent and two of the top Republican presidential candidates in 2024 were Indian American. Nikki Haley, the former governor of South Carolina and United States ambassador to the United Nations, outperformed her rivals and became Donald Trump's main challenger during the presidential primaries that year.

There are also many writers and journalists of Indian descent, and the world of entertainment has seen an explosion of Indian American talent, as Hasan Minhaj, Kal Penn, Mindy Kaling, Priyanka Chopra, and others have become stars. Their contribution has been invaluable in the paths they have opened up for a new generation of Indian Americans, particularly those who are born here.

While all the people I have mentioned are inspirational, the people I profile here have been transformational in the impact they have had, such as Fareed Zakaria in media and Neal Katyal, who has helped to shape constitutional decisions taken by the Supreme Court. Others like Nikki Haley are breaking boundaries in politics, and Ro Khanna is a rising star in Congress.

CHAPTER 17

Fareed Zakaria

I am an American, not by accident of birth but by choice.
I voted with my feet and became an American because
I love this country and think it is exceptional.

FAREED ZAKARIA

The four coordinated attacks on 9/11 by Islamic Jihadists that killed nearly 3000 Americans was a seismic event in United States history. The country entered a period of psychological seizure, terrified by terrorists and Islam and scrambling for answers. Dramatic pictures of the attack were replayed on television screens across the country—the planes crashing into the World Trade Center, the towers collapsing, the horrific scene of civilians jumping out of windows to their death. The towers had turned into burning infernos, with people on the ground covered in white ash from the debris, looking like zombies trying to escape an apocalypse. It resembled a Hollywood movie about the end of the world, and in some ways, it was the end of the world as we knew it. From then on, we would forever live in a post-9/11 world—one with cumbersome security, enhanced identity checks, and long lines. Everyone was looking for an explanation and Fareed Zakaria seemed to have all the answers.

Zakaria wrote a 7,000-word cover story for *Newsweek* called "Why They Hate Us" which sifted through the miasma that had begun to cling to people's perception of Muslims, equating them with terrorism. Page by page he unpacked the failures of Arab leaders to live up to their peoples' hopes and expectations economically and politically, enabling religious leaders and extremists to step into the breach. Zakaria also had policy prescriptions to offer. He warned against pursuing certain policies in haste out of a sense of retribution for 9/11. He urged policymakers to work in tandem with international coalitions before embarking on precipitous actions that would be complicated to execute. He also argued for a cultural strategy to promote open societies and encourage moderation among Arab rulers.

Henry Finder of *The New Yorker* called it the most "widely read, widely photocopied, widely envied" essay. It was broadly circulated within the government; generals and admirals made it recommended reading. "That was the moment," recalls *Newsweek* editor Mark Whitaker, when "Fareed became a rock star."[102]

As an educated Muslim living in the West, Zakaria conveyed a certain authority; he offered himself up as the "interpreter" of Islam as it related to current world events.

My meeting with Zakaria had been difficult to arrange and required some persistence due to his demanding schedule. We had several friends in common, although our paths had only crossed a few times at formal settings, such as a sit-down dinner in Manhattan or a talk he gave at a think tank, so it would be a stretch to claim I knew him before our interview. I had been warned he was overstretched, but it was only when I began the process of trying to schedule our meeting that I got a glimpse of the carousel of commitments he juggled, from commencement addresses, other speeches, board meetings, and interviews for his own CNN program to trips to East Asia to meet a head of state, with a visit to China or a side trip to Ukraine on the way back. It was head-spinning. The Aspen Security Forum? He was there. Davos? He was there. When I finally got a time scheduled, I felt like I'd won a race.

In contrast to the lead up to meeting him, the interview was intellectually stimulating and an unexpected pleasure. Mr. Zakaria has an old-world elegance and surprising warmth; he was open and unhurried during our conversation, which took place in his stately brownstone on the Upper West Side. Decorated with comfortable chairs, beautiful carpets and artwork, and, of course, floor to ceiling bookcases, the house was tasteful but not overdone. It was very much a home, with his friendly dog Brody sitting curled up next to him throughout.

Zakaria is short, trim, and fit, dressed in what I call Manhattan casual chic—dark, beautifully tailored pants and a white cotton shirt. It was mid-August, and a hot and humid day. I had offered to bring sandwiches, as our meeting was scheduled for midday, but he waved me off, saying something light would be prepared for us by his cook. I was impressed. I suggested we conduct the interview first, and then have lunch and discuss the last remaining questions. Lunch was two different salads, and we agreed that we may need to pick up the conversation on China in two months to see if the economy had rebounded.

Any American journalist who has made it to the top, whether Barbara Walters or Peter Jennings or Anderson Cooper, will tell you it takes hard work and a lot of luck. Zakaria, unlike some stories where people come from nothing and make it to the top through grit and brilliance, came from privilege. Not the sort one associates with America, where the scale is quite different, but in India he came from a well-known family that bestowed on him access to a great education and, most of all, confidence that you can conquer the world. His father, a lawyer by training, was educated in India and London and represented India at the United Nations. He served in the Indian parliament and was president of a local university in Mumbai. His mother was the editor of the *Sunday Times of India*. Zakaria's home is lined with photographs of his family with various presidents and prime ministers of India. It is a message to himself and his friends about who he is. One of his identities, being an educated Muslim from an elite background, catapulted him to fame. Zakaria is of course much more than that, as the world quickly understood. What follows is a conversation that unwraps his ascension in America's public intellectual arena.

MA: After 9/11 you were sought after to explain the source of Islamic terrorism to the world. Was that uncomfortable for you?

FZ: It was actually a very uncomfortable position for me to be in. Until 9/11 and for most of my adult life intellectually, being a Muslim had never been part of my identity as a scholar, a writer, or a journalist. Now, all of a sudden, this world of Islam comes crashing into America and to my doorstep and I'm asked to make sense of this. And so, for me, the challenge was to find a way to do it. At some level I felt I knew this world so intimately. I'd grown up with it. My father knew a great deal about Islam and wrote a lot on the subject. I knew the Islamic fundamentalists because I'd observed them in India. The original Deoband school came out of India, and although I knew that world well, I'd never had to grapple with it. I had to think about how to frame the subject in a way that was balanced. I pictured my father reading what I wrote and wondered how critical should I be? Would he think I did the subject justice? I had to weigh if it came across as too anti-Muslim. It was personally very challenging. I was at *Newsweek* and also dealing with a difficult deadline. We were going to run half the magazine on my essay. It was going to be 7,000 words and I wrote it in three days. At one point I wrote non-stop for 36 hours. In the end I just wrote what I knew.

MA: Did you lose any friendships over this? What was the response from Islamic scholars or the Arab world?

FZ: I had a few tense conversations with my father after and a few friends whom I lost who felt I was anti-Muslim, which is ironic because it wasn't anti-Muslim but acknowledging that there was a problem in the world of Islam, that it had not found a way to come to terms with the modern world. Scholars like Bernard Lewis and Fouad Ajami were very supportive, but the Muslim world feels betrayed when they feel you say things to the West that shouldn't be said even if it's true. Nobody could dispute what I was saying, but there was this feeling of "Why are you talking about this?" Like I was revealing house secrets.

MA: In your book *The Post-American World*, you write that the fanatics and terrorists were essentially a small minority feeding on the dysfunction of the Muslim world and easy access to technologies of violence and it doesn't rank on the same level of threat to the world as Germany's drive for world domination in the first half of the twentieth century.

FZ: I have said, there is a problem in the world of Islam, but one of the points I kept trying to make to people was that if these guys were really popular in the world of Islam, they'd have a million people on the streets of Cairo. They don't, that's why they use terrorism because they actually can't win elections and bring out millions of people. Ironically, I have been criticized by the right who go on about Islamofascism being the new great threat to the world. These guys are a bunch of rag-tag crazies, many of whom are deeply unpopular within their societies. When I look back on what I said I think I have been vindicated as the Islamic terrorism problem fizzled out much more quickly than even I would have guessed. But the degree to which the neoconservative right has a desire to conjure up this great moral political and ideological challenge that the United States has to face is difficult to remember now, but I was calling their bluff, putting it in perspective by saying, "Look, this is not in any way similar to the ideological battle we waged against the Soviet Union or Nazi Germany."

Zakaria had gone to Yale for his undergraduate degree and studied history, graduating in 1986. One of his friends, Boykin Curry, who overlapped with him at Yale, said that Zakaria was a "big man on campus" and obviously ambitious, but in a very genial, charming way. "Fareed became the President of the Yale Political Union, which at the time was pretty moribund," Curry recalled. "He realized he could use it as a vehicle to develop relations with powerful officials who were Yale alumni, who had fond memories of their days at Yale. He understood it would be very difficult to arrange meetings with these people once he graduated, so he created trips with a select group of students including me, to meet with an array of important officials. He called every important person who had been to Yale from William Buckley to George Bush and asked them to be on the board of the political union. They all said they didn't have time, but he assured them all they were required to do was put their name on the stationery, and they agreed. So now his letterhead had his name and the most powerful people in America. Now when he wrote requesting a meeting, it was both charming and impressive. We met people ranging from government officials to thought leaders to media personalities. These were people who would never have taken the time to meet with a 24-year-old two years after graduation, but he is so magnetic he now had enviable relationships and an A- plus rolodex that no one else his age could have assembled. He had a truly compelling personality in addition to being smart. Later on, Fareed became a hub.

If he had a dinner party, you went because you meet all the interesting people there from Henry Kissinger to Eric Schmitt, Gillian Tett or the governor of New York."

Zakaria enrolled in a PhD program at Harvard to study political science under Samuel Huntington. He initially gravitated towards a career centered around academia, directing a research project on American foreign policy at Harvard where he met Walter Isaacson. Isaacson found him impressive and recommended him to James Hoge, the editor of Foreign Affairs at the Council on Foreign Relations, who hired Zakaria as managing editor of the magazine in 1992. Zakaria moved to New York and in 1997, they published a book together called *The American Encounter* that was a collection of the essays of some of the legendary contributors to the magazine. Zakaria had also begun teaching at Columbia University as an adjunct professor, juggling several commitments and establishing his credentials among the intellectual set. He caught Kissinger's attention, who was impressed by him. In 1998, Zakaria published *From Wealth to Power*, an expanded version of his dissertation.

MA: By 34 you had two books to your name, degrees from two Ivy league schools, and an editorship at a prestigious journal. You had taught at Harvard and Columbia and published op-eds in major papers. What was driving you and where was the young Fareed headed?

FZ: I was very driven to be intellectually influential in the world. I was never motivated by money. When I look back on it now, I am sort of puzzled at the impracticality. I just never thought about it. The people my parents spoke of with respect were intellectual and political figures, such as the editor of the Times of India, Khushwant Singh, or Nehru. My aspirations were purely intellectual.

MA: You came from a well-known family, by the time you graduated from Harvard, India was opening up, you could have had any number of prestigious jobs in India, did you consider going back to make your mark as some of your contemporaries did?

FZ: I wanted to make a mark on a much larger canvas, and I suppose I was determined to do it. I never thought about the fact that I was Indian. I was not writing about Indian issues; my dissertation is about American foreign policy from the Civil War to World War I. Sam Huntington always said a great scholar, a great intellectual asks himself, what is the big problem out there and then tries to address it, not what problem am I connected to by reasons of race, religion, or ethnicity. I was very much trying to have that impact. There was a certain confidence or even hubris in doing it. When I was a columnist for *The Washington Post*, someone remarked that I was the first Muslim columnist they had. I'd never seen it that way, but I think I'm a lot of firsts—the first Muslim, Asian, brown-skinned, and immigrant columnist.

MA: Your job as managing editor of *Foreign Affairs* put you on the path to journalism. How did you make that move from academia and how much credit do you give the "Clash of Civilizations" essay for your early recognition there.

FZ: I met Walter Isaacson at Harvard and he mentioned that there was a job at *Foreign Affairs* and suggested I apply for it. I distinctly remember telling him I had no interest in it. He wanted to know why not. Well, at the time I was focused on an academic career, and I explained to him that Sam Huntington had told me he was going to arrange a teaching position at Harvard for me. Isaacson said, "You know I am talking of managing editor of *Foreign Affairs*?" and I responded yes, and I am talking about a position on the faculty of Harvard University. You could tell we were both socialized by our respective worlds. Later, at home, I mulled it over and I realized that I had always loved journalism. I had started a magazine in high school in India, my summer jobs had been in journalism, I had worked at *The New Republic* and *Harper's*, and loved it, so I called him up, said I'd made a mistake and was willing to throw my hat in the ring. I was by far the youngest applicant by 25 years and had to hustle to persuade them I could handle the job. When I told my mentor, Sam Huntington I was going to accept the job, he said it was a terrible idea and tried to dissuade me. I discovered, like Kissinger, academics also want you to replicate their path and the mark of success in academia is who your great students are and which prestigious universities they are teaching at. For him, it was a kind of betrayal, he tried to convince me if I stayed at Harvard,

I'd get tenure and argued I could enter government someday. I told him my mind was made up and I wanted to publish the essay he had sent me the other day for my comments called the *"Clash of Civilizations."* He said he had promised it to someone else, but fortunately for us, they had not committed to publishing it. I told him I was committing to publishing it right then and so I got it. It was a huge success and helped me enormously. I had told everyone from the editor in chief to the head of the council that it was going to have a big impact and I made it the lead essay. It was the first time we did something like that and I was right. It was an international sensation and gave me a lot of credibility as someone who had a feel for what was important.

In 1999, *Newsweek* came calling and recruited him to become the editor of *Newsweek International*. By then, Zakaria had begun to make a name for himself. He was a frequent guest on the Charlie Rose show and had written several op-eds for the *New York Times* while he was at *Foreign Affairs*.

MA: Kissinger advised you to move to *Newsweek*. Can you tell me about your relationship with him and why he took an interest in you?

FZ: At some level my friendship with Kissinger was natural. He is a policy intellectual. We had an enormous amount in common intellectually. Sam Huntington and Stanley Hoffman, my mentors at Harvard, were colleagues of his. We had both got our PhDs in the same department at Harvard and gone through a similar experience. The first time I met him in 1993 over a breakfast, there was a real mind meld. I had read everything he had written, and I had just moved to New York as the managing editor of *Foreign Affairs*. I think he saw in me somebody similarly interested in ideas, but also interested in policy, and practical. He always hoped I would go into government, because in a way it mirrored his own experience. There was definitely a part of me that thought I might end up in government but there was a part of me that had watched people like Kissinger make intellectual compromises as well as moral compromises in order to hold onto office and stay in power. In order to do that you have to please people and forego your independence, which I prized. I had seen this with my father growing up in India and found it distasteful and that played on me. I felt I would not be able to live with myself if I had made similar compromises. So, Henry and I had this tension between us as well, where he would always be trying to push me towards serving in government and I preferred the ethical independence I got from just being called a public intellectual.

During an interview for *New York Magazine* in 2003, Zakaria said "my friends all say I'm going to be Secretary of State, but I don't see how that would be much different from the job I have now." It sounds arrogant, but at the time there was a great deal of speculation about him joining government. He seemed like an obvious choice.

MA: There has been speculation on more than one occasion that you were offered a position with the administration. Some people thought you should be Secretary of State, but I assume if that had been offered you would not have refused.

FZ: Colin Powell asked me to be his director of policy planning. It was an interesting idea, but I didn't do it because I did not agree with President George W. Bush. It would have been an odd fit. Powell himself was an odd fit. I would feel compromised trying to help someone who was basically losing every policy debate within the administration. It would have been awkward and difficult. Obama asked me as well, but I realized I valued my independence. At some point, in order to have political power, you have to become part of the court. Maybe under the right circumstance I would do it, but it seemed a heavy price to pay.

MA: Which presidents have read your books?

FZ: President Obama for sure, I believe Biden read my last book and Clinton is a voracious reader and has read my books but not when he was president. We discussed *The Future of Freedom*, which he liked a lot.

MA: Kissinger pushed you to join *Newsweek*, that was a definitive move away from the world of academia into journalism. Did you ever look back?

FZ: If you look at my career, I started out as an academic, I then went to Foreign Affairs which is quasi academic as it's affiliated with a think tank, and the intersection of academia and journalism and when I joined *Newsweek* it was a leap into mass journalism. Kissinger did persuade me to take the offer as he felt that *Newsweek* would offer me a bigger canvas, and he was right. He pointed out that I had made a name for myself at *Foreign Affairs* and done an extraordinary job there, but as the editor of *Newsweek*, when I go to Japan, I get to meet the prime minister. It gave me high visibility and an international platform. People may not remember today, as the world of publishing and newspapers and magazines have changed, but *Time* and *Newsweek* had a wide global reach and enormous prestige. Journalism provides us with a way to engage with the world in a very active way, which is very different from being an academic, and you're able to influence events in a way that nobody from the inside of government or academia can, so I believe it was the right path for me.

MA: What was your mandate at *Newsweek* and how did you change things?

FZ: *Newsweek* was a challenging problem. The magazine needed to be more intellectually provocative, serious, and well-written, but we were now entering the digital age where people got their news instantly on phones and computers so finding the value added was a challenge. How do you take superb reporters and help them go a level deeper? Higher? You can't just tell the new like in the past—people already got it on their phones four hours ago. They need something else. Not just the who what and where, but the why—finding the value added. That became my overriding mission at *Newsweek*.

After 9/11, everything changed. It was a pivotal moment for America as well as for Zakaria's career. At 37, he had already gained international recognition with his *Newsweek* cover story "Why They Hate Us." Now, in March 2003, he once again got on everyone's radar with another attention-grabbing headline "Why America Scares the World." It was published as the United States began to bomb Baghdad. In it, he admonished the administration for its unilateral actions with minimal international support, that sent ripples of anxiety through the world about American heavy handedness. In particular, he singled out the administrations abandonment of diplomatic avenues to solve problems, resorting instead to military might against a much smaller country that frightened even its traditional supporters. Zakaria was articulating what many countries felt but were reluctant to openly express and risk incurring United States displeasure. He came to be regarded across the world as a genuinely thoughtful journalist.

Zakaria emerged both as a public intellectual as well as a prominent journalist. His global outlook and multicultural perspective bridged the gap between East and West, shedding light on geopolitical complexities that had the virtue of coming across as being balanced. His contributions extended far beyond the confines of traditional news reporting. Zakaria was assiduously courted by NBC and ABC in the months following September 11. George Stephanopoulos had him join his show *This Week*.

Zakaria coined the term "illiberal democracy" in an article he wrote for *The Journal of Foreign Affairs* in 1997, pointing out that democratically elected leaders often undermine the very institutions that are typically associated with a true democracy and often prioritize their own interests and retention of power over the rule of law and the rights and freedoms of the individual. In 2004, he wrote a thought-provoking book *The Future of Freedom*, expanding the idea. He pointed out that democracy and capitalism had expanded across the globe and become the de facto choice of newly independent countries, but while many leaders in countries like India and Iraq paid lip service to elections, they did not always observe the rule of law. Even in the West, democracy was flawed—in 1933, the Nazis came to power in Germany via constitutional means. The book also finds American democracy far from perfect. Zakaria writes that democracy is flourishing but liberty is not[103] and he points out its flaws and calls for an examination of its past in order that we may understand the needs of the future. The book was, an instant bestseller and established him as a leading political thinker.

MA: In *The Future of Freedom* you said that communism had been discredited, but under Xi Jing Ping and Putin it seems fairly firmly entrenched. Xi seems to have reversed the more liberal path that Deng and Wen Jx had begun to pursue? Would you revise your earlier view?

FZ: It's a good question. What I was referring to there was the contest of ideas that was so central to the way the world was organized then. If you remember, we grew up in India and the issue of which direction India would take was foremost in peoples mind. It got resolved in the nineties in favor of capitalism and liberal democracy. There has recently been some push back against American hegemony and its idea's but I don't know that we have an alternative set of ideas. When we talk of Chinese communism, and you examine it—half the economy is in the private sector, its tech companies are less regulated than ours and they have embraced markets. Chinese growth over the last thirty years happened because they embraced the private sector. The Chinese model is hard to pigeonhole. It's some strange combination of Leninist political control, which is absolute dictatorship, combined with some market orientation and some state control over that. It's hard from the outside to understand if it's a coherent alternative or a collection of practical accommodations to some evolving reality defined by Xi Jinping's desire for both political control and growth. Call it quasi communism or quasi capitalism.

In 2008, CNN offered Zakaria a platform that gave him global visibility and influence. His Sunday morning talk show "*Fareed Zakaria GPS,*" where the GPS is an acronym for Global Public Square, featured in-depth interviews with world leaders, experts, and intellectuals. The show gained in influence and Zakaria interviewed every major world figure on the show, including Presidents Barak Obama, Emanuel Macron, Wen Jiabao, Vladimir Putin, and Benjamin Netanyahu. He had become a brand. In 2023, at the height of the Ukrainian war, President Zelensky only agreed to be interviewed by Zakaria.

MA: Who was your first guest on Fareed Zakaria GPS? Were you nervous? Who are the two most impressive leaders you have interviewed? Has there been anyone you ended up disliking by the end of your interview? Did you ever regret giving someone a platform on your show?

FZ: Tony Blair was my first guest. I don't know why, but I have never been nervous. Growing up in a politician's family and watching my father at work gave me a familiarity with big personalities that helped. It made me confident. Lee Kuan Yew of Singapore was easily the most impressive leader I've interviewed. He's intelligent and a thoughtful, strategic thinker, but has the rare combination of being a doer as well. The other person that comes to mind is President Bill Clinton. At his best, he had a feel for politics like almost nobody I've ever seen. In terms of misgiving about having someone on, I had some Jihadis on and always wondered whether if that was the right thing. I've always believed that Islamic fundamentalists were more charlatans than true believers and preyed on people's fears, so I wished I had not provided them with an audience. I had Putin on, but I didn't feel that way about him because I felt it was important for the West to try to understand him. He was very intelligent when I interviewed him. He did not display the weird irrational aspect of his persona that you now see, which makes you realize what can happen when you are in power too long. When I interviewed him, he was well briefed, clear and a disciplined thinker but very anti-Western, incredibly so. It came through during the interview, but even more clearly in private in the green room conversation. Kissinger's view is that after 20 years in office and two years in isolation due to the pandemic, when all he did was spend time with his closest most conservative advisors, something changed in him. I essentially agree with that view. As Lord Acton said, power corrupts, and absolute power corrupts absolutely.

In the old days, Americans got their news through legendary anchors like Walter Cronkite and Peter Jennings. All of a sudden there was a fresh new lens through which they were being shown world events. It was a transformative moment for American news. The news business had a reputation for being highly competitive—some would say cutthroat. For an immigrant upstart to have his own platform was remarkable. The success of the show rested on Zakaria's ability to synthesize complex geopolitical issues into digestible narratives that resonated with a wide audience.

Zakaria was now beamed into the living room of an Egyptian family in Cairo as well as a Midwestern family in Des Moines, Iowa, offering viewers a unique opportunity to delve into the nuances of international events. Every Sunday, a non-white Muslim male with an Indian accent and a strong command of the English language and American security interests was in their living room explaining the world to them. For many people around the globe, they felt they could trust this man who looked like them to tell the truth and provide a balanced perspective, but he also resonated with Americans. He was becoming the communication bridge between cultures.

FZ: America is this very unusual beast, which is the most powerful country in the history of the world. It has more impact on the world than any country since the Roman Empire, but it knows very little about the world. You really need to understand what the world looks like, not from the view of the world from the perspective of the 800-pound gorilla, but from the point of view of the little rabbit in the room looking at the gorilla.

David Bradley, publisher of *The Atlantic* when Zakaria wrote for the magazine, said, "I don't think there is anyone who speaks to elite America more persuasively than Fareed Zakaria. If you assign all the prominent media people in the country to convince Washington and the other media of whatever your worldview is, I don't think anyone would do it as effectively as Fareed Zakaria. He takes the facts of a situation and provides a frame for them that is completely compelling in a language that all of us speak. I was on the board with him at the Council of Foreign Relations. The room was full of cabinet secretaries and four-star generals and billionaires, and everyone would still be quiet, waiting to see what Fareed had to say on a topic; and when he spoke it was as if you had already thought it—he's extraordinary at how much detail he's mastered. He goes global, then horizontal, and then he goes back 300 years. There is some journalist envy of him because he's shot past so many print journalists, but everyone I know likes him. What he has in abundance is a combination of grace, humility, and intelligence."

MA: How did you get your own show on CNN? The Global Public Square became one of the most widely viewed and influential news programs internationally.

FZ: My TV career started when George Stephanopoulos asked me to come on his show. That was my first break. He had read my work and asked me to join his roundtable and I became a regular, which was considered a big deal as it was mainstream American TV. The viewership was three and a half million. After a while I was approached by PBS to do a show on foreign affairs, but PBS has no money. I came up with an idea to do a show out of Washington. All the best foreign correspondents of the world's media outlets are there as well as the top diplomats as it's the ultimate posting. Add in the smartest people in the foreign service, IMF... it's a long list of people whose presence no one is taking advantage of because the American debate is so parochial. So, to keep things economical, I'd fly down every three weeks, book a studio for a few hours, and tape three shows. It was called *Foreign Exchange with Fareed Zakaria*, and I did that for four years and then Richard Plepler of HBO intervened. Richard was obsessed with the idea that I should have my own show and spoke to Jon Klein, the head of CNN. We had lunch and worked out a deal. My one requirement was that I should be free to do the show I wanted and if they didn't like it or it didn't work, they could cancel it. But I did not want them dictating to me in week three that I should do a segment on O.J. Simpson or something similar. I believed there was a market for an intelligent show about the world and I wanted to build the audience. To their credit, they agreed. At the time, everyone on TV doing the news looked like Tom Brokaw, but they backed me. It worked out and our show regularly gets one to two million viewers on each airing, and that's several million in the United States and CNN goes to 220 million households internationally. I've seen estimates that say 20 to 30 million viewers internationally, but we quickly became the number one taped show on CNN.

In 2010 Zakaria became a lead columnist for *Time* and *The Washington Post* carried his column every week. Zakaria was everywhere to "help people think about this fast-moving world." He had taken his place among the most celebrated journalists—

James Reston, Walter Cronkite, Peter Jennings—and he had done it by bringing a fresh new perspective to the global order.

MA: You started out as a conservative, but now call yourself a centrist. Can you describe the debate in your head that made you shift? Do you second-guess your views?

FZ: When I came to America it was the early eighties, and the dominant issue was the Cold War. I was not in step with the prevailing liberal consensus of a nuclear freeze, unilateral disarmament, and unilateral no-first use [of nuclear weapons]. I was heartened to see Reagan bringing some much-needed moral clarity to the issue and I believed the Soviet Union was in fact "the evil empire." I had grown up in India and seen the non-aligned bullshit and experienced the dysfunctional socialist economy. I felt there was a power to free markets and free trade. By the Clinton years the Cold War is over, and he moves his party to a much more sensible economic place. It struck me as the right balance of using the market but also using the government to redistribute wealth to give everyone an opportunity. It seemed like the right formula. The right got increasingly obsessed with cultural issues, which never appealed to me as I am socially liberal. I found myself more in the center as I'm socially liberal and a fiscal conservative. Today the protectionism has pushed me further right as I firmly believe that the best solution is to let markets create wealth and have governments distribute it. I'm all for pluralistic societies.

In 2012, at the height of his career, Zakaria was accused of plagiarism and for a brief period suspended from *Time*, *The Washington Post*, and CNN. He quickly apologized, accepted responsibility, and despite the temporary flap, recovered and moved on. At the time, the book publisher Peter Osnos, in an article for *The Atlantic* titled "Fareed Zakaria and the Perils of Modern-Day Punditry" wondered if Zakaria the polymath could do so many things at once—columns, daily blog posts, television appearances, internet videos, books, and speeches.[104] Osnos pointed out that this overprogramming of an individual could lead to lapses.

      Zakaria has written a book once every five or six years and five of them have been *New York Times* bestsellers. In 2009 he wrote a bestseller called *The Post-*

American World about the "rise of the rest" and the rapidly shifting role of the United States from the dominant superpower to a multipolar world. The *Washington Post* reported that it was one of the few books that President Biden had read this year. Zakaria's book makes the case that the traditional mechanisms of international cooperation such as the United Nations—with their outdated configurations of power distribution—are relics of another era. He cites as an example the permanent members of the UN Security Council as being victors of a war that ended 70 years ago.

Zakaria points out that 20 of the fastest growing cities are in China and that the economy has doubled every eight years for three decades and decisively broke with poverty, making it the dream of every third world country.

MA: In your book you warned that although in 2009 China was rising "peacefully," as its power increases, it will be tempted to increase its own security and expand its political, economic, and territorial control and change the international system in accordance with its interests.

FZ: Fifteen years ago, Lee Kuan Yew once said to me that he wasn't worried about the current generation of Chinese leaders because they had lived through the craziness of Mao's cultural revolution and understand the importance of a peaceful rise. But then he added that he worried about the next generation as all they have known is prosperity, and it could lead to arrogance. Xi Jinping is not quite the next generation, but there is clearly a shift. He has alienated all his neighbors, something the Chinese worked so hard to maintain good relations with, and China's prosperity and growth has slowed under him.

MA: Turning to India, in your book *The Post-American World* you write that it would be hard for any prime minister to command national power in the way Nehru did and that all politics were local. After seeing the rise of [Narendra] Modi, do you still hold that view?

FZ: I have been surprised by the Modi phenomenon. I think it's a backlash against modernization, globalization, liberalism, call it what you will. Modi, Erdogan,

Bolsonaro, Putin understand this backlash. There is a group of people in India who resent the urban elites. Modi has ridden this particularly effectively. India is a traditional society. All the populist leaders have used religion. I met with Bolsonaro's chief ideologist once and asked him what was at the heart of his project, and he said the revival of Christianity and Christian values in a society that's become too secular, too liberal. Erdogan has used the same tactic against the Istanbul elite. These leaders understand that the people in rural areas resent the cultural dominance of the urban elite and have mined that for political purposes. It's a far more powerful phenomenon than any of us realized. Modi has perhaps been the most skillful politician in the world in understanding this channel and manipulating it, but his appeal in the south is limited. India is a diverse country, and pushing Hindi in the south is creating resentment. You can't do in India what Xi can pull off in China. There will be resistance to Modi, and it will likely come from the south over the language issue. There will be a backlash against Hindi imperialism.

In his book, Zakaria credits Great Britain with the wisdom of recognizing early on that the balance of power had shifted to its former colony—the United States. After 1880, it began to cede power in the Western hemisphere to the United States and was able to focus its efforts on its colonies elsewhere, maintaining its influence until World War II.

MA: Are you suggesting that the United States derived some lessons from the British in the way they accommodated the rise of the United States? How does this play out?

FZ: The analogy is not perfect because the British Empire was a bizarre phenomenon and the product of an extraordinary industrial revolution. In the nineteenth century it was the only game in town and 5 percent of global GDP in 1945, but it was getting harder to maintain its far-flung empire. The United States is much more powerful than the British were and is a quarter of the world's GDP and the world's most powerful military power. It need not appease China in the same way. The best strategy would be for the United States to establish a powerful deterrence and redlines, such as no to invading Taiwan and bullying neighbors. At the same time, offering an economic carrot, agreeing to supporting their power in international organizations, and expanding trade. If you keep it like a caged tiger, one day it will break out. I don't question who will win the contest should that happen, as my bet will be on the United States, but it will cause enormous international tension, turmoil, and instability, and no one benefits from that. You have to provide China with some legitimate path for expansion or there will be constant friction.

In 2015, Zakaria made a case for the pursuit of a liberal education in the swirl of technology that had begun to surround and shape us. Apple, Google, and Microsoft had become the new Goldman Sachs, Disney, and White House internships. Tech had become sexy, Stanford the ideal school, and Silicon Valley the destination, not Wall Street or Hollywood.

MA: What inspired you to write *In Defense of a Liberal Education*?

FZ: There is a part of me that is a contrarian. We are going through a period in America where everything is dominated by tech. It is true that its impact on the world is huge, but what people are missing is the much longer story of human empowerment and learning. It's a story about us understanding history and culture and philosophy. Technology and science is part of the story but not divorced from it. I wanted to go back to understand how it all started. When did the Greeks come up with the idea of a liberal education? I gave a commencement speech at Sarah Lawrence about it and it went viral. I realized other people felt the same way and suggested the idea of this book to my publisher, who loved it, and I wrote it in six weeks. It was a passionate argument that came from the heart.

MA: The investor Vinod Khosla might argue that a liberal education is a waste of time. He has in a speech been dismissive of English majors, for example.

FZ: He is a brilliant guy and tech does play an important role and has solved many problems, but not when it comes to human values and ideas. Nuclear weapons that are untethered to a conception of a human construct of stability and peace can be dangerous. AI can be equally dangerous. I think it's limited to say that technology has all the answers. We can't dismiss traditional areas of study because technology came out of these fields. It emerged from the world of enlightenment and rationalism using science and rationality to solve problems. A meteor didn't suddenly strike Silicon Valley in the seventies and create technology. What makes and changes a world is not just technology but how we use it. Steve Jobs understood this.

In 2021, Zakaria wrote another bestseller, *Ten Lessons for a Post-Pandemic World*. It is an attempt to give our post-pandemic existence historical context.

As bad as the pandemic was, the Spanish flu and bubonic plague wiped out a significant part of the world's population. We risk poor outcomes if we ignore experts and science and give in to populism and politics. Zakaria differentiates between quality over quantity in government and worries that the erosion of trust in public officials leads to chaos. He cites Denmark as a country that works well and has a responsible government aligned with the interests and concerns of its people. He attributes Germany's successful management of the pandemic and other social and economic crises to the trust people have in their government. Despite America's problems with its domestic divisions and rising inequality, he still feels its basic institutions are strong—but in a highly interdependent world due to globalization, to succeed as a planet we need to find ways to cooperate.

His most recent book, *Age of Revolutions: Progress and Backlash From 1600 to the Present*, is a sweeping survey of the tumultuous path the world took as it lurched its way towards modernization. Zakaria traces the industrial and cultural revolutions that transformed western society and examines its evolution into the world we know today. The book immediately made the *New York Times* bestseller list. It was published shortly after we finished our interviews, and I regret that I was unable to ask him about his prescriptions for resuscitating the liberal international order. I know that he has an underlying cynicism about democracies and good intentions that grows out of his experience as a young person in India, where he was disillusioned by the rampant corruption, nepotism, and submission of political institutions to political power under Prime Minister Indira Gandhi.

Zakaria's rise to fame is not of some obscure person who came from nothing and made it on his own. He freely admits he came from privilege. Zakaria was born into an upper middle-class family in Mumbai, India. His father was an Islamic scholar, but although they were practicing Muslims like several elite educated Muslims of his generation, they were liberal and secular. His mother, who he adored, was a well-known journalist and editor of the *Sunday Times of India*. Both he and his older brother Arshad attended the elite Cathedral School in Mumbai and would often hang around their mother, helping her come up with titles for her articles. In a moving tribute to his mother when she passed away, he said he was the person he was because of her.

MA: Can you talk a little about your mother's influence in your life that you so eloquently referred to in your tribute to her on *CNN* on the occasion of her passing? How important was it that your parents were able to see you achieve success?

FZ: My father was a formidable man. I could never achieve success in the way he did. He was orphaned at six in a small town outside Bombay but gets a scholarship to attend high school and university. He manages to go to England in the middle of World War II and studies law and obtains a PhD. He returns to India to practice law and becomes the chief public prosecutor and from there becomes a politician and through it all writes several books. Think about the distance traveled. I on the other hand was born in comfortable surroundings. My mother was my rock. The two things a mother can do for her child she did in spades. One, is unconditional love, and my mother was the absolute avatar of that idea. If I murdered somebody, there was no question in my mind that my mother would support me; she had that absolute unyielding loyalty and love for her children that transcends everything. Knowing that is one of the great force multipliers in the world, that there is somebody out there who believes in you no matter what, who loves you no matter what, at least for me. When I came to America, I had no money, a funny Muslim name, brown skin, and did not know anyone. The only person I knew was my brother, who was also a scholarship student at Harvard. I remember seeing the prep school kids at Yale from Exeter and Andover and they were so well prepared, it was intimidating, but my mother's love got me through all that very well. She also gave us an enormous amount of respect and treated us like adults. This gave me a great deal of confidence. When she was the No. 2 journalist at the *Illustrated Weekly* she would bring her work home and we'd all sit around the dining table telling her which photographs to use for a story. It was fun being with her.

MA: How important was it for you to have achieved success while your parents were alive?

FZ: It was very important. They were both so proud of me and I'm very glad and grateful I had the opportunity to share my success with them, but it was complicated as well. My father being the self-made, driven man that he was used to drive me crazy when I was younger and always pushing me to move to the next challenge. An example of that is, when I joined *Newsweek*, I made a deal that my column for them would be considered by *The Washington Post* as well. They did not guarantee it would run every week, but they agreed to run it as appropriate. Every week when I spoke to my father, he asked, "So did the *Post* run your column?" It drove me crazy because of course it was something I hoped for and was concerned about, but it exemplified his drive. When he would get an award and I congratulated him and asked if he was happy, his view was that you need to have your eyes on the future and not focus on rewards for past accomplishments. I took that on and it was not good because I now think there is an enormous benefit to recognizing what you have been able to accomplish and giving it resonance by taking pause and absorbing it.

MA: In your book *Ten Lessons for a Post-Pandemic World*, you talk about how we as a people have become incapable of learning and knowing the same things and acting in a coherent fashion. That getting facts and reading the news are no longer neutral acts but loaded with political meaning. You refer to Hume's theory that "reason becomes a slave of the passion." People construct their arguments to come to a preferred conclusion. Contrary to what one would think that people believe certain things out of ignorance, those who read widely and are highly informed are more guilty of partisan thinking. Partisanship ahead of truth. It's called rationalizing voters. The rise of populism, deep suspicion of elites, relying on one's own sources and one's gut is a global phenomenon.

FZ: It's a very difficult problem and what's at stake is the whole liberal enlightenment project, which believes that humans beings have the capacity to reason and think through things and not give in to naked dogma, self-interest, and prejudice. But the speed and power of the technological, economic, and global transformations that are taking place are making people feel they are losing their community and sense of place in the world. AI is going to put all this on steroids, and we don't know what to do about it. In a weird way what we are seeing is the power of the enlightenment project produce this intense backlash. While the liberal enlightenment project creates greater efficiency, better government, more prosperous societies, and provides enormous choice, it leaves people feeling empty. Pascal wrote about this and called it leaving a heart-shaped hole in the chest. Tribalism, religion, and nationalism then fills that hole.

MA: What keeps you up at night?

FZ: The challenge of nationalism, populism, and what I mentioned above could undermine democracy, liberty, and the nature of the world we live in. It's a place that has been hospitable to immigrants and people who are different and rests on enlightenment values. If we end up in a world dominated by naked power nationalism and populism it will be an unpleasant world for minorities, for people who look and sound different, and, in my mind, tensions inevitably lead to war because it's all about enemies. People cling to their tribe and going down that path, as we've seen from the past, produces international tension.

MA: When you look back on what you have already accomplished—more than most people—do you feel it's not enough? Is there something else you want to do?

FZ: I built this multi-technology media platform with print, TV books—it's taken a lot of work and been hard to do, but I believe I built something that has credibility. What I'd like to do going forward is help Americans think about the world and engage with it in a more serious way. I'm not looking for new job opportunities for myself, but I want to take the trust that people have in me and the mandate I have to do it.

Zakaria seems to have no regrets about not having joined the government. He believes the world is changing in profound ways and relishes his status as a public intellectual. He is a trusted and established brand, and his relentless energy and piercing intellect continue to investigate and bring all the important issues of the day to our attention through his books, his speeches, and his platform on CNN.

CHAPTER 18

Neal Katyal

I've realized that the question isn't how to win every argument.
It's how to make sure that, even when you do lose, you stand back up
and keep on fighting for what you believe in.

NEAL KATYAL

The decision to profile Neal Katyal was an easy one for me, but I was inevitably asked by people about the "other" well-known Indian American lawyer, Preet Bharara, who as the United States attorney for the Southern District of New York had made a name for himself by aggressively targeting public corruption and Wall Street crime.

Bharara had also gained notoriety in India for prosecuting high profile South Asians for insider trading, including Rajat Gupta, the CEO of the consulting firm McKinsey and Co. In 2013, he created a diplomatic headache for Washington and came under intense criticism from Indian officials when he arrested Devyani Khobragade, an Indian diplomat in New York, on charges that she made false statements on her visa documents relating to her domestic worker who claimed to have been underpaid.

Bharara was fired by President Donald Trump in 2017 and went on to teach at New York University School of Law, author a book, and launch a podcast. He is currently a partner in the law firm Wilmer Cutler Pickering Hale and Dorr. Bharara had a reputation as a dedicated public servant and a brilliant and accomplished lawyer.

Neal Katyal has all these qualities, but he is an idealist. He is on a crusade to preserve American democracy and the integrity of its constitution. His writ extends to the heart of the law itself and he has elected to put himself in the middle of controversial cases that have even challenged the president's authority, all in order to uphold what he considers fundamental constitutional values.

In a recent Supreme Court case, *Moore v. Harper*, which Katyal won in a 6-3 decision in 2023 in a court dominated by conservative judges (three of whom were Trump appointees), he made history. The ruling put a stop to the politicization of elections by state legislatures by maintaining checks and balances. This had become an issue when Trump lost the 2020 election and his supporters tried to overturn the results in some states. The retired federal judge J. Michael Luttig,[105] a respected conservative on the United States Court of Appeals, hailed the ruling as "the most important case for American Democracy in the almost two and a half centuries since America's founding."

Katyal gets emotional when he talks about the case. "This was one of the most significant cases of my career because the stakes were astronomical. It gets to the very heart of democracy. If you can have fake electors by state legislatures, which was Trump's theory, then you no longer have checks and balances—and that to me is not a functioning democracy. *Moore v. Harper* was what I had taught, written about, and thought about for 20 years. This was the case I felt I was put on earth to do. Even though some people felt I would lose, I always thought it was winnable."

Katyal felt that had he not won the case, he would have given up practicing law. It was for him an intensely serious case, and he was willing to put his career on the line for it. The historical importance of the case cannot be underscored. Its significance was monumental. The Supreme Court agreed with Katyal and was persuaded by his argument and held that state legislatures remained subject to state judicial review and to their state constitutions.

But it was Katyal's first Supreme Court case in 2006, *Hamdan v. Rumsfeld*, that changed his life forever. He went from being an academic teaching constitutional law to an activist lawyer. Walter Dellinger, a former solicitor general and law professor at Duke University, called *Hamdan* "the most important decision on presidential power and the rule of law ever."

For Katyal, the *Hamdan* case was an affirmation of everything good about America—a country where you could expect justice to be dispensed without prejudice. In his statement to the press, he said, "What happened today, a man from Yemen with a fourth grade education accused of conspiring with one of the most horrendous individuals on the planet (Osama bin Laden), being able to sue the most powerful man in the world, the president of the United States, and have his case heard—that is something that is fundamentally great about America and something we should be celebrating to the rest of the world. In no other country would that be possible."

Katyal has argued more than 50 cases before the Supreme Court. In 2017, he made history when he argued his 33rd case, surpassing Thurgood Marshall's record of the most cases argued in the Supreme Court by a minority. He has distinguished himself from among the 1.3 million lawyers in the United States and become one of the most formidable legal minds in the country. His peers have acknowledged his contributions by bestowing several prestigious awards on him. The list is long and started with several awards recognizing his abilities in the under-45 category.

In 2004, Katyal won the *Financial Times* Innovative Lawyers Award for both public and private law and was listed as one of the 40 most influential lawyers of the decade by the *National Law Journal*, winning their pro bono award the same year. In 2011, Attorney General Eric Holder presented him with the Edmund Randolph Award, the highest award given to a civilian by the United States Department of Justice. In 2011 and 2014, Chief Justice John Roberts appointed him to the advisory committee on federal appellate rules. Katyal was named as one of the 500 leading lawyers by *Law Dragon Magazine* and one of only four lawyers to be included every year from 2005 to 2023. In 2017, *American Lawyer* named him "Litigator of the Year." Jeffrey Rosen, the CEO of the bipartisan National Constitutional Center in Philadelphia, said that "Neal is the most important Supreme Court advocate of our time." He continued: "Neal combines exhaustive preparation with complete mastery of factual details and the ability to think strategically about constitutional concepts. *Moore v. Harper* was a landmark case and the consequences for democracy couldn't have been greater. He argued that a state legislature cannot overturn the result of an election. *Moore v. Harper* will be quoted for generations as a vindication of the Supreme Court's devotion to the rule of law. It was a virtuoso performance and a historic argument that went on for many hours—much longer than normal—with many memorable exchanges with the justices. Only Neal could have handled it with such skill. His first case, *Hamdan*, which established the authority of courts to subject military courts to constitutional review, was also first rate." Rosen and Katyal were introduced by their mutual mentor at Yale law school, Akhil Reed Amar. Katyal is married to Rosen's sister Joanna, a physician.

The *Hamdan* case provides a useful window into the secret to Katyal's extraordinary success. He leaves nothing to chance, but it is the rigor with which he handles each case and his unflappable tenacity in the face of reversals that pushes him past the finish line to success. A wonderful book called *The Challenge*, written by Jonathan Mahler, covers the case and its main characters. Much of the information in the next few paragraphs are based on a combination of what I learned from the book and my conversation with Katyal. I have provided some details to illustrate what distinguishes him from others in his profession.

Katyal did not wait to be asked to defend Hamdan. When he learned that detainees from the 9/11 aftermath were to be tried by military tribunals under the jurisdiction of the executive branch and outside the United States court system, he was sure it was illegal. He went on the White House website to study the full text of the order and was stunned by the blatant attempt to use a national tragedy to expand presidential power.

Katyal, who taught constitutional law at Georgetown when he moved back to Washington, distributed the orders for his students to study and pick apart. When Congress questioned other measures that the president was pushing through to monitor people, prompting the judiciary committee to hold hearings, Katyal volunteered to testify. His written testimony included 24 footnotes citing case law going back to 1863. Congress was not persuaded.

Eighteen months later, he heard that military commissions were being set up to try detainees and would be headed by Colonel Will Gunn who was named the first ever Chief Defense Counsel in the Department of Defense Office of Military Commissions. Gunn supervised all defense activities for Guantanamo Bay detainees at the prison. Katyal took the initiative and tracked Gunn down to offer his help. Gunn, understaffed and overwhelmed, immediately accepted. In 2003, Katyal met with the two JAG officers assigned to the project. He would provide his knowledge of the Constitution and they would bring their knowledge of the Uniform Code of Military Justice and combine it into a strategy. Over the course of six years, Katyal quickly transitioned from an advisory role on the outside[106] to writing all the amicus briefs to eventually deciding the entire strategy of the case.

The *Hamdan* case took six years as it wound its way through military courts to civilian courts and all the way up to the Supreme Court. Katyal had bonded with his students at Yale Law School when he taught there for a year in 2001. Together they drafted 22 petitions and, thanks to the connections of another former student, he was able to recruit Perkins Coie, a law firm in Seattle, to work on the case on a pro bono basis. Even after Katyal moved to Washington, he continued to work with his students at his alma mater.

According to the book *The Challenge*, the lawyers at the firm often disagreed with Katyal about the style and content of the petitions they filed, but Katyal always had the last word. The lawyers always wanted to simplify the arguments while Katyal tended to be far more detailed with obscure citations and historical references. One 74-page memorandum of law that argued Hamdan's treatment at Guantanamo was illegal included 113 precedents and 22 statutes, as well as several treaties and acts to support the argument. According to Mahler, Katyal did it his way over the disapproval of the others. Katyal told me he learned a lot from the disagreements and tried to incorporate their suggestions as much as he could and, in the end, he appreciated that it was a better product as a result of the discussions. In another filing in September 2004, Katyal was so tenacious in his commitment to get things right that he worked on 26 drafts of one of his briefs. He was relentless.

Katyal's energy was prodigious. He had three small boys all under the age of five, and it was around this time that his father—who had been diagnosed with glioblastoma, a type of brain cancer—began to deteriorate. In between teaching, working on the *Hamdan* case, and sharing responsibilities for the children with his wife who had a full-time job as a physician, he had to make several trips to

Chicago to help take care of his father, who died a year before the case went to the Supreme Court.

In the summer of 2005, Katyal prepared his petition for the Supreme Court. All his colleagues who had read it almost unanimously urged him to start over, but Katyal was convinced his argument was the right approach and would get a hearing. Katyal was challenging the Supreme Court to provide guidance and clarity for basic ground rules that govern military commissions so that the sweeping authority that had been given to the president did not become entrenched.

Anxious that the court hear the *Hamdan* case, Katyal went on the offensive.[107] He contacted his entire professional network of law professors, legal journalists, and human rights lawyers to write *Hamdan*-related pieces on blogs, journals, and newspapers. Articles began appearing in a range of publications putting pressure on the court to hear the case. One of his researchers even gathered signatures from law professors. He then pulled an ace out of his bag. He found a way to convince Milt Bearden, a highly regarded CIA official who had been awarded the Distinguished Intelligence Medal, to write an op-ed in the *New York Times* focusing on the importance of honoring the Geneva Conventions and referencing the *Hamdan* case in his article. The Supreme Court took the case.

Joseph McMillan, the partner at Perkins Coie, had often been dismayed by Katyal's longwinded approach in his arguments, but often saw him win and let him have his way. Katyal thrived on his colleague's criticisms; he told me it helped sharpen his argument and he always learned from them. For Katyal, it was to become his signature preparation style.

But McMillan was worried.[108] The Supreme Court was the ultimate argument, and an added concern weighing on everyone's mind, in addition to Katyal's unwillingness to include some of their suggestions, was that this was Katyal's first case before the court. The prosecutor who would be opposing him had argued 35 cases before the Supreme Court, while Katyal had yet to turn 35 years old. Perkins Coie had invested 4,500 pro bono hours at a cost of $1.2 million in the case, and rightly felt they should have a say. McMillan had personally spent at least 2,000 hours on the case, including many nights and weekends. He had every right to feel resentful, but Katyal's dedication persuaded him. Until now, a majority of the burden of presenting the cases at court had fallen on Lt. Commander Charles Swift from JAG, but although Katyal considered enlisting some experienced lawyers including Ken Starr, and reached out to him, it did not work out and he decided he would argue the case, and no one dared oppose him.

Katyal now dug in to prepare for the challenge. Beside his bed was the complete 600-page case record of Hamdan, which he methodically studied every night. In the car and on his iPod, he listened to tapes of Supreme Court arguments, but most important were the dry runs or moots—testing out arguments on one's peers. Lawyers do it for one another for free as a professional courtesy.

Most people do one or two to determine the weaknesses in an argument and then refine it. Katyal did 15 moots in five different cities across the country. If there was a lawyer who intimidated him, he asked them to moot him. He even agreed to his colleagues' suggestion to train with an acting coach. Skeptic about this particular arrangement at first, he discovered it added the magic touch to his delivery, and he became a convert.

By this stage, Katyal had been sleep deprived for months, working till 3 a.m. most nights and seldom getting more than five hours a night. Despite everyone's trepidations, he argued the case flawlessly and won in a 7-2 decision that catapulted him to the status of celebrity lawyer. He was inundated with interview requests, offers from prestigious law firms, and speaking engagements. His meteoric rise had begun.

Katyal's rise has two parts to it. The first is undoubtably the foundations he laid—his outstanding education, remarkable mentors, and strategic career choices. But the second and most critical component of the equation was Katyal himself—his brilliance, his strategic approach to arguments, and the sheer volume of work that he puts into each case, polishing his points until he is sure his presentation is flawless.

What follows is an interview with Katyal that traces the arc of his career and probes some revealing secrets about the tactics he employed to win a few of his most high-profile cases.

MA: What persuaded you and your sister both to study law?

NK: When I was growing up, I was told there was only one profession to aspire to and that was to become a doctor. My mom was a pediatrician and my dad was an engineer. They had both been educated in India and arrived here with their degrees and $8 in their pocket, which is all that they were officially allowed to take with them. They had worked hard to create a comfortable life for us. We lived on the north side of Chicago in a mostly white, middle-class suburban neighborhood called Northbrook, but when I was 12, our lives went through a downward spiral. My dad was fired for unjust cause a few months before his pension vested. The case was a humiliation for him, full of racist accusations about his foreign accent, etc., that were spurious. My dad had a breakdown due to his dismissal and was in the hospital, and my mom had to work three jobs as the breadwinner. I was young and just wanted us to be a normal family and was upset about our changed circumstances. A year later, I was on my high school's debate team and my dad, who was home most of the time and had filed his own complaint, had no one to help him fight his case and would ask me about the law and questions about his case and I didn't know how to help him, [and I] was embarrassed by his situation. It weighed on me for years afterwards that he had asked for my help and I had not been there for him, but I was just 13 and angry about the situation our family was in. My father got a lucky break in the federal judge that was assigned to his case. I still remember him. He appointed a lawyer for my dad and the case was settled for $30,000 in my dad's favor, which was a lot of money back then. But more important than the money was the dignity that the lawyer restored to my dad, which changed everything. Until this moment, my parents had been convinced that lawyers were liars. I watched all this and it left a lasting impression on me, and it must have on my sister as well although she was younger at the time. I saw that lawyers can protect people and that justice can be served through the courts. My parents put a lot of pressure on me to study medicine. In my senior year my mother wanted me to apply to the six-year combined medical college programs and was even willing to bribe me by throwing in a car. I did apply and was accepted when I was 17. I'll never forget that when I decided to go to Dartmouth, she was heartbroken and cried. I had seen that medicine was not the only way to protect people. I also did psychological evaluations that told me about other ways I could help people besides medicine, such as doing pro bono work as a lawyer.

MA: You said that Ken Strange, your debating coach at Dartmouth, was an early mentor. I read that you started debating in high school to overcome shyness. Can you talk about that?

NK: When I was young, I was the shyest kid ever. My mom, who did not know much about sports, wanted me to get into an activity and, starting when I was six, pushed me to try out for everything—basketball, football, baseball, swimming, skating... I was at a disadvantage as I was a year younger than everyone and smaller. I was reasonable at speed skating and swimming but not good enough to be on the high school team. In ninth grade, a close family friend suggested I try the debate team, which I thought was a ridiculous suggestion as I was shy and sure I'd be terrible at it, but there weren't that many alternatives, so I joined the club. We had to raise money for the team in order to go to tournaments and I had to go door to door to sell candy to fundraise. I took this task very seriously. I had doors slammed in my face, but I did it every day for three hours a day. I was tenacious and raised 10x more than everyone else. The coach was so impressed by my fundraising skills, he took me under his wing and taught me how to debate. I realized that if you put an enormous effort into something, it works. The lesson I took away from this helped me not just in debating but academically. I had been a B-student until then, but I started putting in the work and by sophomore year I was debating at the national level which helped my self-confidence considerably, and I also started getting all A's in school.

By his own admission, Katyal admits he had plenty of fun as an undergraduate at Dartmouth, a school that is known for its social life, but combining fun, competing on the debating circuit, and excelling academically would be a pattern he would repeat later in life. He graduated with Highest Honors. A member of Phi Beta Kappa and a Dartmouth Presidential Scholar, he also graduated *magna cum laude*.

When he arrived at Yale Law School, Katyal said he was ready to get down to serious work, although by any standards his academic achievements at Dartmouth were exemplary. Akhil Reed Amar, one of his professors and a leading authority on constitutional law, said he was the most memorable student he had ever taught.

Katyal's law school internships were the perfect launching pad for his future career. The first summer he worked as a legal intern in the office of Vice President Al Gore. His connections would lead to an invitation to participate in the Florida recount of the contested presidential election in 2000 as co-counsel for the vice president.

MA: How did you get invited to be co-counsel for Al Gore on the Florida recount? Did you make those connections during your internship at the vice president's office?

NK: When I first arrived as a summer intern, there was hardly any work to do besides opening mail the first month, but then Jack Quinn, the counsel to the vice president, asked if we wanted to help Ruth Bader Ginsburg, who had just been nominated to the Supreme Court, to help with her prep sessions. It was an incredible opportunity, and I worked my tail off and impressed them. Jack was then promoted to become Al Gore's chief of staff and we stayed in touch. After graduating from law school, while I was clerking for Justice Breyer at the Supreme Court, Jack called and told me they were about to nominate someone to be deputy attorney general, and would I like to be their special assistant? At the time, I did not even know what precisely the deputy attorney general did. They planned to name Eric Holder, a prosecutor in D.C. who I had never heard of, for the position. We liked one another immediately, but Eric did not know I was clerking for the Supreme Court and was just explicitly told to hire me by the Gore people. I basically got the job through political connections and later I got the call to help on the election dispute. I was teaching and I put a team together with 11 Yale and Harvard law students and researched the hell out of the legal issues on the case. I had just fallen in love and started teaching and I went from hanging out with Joanna to spending 36 days and nights non-stop working on the case.

His second summer, Katyal worked as an intern in the Office of the Solicitor

General, an office he would one day be intimately connected to. For his last summer, he worked at Hogan and Harston [lovells], for the then-Supreme Court litigator John G. Roberts, who is now the chief justice. In 2011, Katyal would take over the firm's Supreme Court practice.

After graduating from Yale Law School in 1995, Katyal clerked for two judges. The first was Guido Calabresi with the United States Court of Appeals and the second was the most coveted of all clerkships—a Supreme Court justice clerkship to Justice Stephen Breyer. Supreme Court clerks are so highly prized that after their clerkships, the job offers pour in. Most important law firms today have Supreme Court practices, and the market-rate sign-on bonus is $300,000.[109] It is a selling point for clients to have former Supreme Court clerks on staff who understand the justices and the peculiarities of the court and can help them win their cases or get their cases heard.

Katyal took a different route after his clerkship. Initially he went the academic route, He taught for a year at Yale Law School in 2001 then accepted a professorship at Georgetown Law School. It would become an anchor for him in Washington as he stepped in and out of high-profile jobs on his rise to fame. He was the youngest professor to get tenure and in 2008 was named the Paul and Patricia Saunders Professor of Law at Georgetown. He was granted leave to work for the government and even to teach briefly at Harvard and Yale as a visiting professor from 2001 to 2002.

MA: You could have gotten a job with any of the top law firms in the country, but you chose academia and government. Why?

NK: I love to teach and never thought I'd be a practicing lawyer. I also love the national security side of things. My dream job is national security advisor at the White House, the job Jake Sullivan currently has. That's the one job that I'd still love to do. Money was not my focus. Even now, it gives me the ability to do what I want to do.

MA: I read that you now charge $2,450 an hour. Is that accurate? How do you balance your pro bono cases with your corporate cases?

NK: I actually get paid more. When I started my career, I chose to be an academic and then went into government as just making money held no interest for me. It was only after I left government and made some money that I realized how stressed we had been about money, tuition and stuff. It felt great not to have to worry about money all of a sudden, but it is not what drives me. Half the work I do is for free, and the other half pays for it. I do get paid a lot by the hour and don't discount my commercial work for that reason, so I can take on the extensive pro bono caseload.

MA: How many of these cases are pro bono?

NK: *Hamdan*, the Muslim Ban, *Moore v. Harper*, the George Floyd case were some of the well-known ones. I also won the voting rights case at the Supreme Court by an 8-1 decision and the constitutionality of the Affordable Care Act, which was a unanimous decision. These were done while I was in the government, so I represented the government.

MA: You worked for President Obama as deputy solicitor general after the *Hamdan* case. Is that what brought you to his attention?

NK: I got a lot of offers from the top law firms after the *Hamdan* case. I agreed to represent an Indian woman in an employment discrimination case and it became my second case in front of the Supreme Court. Nina Totenberg of NPR did a profile on me around this time that Barack Obama, as a senator, heard. He called me into his office and we spoke for three hours. He then brought his staff in, and we had a debate about what to do about Guantanamo. At the end of it he said, "Neal, this has been great. At one side of the room you've got all these people telling me, don't listen to Neal." And it's like everyone in the room. On the other side is a solitary Indian woman, Ruchi, who is the only person who agrees with me. The senator asked me what I thought he planned to do and I said I wasn't sure, but I hoped he would do the right thing. When I walked out, I was convinced he would double down on Guantanamo and try to reopen it, given that he had launched a presidential bid, but he did the right thing. When I saw him later, I congratulated him on taking a principled stand. He told me he planned to announce his candidacy for president and invited me to Springfield, Illinois for the announcement, but I didn't go. Later he put me on his legal team with Eric Holder, Larry Tribe, and Martha Minow. When he won, Eric and Obama called me and offered me a job at the National Security Council or the Justice Department, saying they both would love for me to join them. I picked the latter because I could bring my work home. When you work at the White House, everything is classified so you have to work there. The hours are long, and I would never have seen my family. I made the decision to become deputy solicitor general.

MA: Given how close you were to Eric Holder, who was part of the president's inner circle, and how highly regarded you were by the president, why were you not made solicitor general when the position became available after Elena Kagan was appointed to the Supreme Court? You were acting solicitor general for over a year. I heard that defending Hamdan may have made it more difficult to get you confirmed.

NK: I'm sure that played some part in it. I was 41 and didn't want to go through a difficult hearing and not get confirmed. It could hurt my career. But there were other reasons the White House did not go out of their way for me, as I had been unwilling to play along with the White House on certain matters. They sometimes wanted me to take positions and do things that I just thought were not right and I wasn't afraid to say so.

MA: Were you disappointed by Obama?

NK: Obama is a once-in-a-generation political figure and I do think he is an incredibly decent, good person and brilliant, but he was naïve when he came in. He listened to people like Rahm (Emanuel) who were experienced Washington hands but had different priorities. On day one I told Eric we had to get great judges confirmed, but he blew it because Rahm kept on saying the only thing that matters is health care and we couldn't do anything else in the first term. We did get some things done in the second term.

MA: Which of your cases was the most significant for you?

NK: Without question the breast cancer gene case because it had a wide impact across the world on patents. Before Angelina Jolie had BRCA1, few people knew much about this form of breast cancer. It cost $6,000 to take the test because it was under patent. It's a blood test and the actual cost is 50 cents. Elena Kagan had just been appointed to the Supreme Court and I was replacing her as acting solicitor general. Right after her nominating ceremony on the morning of May 10, 2010, two cabinet secretaries asked me what my position on the genetics case was. There were 24 different memos by different cabinet officials including state and defense. Elena had not had the time to tell me about it, and it turns out it's an incredibly difficult question. Can you patent the human genome? In this case the BRCA1 and 2? I spent a year studying chemistry to understand it. My mother, who had always wanted me to become a doctor, was getting her revenge. I went to NIH every Monday night for two hours to get tutored in organic chemistry and genetics for a year. Larry Summers taught me about the economics of innovation. The Reagan administration had issued 20,000 gene patents and I decided to invalidate 18,000 of them, which upended the biotech industry. They were up in arms and wanted my head and thrown out of government. We took the case to the Supreme Court and won 9-0, and now a whole new field of genomics has developed because of this. You can do a blood test and run it for 20,000 diseases. It's also about how you metabolize medicine, so its impact on society is huge. When I had no money, we had put $5,000 into a biotech tracking fund. Needless to say, I lost all my money after the Supreme Court win.

MA: Can you share some strategic skills you have employed to win a Supreme Court argument?

NK: Moot court practice sessions are key. Normally I do five for a Supreme Court case, but when the stakes are really high I do more. For *Hamdan* I did 15 and for *Harper* I did 11. When I did the Voting Rights Act case, I probably did eight or nine. You fill the room with people who disagree with you and will give you a rough time. I audiotape and videotape it and watch them over and over to see what I can answer better and, more importantly, can I answer it in a way that does not

invite a follow up question I don't want to get? Then last is the most difficult—can
I answer the question in a way that invites a question I really want us to get? It's
very subtle. Some of it is literally a word I know a particular justice likes to use and
I use it for that justice. I'm trying to invoke a memory in them so that they ask me
a particular question. In the *Hamdan* case, we wanted to bait the opponent into
saying the president had stripped them of the right of habeas corpus and he fell
for the trap and Justice Souter yelled at him. At that point everything in the room
shifted emotionally. Before that, I was Bin Laden's driver's lawyer, and now I was
defending the Constitution. It was a deeply thought-out strategy. I had planned
the trap five different ways, then settled on this approach, and it worked.

MA: What about *Harper*?

NK: I knew Justice Thomas would ask the first question due to seniority. Before
COVID, he had famously not asked a question since 2006. During COVID, the court
had instituted speaker phones, and out of deference to his seniority, it would
have been awkward if he passed every time, so he started asking questions. After
immunizations we moved back to the court, but the justices still waited for him
to go first. So, I tried to use this information and developed a set play in my head. I
don't recall his question, but I had a script right after, which said, "Justice Thomas,
in arguing before you for 20 years, I've been waiting for this case, because it speaks
to your method of constitutional interpretation: and here are the four things you
need to know about what our founders thought about this issue." I was quoting him
back his own philosophy and got it out in six minutes. The court was riveted, the
atmosphere changed, and that's when I knew we had won. I knew the history and
the judges, and I felt I was the right person to argue the case. After the oral argument,
everyone thought we had lost, but I was convinced we had won. Everyone filed briefs
in the Supreme Court after the oral argument to get rid of the case—Biden's solicitor
general, the public interest groups, and the lawyer representing the voters. They
all said to the Supreme Court this case is moot, because they were afraid we'd lost.
I was the only person to file a brief that said keep the case. I knew that if I made
the wrong call and they kept the case, and decided against us, and democracy was

over, I was never going to be able to argue another case in the Supreme Court again. How could you recover from that? My career as a lawyer would be finished if a call like that was wrong. Luckily, it was the right call and we won. Another skill I am learning are classes I'm taking in improv comedy. It helps with shyness but also to overcome my need to have everything planned in advance. I'm learning a lot. I usually game out every scenario in advance, but improv is about spontaneity. It's not about your brilliance but about making other people look good.

MA: How does that help a Supreme Court argument?

NK: It's a massive help. You realize the argument can't be about you. It's got to be about them—the justices. It teaches you never be antagonistic. When they say something, agree and add to it the "yes, and" method. Even when you get hostile questions, you never detract. I'm now more comfortable and dynamic in unplanned situations and even make the occasional joke, like the Lollapalooza joke that went viral on the internet.

Katyal has had his share of disappointments. He represented the State of Hawaii in its suit against the Trump travel ban that targeted people from Muslim countries and won in the Ninth Circuit. Katyal had argued that the ban exceeded the president's authority under federal immigration laws and violated the Establishment Clause of the constitution. Katyal and the other lawyers were successful the first two times in court, but the administration tweaked the ban and in 2018 when it went to the Supreme Court, he lost 5-4. Katyal is philosophical about certain cases. He believes that the arc of justice is long, and good, well-thought-out arguments generally prevail, but you sometimes need history on your side—such as in the case of *Korematsu v. United States*, which he felt was a miscarriage of justice toward Japanese Americans during World War II.

NK: I was devastated when we lost the case 5-4. I was shocked because it was so inconsistent with American values and I am still shocked today, but the Supreme Court is deferential to presidents' signature initiatives early on and the travel ban was Trump's. Now the chief justice wrote the opinion, and in that opinion, he overruled *Korematsu*, essentially saying it was bad law and rights a wrong. I remember getting a call from the career deputy solicitor general saying he was sorry I lost the Muslim Ban case, but I got what I really wanted because I'd been fighting for years to overrule *Korematsu*. It was a small consolation. The Muslim Ban case was very much like *Korematsu* in that it demonized a whole group of people in such broad strokes and was so antithetical to the founding values of our constitution. The idea that everyone is an individual and is treated as such, and it doesn't matter who you pray to, when you come to America's shores, you can be expected to be treated fairly. I feel the security rationale was flawed and I took the case seriously as I felt our fundamental values would say otherwise.

Recently, Katyal offered his services to the State of Minnesota to act as a special prosecutor on behalf of the defense in the high-profile murder case of George Floyd. This time, they won.

MA: Did any case change you?

NK: The *Hamdan* case changed the trajectory of my career and my self-image. I'd always thought of myself as a theoretical law professor writing articles for law journals. Even once I began work on the case, I thought of myself as an academic with a constitutional conscience. It was a cause. After *Hamdan*, people wanted to hire me as a professional lawyer. I had never thought of myself that way.

MA: Did people advise you not to get involved in the *Hamdan* case?

NK: Everyone! Quite honestly, I don't know if there is anyone I can think of who wanted me to get involved in the case. People said to me, "Do you really want to be defending Osama bin Laden's driver?" Akhil Amar, my mentor at Yale, told me not to take the case, but I believe the first judge I clerked for who is like a second father to me, Guido Calabresi, would have wanted me to do it. Like me, he is the son of immigrants. His family fled the Nazis in Italy, and he is highly principled and was a good counter in my head, although I was unable to discuss it with him. My wife, Joanna, was also very supportive, although she worried about the threats and the hours and stress.

Katyal seems to have at least four full-time jobs at any given moment. He teaches at Georgetown Law School; he runs the Supreme Court practice at Hogan Lovells (the successor firm to Hogan and Hartson), which was Chief Justice John Roberts's old job; he established a nonprofit out of Georgetown's Law Center called the Institute for Constitutional Advocacy and Protection (ICAP), which has 10 attorneys working on 15 pro bono cases; he is a commentator on MSNBC and produces his own podcast. This is not counting the various congressional testimonies, *New York Times* op-eds, and legal articles he writes for various publications, in addition to his speaking commitments and the boards he is on.

MA: How do you manage to balance your work and home life?

NK: Joanna is the key to everything. Last year I worked seven days a week, 14 hours a day for at least 355 days. I had 10 major cases to argue in a 10-month span. That's not a schedule any human being should have to do, but I did, and five of those cases were at the Supreme Court. I had no choice, so inevitably on the home front, a lot of the responsibility was carried by Joanna, and she has a full-time job as a physician. Fortunately, she has set hours while mine is unpredictable, so we reverse-engineer our schedule. When COVID hit, she had to move out of the house to protect her patients, and it was just me with the three boys. The enforced time at home and remote work turned out to be a blessing as I got to spend time with my boys. I usually talk to my kids before every Supreme Court argument. I've always done that because if they can understand the points I'm trying to make, I feel I've achieved clarity. Two of them have left for college so it's harder to do that with them now, but it's been a very bonding experience and one that I hope they've enjoyed.

People who are used to seeing a conservative-looking Indian American in dark suits and rectangular wire-rimmed glasses with a somewhat intimidating piercing gaze in front of the Supreme Court speaking to the press, or a slightly more casual dress code of a cashmere sweater and open-neck shirt on MSNBC—but still very much in Washington mode—may have been shocked to see Katyal surface at the music concert at Burning Man in Nevada in 2023. He took many people by surprise in a flowered shirt and funky hat, including friends who know him well, but those who are close to him are familiar with his passion for music, skiing, and good wine.

As hard-driving as Katyal is at work, he is an exceptionally loyal friend. How does this hard-driving, turbo-charged, always-on-the-go lawyer find a way to unwind? I found the answer when I met his wife, Joanna. The first time I saw them walk in together, I just saw a very shapely blonde woman and thought, "How predictable. Successful lawyer finds hot babe." I could not have been more wrong. So much for making superficial assumptions. Joanna is a physician who works at the Veterans Hospital and is one of the kindest people you could meet. She has a soothing presence and everything about her is calm and warm. Her questions are insightful but gentle.

They were introduced by Neal's friend Jeffrey Rosen, also a graduate of Yale Law School and Joanna's brother. As Rosen recalls, "Neal and I were both working in Washington in the early 1990s. He was clerking at the Supreme Court for Justice Breyer and I was the legal editor of *The New Republic* magazine. Our favorite law professor from Yale, Akhil Amar, introduced us. I was instantly struck by Neal's legal brilliance and his devotion to the Constitution. He was a very decent human being and shared similar values. We would meet at his house and had great conversations and bonded over great bottles of wine. Neal is an authority on wine, so I felt I should do something for him and decided to introduce him to my beautiful, brilliant sister who was in San Francisco at the time. She flew over and the attraction was instant. They were engaged soon after. You might call it an American version of an arranged marriage, but one I was very proud to have orchestrated."

Joanna told me she had just come out of a relationship when she met Katyal and had been a little hesitant at how quickly it had all happened, but Neal made several trips to California to woo her. I understood after meeting her why Katyal was persistent until she agreed to marry him.

MA: You seem on a mission. What drives you?

NK: We are only on this earth for a short time, and I want to protect the things that I hold dear. Justice Breyer has been a great mentor and a living example of someone who does multiple things at once. In order to do the public-interest litigation that I do and have an impact, I need to have the resources and platform to be able to do it. An affiliation with a good corporate law firm is an important component. My law firm probably puts $10 to 15 million into my war chest for my pro bono cases every year. My nonprofit gives me an additional 10 attorneys—that was founded just after Trump won. We have 15 cases right now. We argued the Charlottesville case, and when Trump claimed executive privilege case over the January 6 committee in the Supreme Court, we won it 8-1.

MA: Is there anything you would like to accomplish that you haven't?

NK: I have always felt that the death penalty was unconstitutional as it was cruel and unusual punishment under the Eighth Amendment. From 2014 to 2016 I was convinced we could win this argument. Justice Breyer had arrived at this view for the first time during this period, and I felt Justice Kennedy would be the fifth vote. I looked for the ideal case; then fate intervened and Justice Scalia passed away, and it delayed the court from taking on difficult issues. Justice Kennedy then retired and was replaced by Justice Kavanaugh, which was a much harder vote to win, and I put the plans in abeyance. I have brought cases that challenge a particular application of the death penalty with considerable success such as *Cruz v. Arizona*, potentially saving 30 lives, but rescinding the death penalty is something for the future. I have a dream that I hope can one day become a reality, and that is to establish a museum dedicated to immigrants near the National Mall. I want a place that tells the story of the pathways that people found to come to this country, how they've been treated, and how they benefitted this country and thrived here. The Trump era demonized immigration and the museum can tell a different story. We have the African American Museum, the Native American Museum, and we will soon have the Latino Museum. We are a nation of immigrants. That story deserves to be told in full.

CHAPTER 19

Nikki Haley

I am the proud daughter of Indian immigrants who reminded
my brothers, my sister and me every single day
how blessed we were to live in this country.

:::

Some people think you have to be the loudest voice in the room to make a difference.
That is just not true. Often the best thing we can do is turn down the volume.
When the sound is quieter, you can actually hear what someone else is saying.
And that can make a world of difference.

NIKKI HALEY

Nikki Haley was very fortunate that her parents chose to give her an Indian nickname. Bestowing names on their children that are considered endearing but have little connection to their formal names seems to be a common affliction among Indian parents. Within the Punjabi community that Haley and I both belong to, it is endemic. The overriding characteristic of these nicknames is that they all end with the "e" sound. Haley's siblings, Mitti, Simmi, and Gogi, all conform to this enduring tradition. Haley's parents chose Indian nicknames for their children, which are far nicer than the common anglicized ones, such as the countless Candys, Bublees, and Sweeties I have encountered among my cousins and school friends growing up.

You might ask, what's in a name? Well, a lot, it turns out. Nikki means "little one" in Punjabi. Had Haley's parents called her "Tiny" or "Teeny" (as ridiculous as it sounds, people actually are known by these nicknames), Tiny Haley would just not have had the political cachet that Nikki has. Neither would another close Indian version "Choti," which also means small and is quite common among Hindi speakers. "Nikki" not only has the advantage of spanning the cultural divide, but conveys determination and warmth simultaneously, although Nikki Haley is anything but little in stature.

Haley has broken the proverbial glass ceiling not just once but again and again. She has risen within the Republican Party against all odds and won elections in a deeply conservative Southern state as a woman and an immigrant, proving herself to be a transformational politician. She was the first woman of any color and ethnicity to be elected governor of South Carolina, but to be elected as a minority woman was doubly significant given the state's history of segregation.

Haley's parents, Ajit and Raj, had come from upper-middle-class families in India and her mother was a lawyer by training. Haley's father had moved to Canada to pursue graduate work in biology, but life overseas had not been easy. In India, Haley's mother grew up in the shadow of the Golden Temple, the holiest shrine for the Sikh religion that they belonged to. Her home was full of family and household staff. In Canada, she had to manage the children and work two jobs to support them all while Haley's father finished his studies.

America was always the place they wanted to be, but Haley's father was unable to find a job and decided to return to India. He was discussing his situation with a close friend on the phone who suggested he apply for an opening at Voorhees College, a mostly African American college in Denmark, South Carolina, that was looking for an associate professor of biology.

It was sheer serendipity and thanks to the intervention of a good friend that Haley was born a United States citizen and has become the embodiment of the American Dream. Her older brother Mitti, a naturalized American citizen, had been born in India where her parents had married, and her older sister, Simmi, was born in Canada. Namrata "Nikki" Randhawa, their third child and the first to be born a United States citizen, arrived in January 1972, two years after they moved to South Carolina. Had Ajit Randhawa's friend not helped get him the job, Nikki Haley could very well have been born in India.

Nikki was strong and determined from a young age. When she went to college and met her husband, he was known as Bill Haley. She decided he looked like a "Michael," which was his middle name, and made him change his name. Her parents did not approve of her dating Michael. They made it clear that they wanted their children to marry within the community. Haley had observed the fracture that had taken place in her family when her older brother, who she adored, had rejected the woman her parents had chosen for him from India. In her biography she wrote that "At first he went along with them, but in the end he broke off the engagement and married an American girl, Sonya, whom he had met in Alabama. ... The year after he was married was the first year we didn't have Christmas at the house. Mom said that if the whole family couldn't be together, we couldn't have Christmas." Haley's parents refused to speak to her brother. They would eventually reconcile after his daughter was born and he was deployed to Iraq during Desert Storm.

Haley refused to give up her boyfriend and eventually sat her parents down to tell them she was going to marry Michael, and she managed to convince them that he was the right person for her. In what must have been a very disappointing decision for the Randhawas, Haley also converted to Christianity, her husband's religion. It was a decision that undoubtedly helped her politically and her need to "fit in." Her parents had instilled a sense of confidence in Haley, and she had grown up seeing her mother as an entrepreneur and professional working woman as well as her own boss.

Haley remembers being stunned as she sat down for a meeting when she started her first job out of college. When the meeting began, one of the executives turned to her and asked her to get a cup of coffee for the CEO. Knowing her response would determine if they would treat her as an equal, she coolly said "Okay," and dialed her secretary to ask her to bring in the coffee. No one ever suggested she get them coffee ever again.

Haley spent 14 years in public service as a legislator, a successful governor, and President Trump's ambassador to the United Nations before she decided to announce in 2023 that she was running for president. Despite her experience and electoral successes, *The Hill*, a popular political paper in Washington, D.C., amplified an editorial from the *Wall Street Journal* with the headline "Wall Street Journal Editorial Board Sees 'No Clear Rationale' for Haley Candidacy." The editorial board, while praising her as a popular governor, had said rather condescendingly that when it comes to running for president, "the biggest challenge for Ms. Haley is identifying the rationale for her candidacy beyond a winning persona." It prematurely concluded that Haley did not distinguish herself in any way that would propel her out of her single-digit poll numbers–"Her campaign announcement stressed a belief in America as a force for good, the seriousness of global threats, and the follies of the progressive left. Is there a Republican presidential candidate who believes something different?" Critically, the board also felt "she doesn't have an obvious core of support."

The *New York Times* headline on February 15, 2023, was definitive. "Nikki Haley Will Not Be the Next President: Our Columnists Weigh In." It was followed by several veteran political analysts such as David Brooks, Bret Stephens, and Ross Douthat, among others, listing the pros and cons of her chances–which ultimately pointed to the damning headline. Within nine months, Haley would prove them all wrong. Her numbers began to rise, and she was edging out Florida Governor Ron DeSantis, the only person considered a serious threat to President Trump. While DeSantis's super PAC was slowing down, Haley's campaign war chest was exploding with the Koch brothers throwing their support behind her and Reid Hoffman of LinkedIn committing $250,000.

This would hardly be the first time that Nikki Haley had been underestimated by the political pundits or discouraged from running for office. Ironically, Haley credits Hillary Clinton, a woman vilified by the right, as the person who inspired her to join politics. Haley went to hear Clinton speak at Furman University in Greenville, South Carolina, in 2003: "She was the one that said for all the reasons people tell you, you shouldn't run, those are the reasons you should. ... Everybody was telling me why I shouldn't run: I was too young, I had small children, I should start at the school board level." In an interview she gave to the *New York Times* in 2012, she said she heard the same message from Clinton, who was the keynote speaker at the Leadership Institute at Birmingham University in 2012 encouraging women not to be deterred from running for office. Haley recalls that she walked out of there thinking, "That's it. I'm running for office."

By the time Haley entered the 2024 Republican presidential contest, she had never lost an election, despite having run as an underdog every time. The first time she ran for office in 2004, it was for the state legislature from District 87. Her campaign had an uphill task—they had no money, a candidate that was unknown, and even Haley jokes that she was "Nikki who?"

Haley had decided to enter her first race under the mistaken assumption that Larry Koon, who had represented the district for 30 years, was retiring. Her information was either incorrect or he changed his mind. Once he declared he was running for reelection, Haley had trouble hiring anyone to work for her, as Koon was either related to or friends with many of his constituents. Haley refused to reconsider. She had thrown her hat in the ring and was going to give it her all.

No one should underestimate Haley's grit, determination, and focus on accomplishing her goals once she sets her mind to it. Hers was a grassroots campaign; it entailed knocking on doors with doughnuts and making her own yard signs. Incumbents tend to get lazy—Haley was the opposite. She found her opening when Koon lied during the campaign by claiming that he had been endorsed by Governor Mark Sanford, an influential figure in South Carolina politics with a popularity rating in the eighties. Haley convinced the governor's office to issue a letter to the contrary that she mailed to voters, contradicting Koon's claims and exposing his dishonesty.

Koon then stooped to distributing racist flyers to tar her. This was not the first time that Haley had encountered racism—and some of it got ugly. Posters of her with "Indian female and Buddhist" written below her head shot, and "White Male and Christian" under his picture were widely distributed by her opponent. Haley exposed him as a bully and misogynist and won the voters over, unseating the longest-serving legislator in a deeply conservative red state district.

The state legislature was run like an old boys' club, and Haley describes her experiences in her book *Can't Is Not an Option*. By 2009, Haley was ready to move on, and Governor Sanford encouraged Haley to consider running for governor when his term ended. Haley may have endeared herself to the people in the 87th district, but she was still "Nikki who?" to many in the state. Running for governor of South Carolina in 2010 would be entering the big leagues, and she would need some support from politically powerful backers.

The endorsement of a sitting governor would be an enormous help as her opponents were powerful white men. The attorney general and the lieutenant governor had both declared their intention to run as well. Once again Haley was the underdog, but she did not realize how much until a few months after the race had begun. Her main backer, the governor, went up in flames when it was discovered he had been having an affair. His popularity imploded and cast a shadow over Haley's campaign. Tainted by association, she had lost her most important political endorsement and had to distance herself from Sanford.

Haley wrote in her biography that "I had gone from being an underdog with potential to being the expected endorsee of a political joke. My critics had long called me 'Mark Sanford in a skirt,' but now it held a special sting—and a special stigma. People looked at me with pity. They no longer treated me like a real candidate. Worst of all no one returned my calls. ... Before Sanford imploded, my fundraising had been respectable. ... I had always been a relentless fundraiser. In my state house race, I had walked into rooms full of uncommitted voters and routinely left with thousand dollar checks. But in the aftermath of the Sanford scandal, I couldn't raise a dime."

Haley always performs best when her back is against the wall. She managed to run her campaign on a shoestring budget and a skeleton staff. They had to resort to selling posters and cajole interns into volunteering, but Haley stayed focused on the issues, winning Mitt Romney's endorsement and, more importantly, Sarah Palin's, who has a big following within the Tea Party movement. She says she felt an instant bond with her. "We realized we had a lot in common. But it is also about being moms and wives and daughters and talking about the impact on the family (of public life) and the challenges. She told me that once you start to gain steam, they are going to start attacking you, and once they start attacking you, they will never stop even after you win."[110] Palin came to South Carolina to campaign for Haley, which helped expand her base of support.

As Haley started gaining traction, her opponents resorted to personal attacks on her, including one person who claimed to have had an extramarital affair with Haley without providing any evidence. It was soon discovered that he was on the payroll of one of her opponents. A second person also tried to level similar attacks, but on such flimsy grounds as to constitute harassment that the voters felt she was being unfairly targeted, and it had the unintended effect of making people sympathetic towards Haley. Palin came to her defense. She posted blogs supporting Haley. It cemented their relationship.

Haley even had the aggrieved ex-wife of the disgraced Governor Sanford campaign on her behalf. Jenny Sanford had won the admiration of the people of South Carolina by the dignity she had displayed through her marital crisis.

In a repeat of her campaign for the state legislature, her race against her Republican opponents went to a run-off. She came in just under 50 percent even though her closest opponent, Congressman Gresham Barrett, was almost 20 points behind her. She won the run-off, against all the odds that had been stacked against her, and went on to beat the Democratic candidate, State Senator Vincent Sheheen.

Haley had made history as South Carolina's first woman and first Indian American governor. In her inaugural address she thanked her family and friends. "I am the daughter of immigrant parents who reminded me every day how blessed we were to live in this country, I am the sister of a man who fought in Desert Storm, and I still remember what it was like to know if he was coming home, I am the daughter of a family who, when all this got dirty, all they did was say, 'We love you. You fight. We're here for you.' I am the wife of a man who puts on a military uniform every day. This is what has kept me strong every day for the last two weeks."[111]

As governor, Haley was an outspoken critic of what she considered President Obama's excessively liberal immigration policies. She had tried to crack down on illegal immigration in her state by enforcing Social Security ID checks by employers. She brought in voter ID and resisted Obamacare. She promoted herself as an accountant who was pro-business and was successful at creating favorable conditions for businesses to operate in her state, and even helped facilitate a Boeing factory that created thousands of jobs. Businesses liked her because she was anti-union.

Race relations had been low on Haley's list of priorities, but it was during her tenure as governor that one of the South's most controversial and enduring legacies—the fate of the Confederate flag that had been flying from the State Capitol since 1961 as a protest against the civil rights movement—became an issue she had to confront. On June 17, 2015, a 21-year-old white supremacist, Dylann Roof, gunned down nine Black parishioners while they were at church in Charleston. Among the dead was Clementa Pinckney, a legislator who had been calling for some time for the flag to be removed. Earlier that year, Pinckney had been behind the lobbying effort that pushed Haley to adopt a Democratic plan calling for police officers in South Carolina to wear body cameras. The investigators had found racist literature among the shooter's personal effects, and the murderer showed little remorse when he was apprehended. The media had seized on the story of the cold-blooded massacre and South Carolina's culture of racism, and tensions were running high in the state.

Haley understood discrimination, having been subjected to it herself growing up. When her parents arrived in the small town of Bamberg, South Carolina, in 1969, it had just 2,500 residents and most had never seen an Indian family before. According to the 1970 census, there were barely 51,000 Indians living in America and most of them were in California or on the East Coast. "We were the only Indian family in my hometown of Bamberg," Haley recalled. "... We stood out. I remember the stares. And I remember when the stares became whispers, and the whispers became fear, and that fear showed itself in suspicion and exclusion. ... Once when I was young, my family went to a picnic at a local country club. It hurts even now to remember how no one would sit next to us or even acknowledge us, so we ate and left."[112] Haley was conscious of being followed by police officers when she went shopping with her father, who wore a turban and stood out in the small town. "My heart hurts when I think about the way people would look at my dad in his turban."[113]

Despite its small size, Bamberg was racially divided into Black and white sections. Haley was constantly asked which sports team she was going to be on, Black or white? "I learned early on that the ways in which I was different—my religion, my race, and even my gender—would be a constant in my life." In a story she has repeated often, she and her sister were excluded from a beauty pageant as the organizers could not decide which racial category they belonged to, and there were only two beauty queens, one white and one Black. Haley tried to follow her parents' advice to avoid emphasizing one's differences and focus everyone's attention on the similarities between people. She learned to avoid direct confrontation early in life and deflected racial questions directed at her. She admitted that she was impatient with "victimhood," and almost seemed in denial of the undercurrent of racial tensions in her state. Haley points out her rise to the governor's mansion as testament to the progress the state has made in race relations.

The callousness of the Charleston massacre changed everything. As she wrote, "It shattered my world ... the heart and soul of South Carolina was broken. ... I went to every one of the funerals. Most were held in Mother Emanuel Church. I watched family members fall over their loved one's bodies in complete despair. ... Sometimes I would hold it together, sometimes I would break down. ... Going to these nine funerals is the hardest thing I've ever had to do in my life. On the Saturday after the murders, the killer's ramblings were found online ... interspersed with a twenty-five hundred word racist manifesto were pictures of the killer with the Confederate flag. ... When I became governor, the Confederate flag was a defining issue for how a lot of Americans regarded South Carolina. I made a point early on, of talking to both Republicans and Democrats to see if there was the political will to take the flag down once and for all. Members from both parties pushed back against the idea ... but the images of the Charleston killer with the Confederate flag changed all that. ... I told Michael, I would never be able to look our children in the eye and tell them the flag was still flying on the statehouse grounds. Not after what I'd seen."[114] Haley was exhausted and drained after the mass killing. She wrote that she lost 20 pounds and had trouble sleeping during this period. Six days later, she made the decision that the flag had to go.

President Obama congratulated her, praising her "eloquence." Her critics claim she equivocated for months on the issue of the flag and often deflected questions on race until the victims of the shooting paid for it by their deaths.

Public opinion shifted after the massacre and people were ready to take the flag down. According to Michael Kranish of *The Washington Post*, Haley had placated Confederate groups by calling the flag a part of the state's heritage; when she was campaigning for re-election the previous year, she called a proposal by her Democratic opponent to remove it "desperate and irresponsible." She has also said the Civil War was a fight between "tradition" and "change," rather than slavery.[115] This far-fetched interpretation of the past may have played well in South Carolina but grated nationally. Placating the Sons of the Confederacy and similar right-wing extremists with one set of speeches that sugarcoated the past by acknowledging it as an acceptable part of the South's history while doing the right thing by taking down the flag may have been grudgingly tolerated in her state, but this sort of obfuscation did not go over well nationally.

Haley would be better served taking full credit for removing the flag. Without her decision, the issue may have continued to be a festering sore. It got done quickly once she decided to put her weight behind it and she will always be remembered as showing leadership and moral courage when the situation demanded it. Should she have done it earlier? Yes, but she was being strategic and knew that it was a political landmine that had buried politicians in her state before.

Years later, when she was running for president, Haley was challenged on her views on slavery and the cause of the Civil War at a New Hampshire town hall on December 23, 2023, and her evasive, rambling answer appalled many across the nation—including her fellow Republicans, who accused her of not knowing her history. One of her primary opponents, Former Governor Chris Christie of New Jersey, put it best when he said she was afraid to offend.

Haley ran a tight presidential campaign and made few mistakes until her gaffe on the slavery question. She has managed to tread the abortion debate with skill. Haley has been firmly pro-life; as governor she signed a law banning abortions after 20 weeks with no exceptions for rape and incest. After the Supreme Court's *Dobbs* decision in 2022 reversed *Roe v. Wade*, the backlash from voters made it clear that they disagreed with the court's decision. Many states that held referendums discovered that the public response was swift and unequivocal. They opted to make sure abortion was safe and accessible. Haley, with her eye on national elections, softened her stand, angering the right wing of her party when, during a Republican debate in November 2023, she said that she would not judge women who believed in and made different choices to hers. "As much as I'm pro-life, I don't judge anyone for being pro-choice, and I don't want them to judge me for being pro-life. Let's find consensus. ... We don't need to divide America over this issue anymore." Her remarks played well nationally, as she has come across as less harsh than her Republican rival DeSantis. She also very cleverly pointed out to her fellow Republicans on the debate stage that it was technically implausible for them to promise voters a federal law banning abortion, as they could never procure the necessary number of votes on the Hill—it would require Democrats to agree. "Let's bring people together and decide what we can agree on, but don't make the American people think that you're going to push something on them when we don't even have the (60) votes in the Senate."

Haley can think on her feet and does not let people get away with trying to demean her. On the presidential debate stage, she put Vivek Ramaswamy in his place on foreign policy when he attacked her, but always stayed away from personal attacks. It was when Ramaswamy crossed a line most candidates don't breach—bringing their opponent's children into a debate to attack them; in this case, Haley's daughter—that she called him "scum." His vicious attacks on her backfired and one of the other presidential contenders, Chris Christie, came to her defense in a memorable and laudatory moment during the third debate.

Haley shines during debates. Her performance at each one helped propel her forward. She comes across as well prepared, knowledgeable, and honest about what is actually achievable, making the other people on the stage look like blowhards. She also has warmth, which helped her climb past Governor DeSantis to become Trump's chief challenger. Many big Republican backers who dislike Trump backed her rather than the presumptive favorite DeSantis, and she steadily rose in the polls. Haley's position on foreign policy issues such as support for Israel, NATO, and Ukraine, are more in line with traditional Republicans. She is a hawk on China and Russia, which put her at odds with her former boss, President Trump.

Trump could not have placed Haley in a more beneficial launching pad for a future presidential run than ambassador to the UN, which placed Haley in New York City–where some of the world's richest financiers live. Her conciliatory approach toward traditional allies went over well and countered Trump's erratic behavior that had been so disruptive to relationships with some of America's closest allies. Haley burnished her foreign policy credentials which she had previously lacked and met and impressed many Republican and independent donors who encouraged her to run for president in 2024. Her staunch support for Israel during her tenure at the UN as well as in the aftermath of the October 7 attack has been appreciated among her friends in New York. Several held fundraisers for her in December 2023, including some high-profile ones reported in the press by Dan Senor and Larry Fink as she has continued to emerge as a top challenger to Trump.

A more recent revelation that may destabilize her rise is the whiff of impropriety that has arisen in allegations of her financial involvement in her parents' business problems. Although it is not a new story, it has been dredged out to embarrass her.

Haley's mother, Raj Randhawa, was the driving force in the family. In her recent book about leadership lessons from bold women, Haley paid tribute to her mother in her dedication. "To my mom, who taught me how to dream, how to fight, how to love, but most importantly how to live with a faith in God that would get me through anything." Raj was determined to be a success and set up a clothing business called Exotica once she and her husband settled in Bamberg. The business became an anchor for the children growing up, and they all worked there at some point. Haley became the unofficial bookkeeper when she was a teenager and attributes her decision to study accounting to the skills she learned there. Her first job after she graduated from college was serving as her mother's CFO. Her sister, a fashion designer, worked there on and off as did their brothers, who helped out with computer work.

The Randhawas expanded their business interests and invested in real estate, including purchasing a strip mall for $1.3 million that housed their clothing business. By the time Haley graduated from Clemson University in 1994, they had also purchased a 5,500-square-foot lakefront property for $1.15 million with a $920,000 mortgage.[116]

Raj Randhawa's dreams were being fulfilled. Her children were thriving, and she had been recognized by the community as a small business, even winning an award. But by the time Haley's career as a politician began to soar, her parents' finances began to unravel. Hoping to retire but unable to meet their expenses, they took out a second mortgage on the strip mall and Haley's father sold some real estate investments he had made to raise additional funds. It proved inadequate, as they were in more trouble than they realized, and by 2014 they turned to Haley for help.

Haley and her husband, Michael Haley, initially helped her parents with a loan of $400,000, using the strip mall and lake house as collateral. By the time Haley moved to New York as Trump's ambassador to the United Nations in 2017, her parents were unable to make the payments on the lake house, and Bank of America started foreclosure proceeding. They tried to serve Haley papers at her official residence at the UN because she was listed as a co-defendant. She was released from the suit when she relinquished her interest in the property.

The following year, Haley took over the strip mall debt through a company Michael incorporated and disposed of the debt by selling the property. Shortly after, she resigned from her position at the UN. Soon after she left government, Haley lost no time in making up for her financial losses by giving speeches, serving on corporate boards, and writing a book.

Haley has been criticized by her opponents for trying to make money during this period, but she did nothing different from what most politicians and chief executives do when they leave high-profile positions. From an Indian American perspective, Haley will be viewed as an ideal daughter, devoted to helping her parents in their time of need. Haley and her husband were not wealthy people at the time her parents' misfortunes landed on her doorstep. They both earned salaries and owned a relatively modest home worth $350,000 along with a couple of pensions. Haley was clear about one thing—her parents had been there for them growing up, and she would be there for them when they needed her.

Though Haley did not win the Republican presidential nomination in 2024, what she managed to do was astonishing: she pushed past the obvious favorites to become the alternative Republican nominee were Donald Trump to falter or be found ineligible to run. The polls indicated that she would win hands down against President Biden to become the first female president of the United States. Trump swept the votes during the primary, but he underperformed expectations in every state, with close to a third of Republicans giving their votes to Haley. She exposed the commonly held view that Trump had total control of the party. A significant number of people in his own party, it turns out, do not want him to become president. She likes to say she gave them a voice. She has shown grit and courage, standing up to his insults as he tried to diminish her by calling her "birdbrain" but it did not stick. Though she bowed out of the race, she had proved something to Trump and to the country. She would not be bullied and it is possible to stand up to him.

Haley has shown that a woman and a child of immigrants is capable of being president. She has raised her national profile, established a nationwide political network and demonstrated the ability to raise money from powerful Republican supporters. She is only 52 years old and ambitious. Her political life is far from over. She is well positioned to run for president in 2028.

CHAPTER 20

Ro Khanna

It always seems impossible until it is done.

NELSON MANDELA

The first time I met Ro Khanna, at the home of a mutual friend in 2010, he was serving as deputy assistant secretary of commerce in the Obama administration. Tall, dark, with a somewhat shy smile and still not 35, Khanna was relatively new to Washington. Having started his job the previous year, he still had an earnestness about him that was endearing.

Khanna was single, and with his Ivy League credentials, he was an eligible Washington bachelor by any standards. He was remarkably open and self-deprecating, and we bantered about his declining marriage prospects within the Indian community given that he'd opted for a career in government, where his income could never match the private sector. Khanna had been bitten by the Washington bug, and he seemed to relish being in the city that was the center of power.

Khanna, whose parents had immigrated from Punjab, India, was born and raised in Bucks County, Pennsylvania. He attended the University of Chicago as an undergraduate and went on to Yale Law School. He attributes his interest in public service to his maternal grandfather, Amarnath Vidyalankar, who fought for India's independence movement. Khanna has often referenced him to burnish his political lineage. He was just nine when his grandfather died, but he likes to say that his grandfather, who was a follower of Gandhi and devoted his life to politics, was his inspiration. It may explain some of the positions Khanna has embraced, which favor peace rather than aggression as a way to resolve conflicts. He favors a non-interventionist foreign policy when the United States is not at risk. In 2017, he submitted a bipartisan bill in Congress to halt military assistance to the Saudi-led military campaign in Yemen and followed it up with an op-ed in the *New York Times* citing the human costs of the war. It was a very Gandhian perspective. He pushed to relieve tensions with North Korea and firmly believes that the president of the United States should not be allowed to launch a nuclear strike without congressional approval.

Khanna's parents had hoped their two sons would become doctors or follow their father's career path as an engineer, but both became lawyers. Khanna's younger brother, Vikas, is also highly accomplished, having gone to Princeton and Harvard Law School; he works as the first assistant United States attorney in New Jersey. Their parents recall their older son Ro (Rohit) displaying an interest in politics while he was still in middle school, when he began writing letters to the editor of the local paper protesting the Gulf War.

Khanna jumped into politics early. He volunteered for Obama's State Senate campaign in Illinois, when he was a college student in Chicago. Later, he interned for Jack Smith, Vice President Al Gore's chief of staff. After law school and a clerkship in Little Rock, Arkansas, Khanna moved to California and chose to make his home in the Bay Area.

Initially, Khanna followed a fairly traditional path of a successful Ivy League law school graduate. After clerking for a judge, he took a job with a prestigious law firm working on intellectual property. But his ambitions soon pushed him toward a different horizon, a path with both setbacks and achievements. He decided to run for Congress in 2004 in an ill-fated campaign to unseat the immensely popular Tom Lantos, a Holocaust survivor who had been successfully elected 13 times and would retain his seat until he died in 2008. It was a bold move, and one that was frowned upon by Democratic Party leadership as it was considered a safe district for the Democrats. Khanna was also viewed by the party as the upstart newcomer who hadn't paid his dues, but Lantos, who defeated Khanna easily, harbored no ill will—he took a liking to Khanna and decided to become a mentor. Khanna has no regrets, and still thinks it may have been the most idealistic thing he's ever done.

When I caught up with Khanna several years later, he was no longer the wide-eyed newcomer with a Washington dream. He had taken his knocks on the political battlefield and lost three congressional races, becoming a more hardened politician in the process. He cultivated people in the party assiduously, and Nancy Pelosi became one of his early backers. In 2016, he finally won against Mike Honda, backed by some of the most powerful names in Silicon Valley, and has represented California's 17th congressional district ever since. He is married to Ritu Ahuja, a wealthy Indian American woman whose father, Monte Ahuja, made a fortune in the auto transmission business.

Khanna is now listed as the 14th richest congressman in America at $27 million. He made a bold decision to combat the insidious influence of money in politics and declared on X (formerly known as Twitter) that he would not accept any money from political action committees (PACs), which try to influence politics. "From day one, I refused to take a dime of PAC money or lobbyist money for my campaigns, and I never will," he posted. "But we can't depend on members of Congress to volunteer to do the right thing, we need to pass a law to ban all PAC and lobbyist contributions to political campaigns." Some congressmen have complained that Khanna can afford to turn down PAC money given his newfound wealth through marriage, and his extraordinarily wealthy constituency. Some of those who represent poor districts and have no personal wealth have no choice, given how expensive elections have become.

The quality that remains genuine about Khanna—despite the politician's persona that he has acquired that seems inevitable after spending so many years running for office and living on Capitol Hill—is that he is a genuine nerd. He gets deeply engaged in trying to find solutions to problems. This can be a plus, as it appeals to a certain group that likes analytical solutions, but it can hold him back if he runs for national office in the future. The general public may find him too cerebral and hard to relate to.

Khanna has published two substantive books. The first, *Entrepreneurial Nation*, is an optimistic view of America's manufacturing base and ability to innovate and compete with China—another preoccupation in the United States.

It was written during his initial time in Washington when he was in the Obama administration.

His second book, *Dignity in a Digital Age: Making Tech Work for All of Us*, is a roadmap that lays out his vision for using technology to bridge the geographic, cultural, and economic inequalities between the heartland and the coastal elites. Khanna was determined to find creative solutions to bring communities together and as congressman, has tried to apply some of the ideas he expressed in the book. Although the results were mixed, it did raise his public profile.

Where Khanna has really distinguished himself is reaching across the aisle in a country that seems hopelessly divided. He has shown both leadership and commitment in trying to bring a fractured country together. He arrived as a newly elected congressman in Washington in 2017, when President Trump took office. It was a particularly polarizing moment in American politics, beginning with Trump's stunningly negative inaugural address that talked about "American carnage" and painted a negative portrait of the state of the country. The divisive speech seemed to shock even a past Republican president, George W. Bush, on the podium. It was a challenging time for Democrats. Khanna had seen firsthand President Obama's attempts to win over Republicans with little success when he worked in the administration, and he had spent time thinking about a way to open a channel.

Khanna used the power and glamor of Silicon Valley to reach out to middle America and the Rust Belt–Trump country. He hoped that by trying to connect tech jobs to these regions, he could bring communities together. Khanna has tried to convince lawmakers and investors in Silicon Valley that for democracy to prosper, economic opportunity cannot be confined to the coasts. "It's only by including rural America and Trump's constituency in the share of high-paying tech jobs that we can eliminate the toxicity that has divided the nation," he told me. Khanna has arranged for several tech delegations to visit districts in Kentucky, Tennessee, and elsewhere to set up training programs and discuss job creation. If he succeeds, Khanna will have proved to be a truly transformational politician with bipartisan appeal and raised his national profile in an enviable manner, which will position him for a future presidential run.

In 2018, Pelosi asked Khanna to draft the Internet Bill of Rights, a set of principles that protected United States citizens by giving them control over their own data. He was instrumental in getting the Chip and Science Act passed and was chair of the House Oversight Subcommittee on Environment. He went after the big oil companies for spreading disinformation about climate change and for their role in degrading the environment. During a hearing, Khanna told them, "Spare us the spin today. We have no interest in it. Spin doesn't work under oath." He admonished them and suggested they think of themselves as human beings.[117] Khanna may have been playing to the cameras, but he was stating positions he believed in.

Khanna's meteoric rise within the Democratic Party, his assiduous courting of the press, and his appearances at political events in states far from his own district have painted him as ambitious, but he sees it as an attribute rather than a flaw. "The people who built America were ambitious, the people who built my district and made it into a global powerhouse were ambitious, the people who built Google and Facebook and all the other entrepreneurs in the Valley are ambitious. I make no apologies for being ambitious."

Khanna toys with running for president and asked rhetorically if I thought the United States was ready for "a Rishi Sunak," referring to the British prime minister, the first person of Indian ancestry to hold that post. He has spent large sums of money recently on political consultants with connections to early primary states such as Iowa and New Hampshire, spending considerable time and energy there. He hired Shannon Jackson, Bernie Sanders' former New Hampshire state director, and engaged a Sanders-connected digital advertising firm. He also paid political firms in Iowa and Nevada to facilitate meetings with labor leaders in the state.[118]

Although the United States has yet to elect a woman, a Hispanic, an Italian American or a person of the Jewish faith to the presidency, Indian Americans are attempting to break the glass ceiling. By investing time in trying to help the economy in red states and visiting districts far from his own, Khanna certainly seems to be laying the groundwork for something big.

What follows is an interview with Congressman Khanna.

MA: When you looked at Capitol Hill, what was the moment when you said, I want to be in Congress? That the system is not working and when I get there, I can try to fix it?

RK: Well, I certainly didn't have the audacity in 2009 or when I first ran in 2004 to think that I would change the entire system. I ran for Congress at the age of 27. My aspiration then was for America to have a more just foreign policy, but I lost in a crushing defeat. I was very, very opposed to the war in Iraq. I had a friend from law school whose brother was taunted and told to go back to Pakistan even though he had been at MIT for 10 years because we were in a moment of fear because of the Patriot Act.[119] I was very conscious of being a South Asian male and the impact that was having on the South Asian American experience. I was personally being stopped at every metal detector for advanced screening. I was very opposed to the Patriot Act and the war in Iraq, and decided to run against a congressman who was the one of the most powerful Democrats in the nation—Tom Lantos, who voted for the war in Iraq, as well as the Patriot Act. The campaign lasted just a few months. I got 20 percent of the vote, and it was a sobering lesson in how difficult it is to make a change in foreign policy when you couldn't even get close to winning a race for Congress. It was 10 years before I tried again.

MA: You entered politics because you were concerned about the Iraq War and wanted America to live up to its ideals in its conduct in foreign policy. When did you come to some realization that running for office in America is actually more about domestic politics than about international?

RK: It's a mix. I mean, look, I don't think Barack Obama would have become president if it weren't for the Iraq War. I think that was the salient distinction between him and Hillary Clinton. In Congress, I have had a leadership role along with Bernie Sanders in trying to stop the Yemen War. I believe people care about both, but they prioritize, understandably, their own livelihood and their own aspirations and their own communities. I definitely think domestic issues are a bigger focus for people. But when I first ran for office in 2003, the war in Iraq and the Patriot Act loomed large on many people's minds. Bush was being heavily criticized, and I don't think I lost that campaign because people weren't focused on the war. I lost that campaign because people didn't think they were ready to be represented by a 27-year-old in Congress with all that that entailed, and they were right. I mean, I wasn't ready to be a good member of Congress at the age of 27, so the voters' judgment was probably accurate.

MA: You were going to run in 2012, but then you changed your mind halfway through your campaign. Why?

RK: Tom Lantos decided to mentor me and told me, "You can't just get up and run for Congress unless you're a movie star. You've got to build roots in the community, in the party, and build your resume." Well, for eight years I decided to build. I needed to build my connections within the party, and it began to pay off. Nancy Pelosi began to take an interest in me. I worked hard at the local level, both in the community and with party members. I built support with the tech community and my constituency. I learned the lessons from my early losses, and I wanted to go in completely prepared the next time. I looked at running in 2012, but the district got redrawn in a way that excluded a lot of the tech community, and I was hoping to represent tech. The district I was looking at to run from no longer included tech. It was Pete Stark's seat, and I didn't think it was the right moment or the right district, so I pulled out.

MA: In 2014, you challenged Mike Honda, an established Asian American Democrat who had successfully represented an Asian district in Silicon Valley for several years. That was a big risk. You lost again.

RK: Mike Honda was a formidable opponent. He had been interned during the Japanese internment as a child and was a giant, like an oak tree with deep roots in the community. He had been a city council member and supervisor in San Jose, a state assembly member, and a congressman representing the 17th district for 14 years. He was entrenched in the community and had been around for 40 years. When I came out with all my endorsements, several important tech people backed me. It was the who's who of the tech leaders—the Eric Schmidts, Sheryl Sandbergs, and Vinod Khoslas. People wanted the future, and I felt had a better vision of innovative economic ideas and better technology sense, but I was missing a critical component. Mike Honda told me he knew he would beat me when I came out with all the big tech endorsements because he had the list of all the PTA leaders, the teachers, and all the neighborhood leaders, and there are a lot more of them than there are tech leaders. I lost 52-48, but this time it was much closer.

MA: How did you manage to finance yourself when you were losing all your elections?

RK: Well, there was a year in which I didn't pay off my student loans and I took on significant credit card debt. I had to struggle to keep my apartment. I was paying $1,000 for a one-bedroom apartment in someone's house in D.C. and working on John Kerry's election at one point because I had a passion I was following. It made me aware of what it's like to live on the edge and not make the bills. I considered myself fortunate, as I had the security of always knowing I had a safety net. For one thing, I had a law degree from Yale, and I had parents who I knew would have ultimately been there to support me. Even though they're middle-class and ended up upper-middle-class. I don't dwell on the struggles, but....

MA: When did your fortunes begin to turn for you?

RK: In 2016 I was now engaged, and I told Ritu, "Look, let me try one more time. I've lost once, the first one didn't really count, I was just 27. The race in 2014 was a real loss, but we came close. Let's give it one last try, and if I don't make it, I'll do something else." In 2016, I didn't care as much about being in the front pages of the *New York Times* or being featured in *The New Yorker* or other top magazines. I knocked on doors and had breakfasts and coffees with teachers and parents and community leaders. It was very intentional. I was hyper focused on the local, not about the national press or even the LA *Times*. I had the backing of the tech community and I felt I had youth, energy, and new ideas on my side. This time I won 60-40.

What had also helped Khanna in 2016 was that Honda had begun to show his age and become complacent. *The Mercury News* reported that Khanna raised $801,000 in the first quarter of 2015, much of which poured in when C-Span aired footage of the 71-year-old Honda dozing off during a February 27 House floor debate on homeland security funding.[120] Honda had also lost the support of the tech titans who defined his district. They shifted their support to the younger, more energetic man who was trained as a patent lawyer and seemed to understand their concerns. The contest began to focus on the generational divide, with Honda representing the past and Khanna representing the vigor and energy of the future.

Khanna was a relentless campaigner and aggressive fundraiser. Despite his earlier losses he kept going back and pushing and persuading people to believe in him and his ability to win. I had followed his aborted run in Stark's district and in 2014 against Honda and attended his fundraisers for the Indian community. At the time I wondered if he had the charisma to appeal to non-Indians. He came across as somewhat nerdy and although he was thoughtful, he lacked humor and the dynamism of an Obama or the magnetism of a Clinton. I could see his appeal to the tech crowd, and Indians would vote for him out of tribal loyalty, perhaps, but how would he engage a 65-year-old white postal worker from a small town in his district without that extra element of charisma? But Khanna has won them over, and the seat now seems a secure one for him—and some of it may have to do with his progressive ideas and his dramatic rise within the Democratic Party.

MA: When you discovered that you had won, how did you feel?

RK: Deep joy, excitement, and a sense of perseverance, you know. In retrospect it looks like I've had a lot of blessings in life, but at the time it felt like I was really fighting hard to make it. There was a sense of excitement at the possibility of now, finally, having an opportunity to contribute to the country.

As the son of immigrants, Khanna has always been interested in international politics. He would love to be secretary of state and has taken an active role in foreign policy as a congressman.

MA: You once told me you'd love to be secretary of state. Is your passion for international affairs on hold given your focus on domestic concerns as a congressman? How do you split your time between the two?

RK: When I was younger, yes, it's a job that held a lot of appeal. I spend 80 percent of my time on domestic policy. But the biggest foreign policy impact I've had is with Bernie Sanders in passing the only war powers resolution in the history of the country on Yemen that stopped our refueling of Saudi planes. I fundamentally believe that a stronger America democratically and an America that is more multiracial will be an America that is more thoughtful about foreign policy. So to the extent that I can facilitate that kind of an America to emerge, I can have an impact on a better foreign policy. I stood up in Congress against endless wars and for more restraint in foreign policy. I'm on the China select committee and I'm having an impact there. I serve on the Armed Services Committee and have had significant impact on foreign policy through that. I'm also the co-chair of the India caucus.

MA: You arrived as a congressman at a time when the country was deeply polarized. Were you concerned about how to tackle this?

RK: There are two different approaches to polarization. I fall into the more boring camp which doesn't make me go viral as often. I don't question a person's motives or their patriotism. I try to win the issues through argument and persuasion and a large part of my party (Democrats) doesn't believe in that. They think they are fighting culture warriors on the opposite side, and you need to take the fight to them. That usually gets more media attention. If you look at President Biden, President Obama, President Clinton, and President Carter, I think the country ultimately deeply wants aspirational, unifying figures. After the Biden-Trump rematch in 2024, I think there will be space for new leaders to emerge. Trump is just one data point. When you look at successful models of leadership they tend to be unifying. It's not that they don't stand up on principle, but they look to find common ground where they can, and they try to make an argument based on the issue rather than hurling insults. That's been my approach—whether it works or not remains to be seen.

MA: Do you think that we're too broken? Do you think that we have to break before we can rebuild?

RK: No, I think we're going through a very difficult time because we're so diverse. There is so much ethnic diversity, racial diversity, and religious diversity in America now, and then we've justly seen the rise of women and minorities and people of color and the rise of the LGBTQ community. We have seen them assume positions of responsibility and power and that has posed a challenge for society. It is inevitable when society goes through that kind of rapid change so fast. Our institutions are struggling to keep up. Today, we have a daughter of Palestine serving in the same Congress as a child of a Holocaust survivor.

MA: And when did you decide that you were going to be the person in the Democratic Party that was going to reach across the aisle? Was that an unusual decision?

RK: Others have tried to reach across the aisle—what I tried to do that was transformational was reach out to rural communities in red America. It all began to crystallize for me in the final months of 2016. We were coming off the 2016 election and I could see the Trump campaign and some of the sense of frustration and anger in the communities that he appealed to. I realized that Silicon Valley has to answer the nation's call and that we can't just be thinking about what's good for Silicon Valley. We need to be thinking about how to extend our economic opportunities and prosperity to places that have been left out. It was a few weeks after the election that I started to float the idea that we've got to create these technology jobs in places like Ohio and Pennsylvania. The first place I went was Kentucky. Hal Rogers, the congressman from there who was in his late seventies, came up to me and said, "Come on down to my district." He had heard me speak about it. The press really found this intriguing. Here's this young Indian American, Hindu faith, Bay Area congressman in his early forties being invited by an older white Republican from a heavily Trump district. And they're working together to bring technology jobs to Trump country.

MA: What concrete actions did you take?

RK: You can help lead America to that place by helping provide economic opportunity for people who have been left out, by setting the tone of respect for communities that have been left out, by articulating a vision of patriotism that everyone can buy into. Technology, in my view, is going to be a big part of the revitalization. By 2025, 25 million digital jobs are going to exist in America. Many of those middle-class, good-paying jobs can be in communities that aren't in Silicon Valley. We've seen that post-COVID, a lot of jobs are going to rural communities and smaller towns. People are able to stay and work remotely. I am doing a program with Google and Allegheny Community College and the Benedict community. The kids get a stipend while they get trained with the help of AI and at the end of it they get a $65,000 job and they can stay in their own community. It's a pilot program, but there's no reason that can't be scaled. And some of this scale doesn't even require government. It just requires bringing the tech companies together with the universities and having the right investment.

In his book, *Dignity in a Digital Age*, Khanna explains his vision for a future that is more equitable, with technology being the vehicle that brings communities together through job creation and investment. He argues that globalization has failed most working-class Americans, particularly in poor, rural areas, and has arranged several trips bringing tech executives from Apple, Google, and Intel to Paintsville, Kentucky, and Ohio to train kids with the help of funds and jobs from Silicon Valley. He also proposed a $1 trillion expansion of the earned income tax credit, which would have doubled the money for low-income families. The states that would benefit the most from his plan were not that of his party but red states like Arkansas, Mississippi, and West Virginia.[121]

MA: The Democrats have been steadily losing the working class to the Republican Party since the seventies. Manufacturing went to China and unions were broken and the average factory worker no longer felt secure. Many working-class Democrats have become Republicans. Can you win them back?

RK: The issues of the working class have become more complex. I agree that the Republicans have made too many inroads into the working class. But when it comes to communities of color and the working class, we are still overwhelmingly winning them as Democrats. We have seen erosion among the white working class, but I think we can win them back if we can talk about how to bring economic jobs and prosperity into those communities and convince them that we're serious about doing it. One of the most disheartening things for me when I was talking about making things in America and I started making trips in Trump's America. In Anderson, Indiana, a reporter who was following me talked to one of the steel guys afterwards who said, "I'm surprised this guy's [Khanna] talking about making things in America. I thought that was a Donald Trump thing." We all know that was an FDR thing, it was a Hamilton thing, but somehow we have lost that narrative and we've got to figure out how to reclaim it. The president has been trying to bring it back, but to your deeper point about the polarization, we need a bold vision of bringing economic development, economic prosperity, and economic moonshot of revitalization into those communities; we need to focus on doing that in a big way and it is transformative in the sense that it is rooted in what Hamilton and FDR wanted to do and what Biden wants to accomplish.

MA: You have pushed to bring manufacturing back to the United States and been a sponsor of the Chips Act.

RK: I don't think we can just run the same playbook and manufacturing processes and compete with the cheap labor and deregulation in China and other places. I think you have to have the innovation advantages in steel or aluminum production combined with federal incentives. I think a lot of the technology on robotics, on digital sensors, how a factory floor works, and AI is taking place and will help us understand greater efficiencies and in the process will all contribute to a productivity advantage that ends up allowing America to be more competitive. I visited two factories in Columbus, Ohio, and in upstate New York with Micron, and we're going to see more factories coming across America, more good jobs being created, more of a sense of these communities feeling they're part of the future and new technology, so it's going to create a sense of shared prosperity.

Khanna is very media savvy and decided early on to make himself into a nationally recognized figure. Being a relative newcomer to politics, the mainstream media did not initially elevate him in any way. Khanna, who wanted to be a transformational politician by reaching out to Republicans, appears frequently on *Fox News* to promote his ideas, a channel most Democratic politicians boycott. But if this was the channel all the Republicans were watching, it seemed foolish, according to Khanna, to ignore it.

MA: You have not hesitated to court *Fox News* and appear on it on a regular basis. A lot of Democrats and progressives shun them.

RK: Well, I don't understand why people are so afraid of it. First of all, in the first quarter of 2023, the ratings came out. The top 13 cable shows in this country were on *Fox News*. You have to get to like No. 14 before you get to anything on MSNBC or CNN. So, if the top 13 shows that Americans are watching are on *Fox*, and you have 95 percent of the Democratic Party boycotting it, that makes no sense to me. I think it's one of the most straightforward decisions that you should want to go and talk to voters where they are. I don't go on some of the most inflammatory *Fox* shows, but I go on Bret Baer and Dana Perino. I often joke with folks that the British press is far harsher than *Fox*. I once had an interview with a liberal British TV station that was much tougher on me than most of the *Fox News* interviews I've had. There are some Democrats who will ask, "Why am I legitimizing *Fox*?" We'll get a lot of angry phone calls, but my staff is used to that. I often say, "Well, *Fox* doesn't need Ro Khanna to be legitimized." They're legitimate enough. But overall, I think my goal in going on it is not to get people to agree with me, or vote for me, or even persuade them, but just to get them to say he's a decent guy, he's a patriot, he cares about the country, and is reasonable. I have had some people say, "Well, you know, I'm persuaded that the Democratic Party cares about manufacturing or the economy." Now, maybe it's only 5 to 10 percent that I'm reaching that are being persuaded, but that's significant in a context of the millions of people who watch.

Khanna has understood that in order to reach young people you have to meet them where they congregate. His tech savviness and relative youth give him a huge advantage over the aging demographics of the Democratic Party. "The new generation of Americans aren't getting their news from MSNBC, CNN, or *Fox*... That's just not how millennials and Gen Z consume news or get inspired," Khanna explained. He has embraced streamers and online content creators like Destiny and Vaush, as has the tech entrepreneur Vivek Ramaswamy, who ran for the Republican presidential nomination in 2024. The content creators discuss student debt relief, climate change, and affordable housing on Twitch and YouTube. The forums are powerful and unscripted, and not everyone is comfortable engaging with them in this manner, but those that ignore them risk losing that entire demographic.

MA: You represent some very rich people in your district, then, obviously, some poor people as well. How do you reconcile their interests?

RK: Well, the very wealthy folks give me a pass on some of the policies—they proposed Medicare for all, free public college, childcare for all, which are all about working-class issues, affordable housing, because a lot of them are liberal, because a lot of them understand that income inequality is a huge challenge. They understand that if we don't solve the democracy challenge, their own success and their kids' success is at risk. When it comes to being a champion for talking about technology's good in the world and the importance of entrepreneurship, I've always been there on those issues. They know I understand and appreciate and celebrate technology, that I'm optimist about technology, that when the depositors at Silicon Valley Bank that helped start-ups were threatened to be wiped out, I was there standing up for the start-ups in the Silicon Valley ecosystem. I talked to the administration, everyone in the media, I went on "Face the Nation," I made the case very strongly that these depositors were the innovation pipeline of America; that if you want climate tech, if you want biotech, if you want people who are looking for cures to cancer, we have to make sure that all these small businesses and start-ups don't get wiped out. We succeeded in convincing Secretary [of the Treasury Janet] Yellen to guarantee all depositors by Sunday night. I think Silicon Valley has allowed me to champion the policies I have embraced, both because of their own liberal values, but also because of their recognition that the data integrity and quality matters.

Though Khanna is closely aligned with Bernie Sanders, the left wing of the Democrats, he has managed to be a progressive without alienating the right, which has meant walking a fine line. His philosophy is one of being civil and agreeing to disagree while working to benefit people across the aisle.

RK: There was a backlash, of course, when I chaired the national culture for Bernie Sanders campaign, but you know, my constituents put up with it and Bernie carried my district. I think it was much harder for me to support Bernie Sanders than people from other districts who have constituencies that are natural for Bernie Sanders. It would have been an easier course for me to just be a fiscally centrist Democrat that wasn't speaking about working-class issues. That's one of the things that progressives appreciate about me—that I was willing to uphold progressive ideals while representing a very wealthy district.

MA: Do you think unions should be brought back?

RK: Yeah, in fact, this morning, I was meeting Starbucks workers and I've been leading the fight for Starbucks. I'm one of the few offices of the House that have allowed my own employees to unionize. I have been very much on the picket lines of a lot of unions. So I'm a strong supporter.[122]

MA: Everyone is worried about the impact of AI. What are your views on this? A prominent member of your constituency and an early investor in AI, Vinod Khosla, predicts that labor will be replaced and people will work only if they want to.

RK: I know Vinod is very smart, but I disagree with him on that. John Maynard Keynes certainly was very smart and predicted in a famous essay in the 1930s that we'd all be working 15-hour work weeks. He wrote that technology was moving at such a rapid pace that everyone would be engaged in poetry and leisure and thinking, but that just didn't turn out to be true because the human imagination is limitless. The human ability to create new industries is limitless. When we have the car replace the horse buggy, there was a whole automobile industry that stood up; when the telephone replaced the carrier, there was a whole telecom industry that stood up; when the airplane replaced so much other modes of transportation, that was an analog industry that stood up. I think that new industries will emerge. If you look at productivity, this idea of moving towards the jobless future is just not showing up in the data.

MA: When you have a difficult problem or a political issue that you're grappling with, what is your strategy?

RK: My grandfather once told me that you have to think of your goal and then work backwards. That's quite simple in how it sounds, but it actually is clarifying. If you have a difficult problem and then you think about, What is your goal for something five years from now? And how do you work backwards? You then evaluate which step would help advance that goal. It's a very useful analytical framework for what you should do. I also text and chat with a close group of people and get their feedback informally, and I think about how other leaders may have approached it.

MA: Late at night when you're asleep, do you ever think that you could have had a different career? What would it have been?

RK: No, I love what I do. I've always, since college and law school, wanted to work in politics and I've loved it ever since. I wish I had more time with family, with kids, with my parents, with my brother. But not in terms of what I'm doing now. I've felt that I think I'm doing what I love. It's doing what I'm good at. At times I wanted to be a playwright, but I'd be a C-minus playwright. I could have done it and liked it, but I wouldn't have been good at it. One of the great blessings of life is to be able to do what you love and end up being good at it. I often doubted myself as well, many, many times. It's very important to have people around you who believe in you. It doesn't always have to be family. Sometimes your family is actually not the ones who will believe in you. I think it's very hard to pursue something difficult without people who believe in you—to know whether it was worth continuing. There may be some people who just innately have deep, deep confidence, but most people end up having self-doubts. My very close friends and some family members were very, very supportive and continued to believe in my ambition, my aspiration—my mother, or my brother, my wife—despite my earlier setbacks. I don't think Gandhi had someone giving him pep talks, but for me it was important.

MA: What do you feel you would like to accomplish that you have not as yet?

RK: Well, I would hope that leading an economic renaissance for the nation in different parts of the country, because I think a nation that is dynamic and prosperous and on the move and building things and creating jobs and creating prosperity with people and Indian Americans and Silicon Valley, working with African Americans in the South, working with white Americans in the heartland, will help stitch this country together into a strong, prosperous, multiracial democracy. And in so doing, we would have done something unprecedented in world history. No country has ever done that. And it would be America's unique contribution to human civilization. And in doing so, we would also set the stage for an America that probably pushes for a more just world because the communities that would be empowered and this multiracial democracy would have a sensitivity to the aspirations of people in Africa, to the aspirations of people in Asia, the aspirations of people in South America, and clearly reject the colonizers' model of the world and move towards a world where America leads a model of truly multiracial democracy.

MA: What has driven you?

RK: The American story. I grew up with a love for the Constitution, the founders, the mythology of America. This is such a remarkable country and I still think that what an honor and what a privilege it is to represent the United States of America and the Congress. Growing up in Philadelphia my family would go to Independence Hall and the Liberty Bell. My teachers, actually, were probably one of my biggest inspirations. Mrs. Robb, and my 10th grade English teacher who taught me to love American history. My 9th grade English teacher who helped me publish my first op-ed in the local Bucks County paper. My professors at the University of Chicago, who made me understand the extraordinary achievement of the American experiment and why it was such a consequential achievement in world history and why I want to be part of that project.

CHAPTER 21

GenNext: Born in the USA

Then there's the eternal, original judgment—of my mother, my parents,
their immigrant community, their many friends with advanced degrees. Theirs
was a language of comparison and competition, everyone striving to establish
themselves and get ahead. And there's that overhanging judgment,
of the world my parents left behind in Kolkata. All of which I internalized.

JHUMPA LAHIRI

In 1988, Rageshree Ramachandran, from Sacramento, California, won the Scripps National Spelling Bee Championship with the word *elegiacal.* At the time, few people paid much attention, attributing her success to a unique talent. Today, the spelling bee has become synonymous with Indian talent. Some Indian families told the *Los Angeles Times* that when they watched Nupur Lala, an Indian American girl, win the 1999 contest, it inspired them to enter the competition. The general feeling was, "If she can do it, why not us?" The families trace their interest back to 1994, when ESPN began airing the Scripps National Spelling Bee. Indian parents who were engineers, doctors, and high achievers themselves were excited to have found a platform in which their children could compete at the national level.

The spelling bee quickly became a prestige activity in the Indian American community and spawned a vast network of contests conducted by parents and volunteers to prepare their children for the Scripps National Spelling Bee. The South Asian Spelling Bee sponsors 12 regional contests nationally, and a nonprofit called the North South Foundation runs academic competitions in 35 states.

From 2008 to 2019, 12 consecutive national spelling bees were won by Indian contestants, who have dazzled the judges and audiences with their ability to spell words that even spellcheck does not recognize, such as *prospicience* and *guetapens*.

In 2015, three Indians won the spelling bee in a tie, and the same thing happened the following year. Things reached an absurd level in 2019 when eight children were crowned co-champions, seven of whom were Indian American.

When Zaila Avante-Garde won the Spelling Bee in 2021, it jolted the Indian American community. Avant-Garde had not only made history as the first African American winner, but she had jolted the Indian American community, whose members had begun to take for granted that the title belonged solely to them. Social media lit up with messages ranging from dismay to humor.

- "We lost the #SpellingBee. I am an Indian American and I am devastated."
- "Math Olympics, we still have those... fret not!"
- "Next year will be more suspenseful. The kids who study 10 hours a day will need to up it to 15 hours a day."
- "Aren't nine out of 10 health professionals interviewed on American television of Indian origin?"
- "Being outperformed by others in intellectual tasks is how you know that your identity group has been assimilated into the great American miasma."
- "It is a sign that the third and fourth generation is no longer being indoctrinated as much by Indian parents into useless acts of mental gymnastics."

In 2022 Indian Americans reclaimed the title, and in 2023, they placed first, second, and third. Preparing for the spelling bee is a serious commitment, and the standards have risen as the pool of applicants arrives better prepared each year. The level of difficulty has skyrocketed, requiring hopeful contestants to substantially increase the time they devote to preparing for the competition. Indian parents are as invested as the children in winning, often working along with their children even as the hours of prep required on weekdays has doubled and gone up to 12 hours on weekends. It is a level of discipline and dedication that most American children—and even most American adults—would find challenging.

The amount of time and effort that Indian parents put into supporting their children's efforts give them a clear advantage over their peers. Take the case of Shourav Dasari, a 14-year-old boy from Texas whose engineer parents had prepared a spreadsheet on his computer containing 125,000 words, or Akash Vukoti, who at age seven was the youngest contestant in history. Parents take turns helping their child compile words, practicing with them, and even deploying siblings to help, many of whom will enter the competition themselves at some point.

In the documentary *Spellbound*, which follows several Indian American contestants and their families as they prepare for the competition, one mother says she takes care of all the chores—including cleaning her son's room, doing the laundry, and whatever else her child needs—so that her son can stay focused on the project. The film also includes a few non- Indian contestants from diverse backgrounds. Not everyone's parents are in a position to spend hours coaching their kids, even though they are uniformly supportive of their children's endeavors. The support provided by non-Indian parents is in the form of encouragement, advice, and nurturing more than the hands-on coaching provided by Indian parents. In most cases, competing in the spelling bee is an idea initiated by the student or an encouraging teacher who identified potential in one of their students. But in the case of the Indian community, the idea is primarily promoted by the parents, for whom winning the spelling bee is a family affair. As *The Independent* newspaper reported in 2016, "In Fresno, California, Jayakrishnan spends four to five hours a week with his daughter. They spell out words and he puts her through mock contests. Sometimes, his daughter protests. 'How will spelling help me?' she asks. 'I have a spell checker on my computer.' 'It's for your benefit,' Jayakrishnan tells her. 'Learn the root, the origin of a word. If you go through this at an early age you will grow as an individual and succeed in life.'"[123]

Nupur Lala's teacher said she loved having Indian children in her class because the support the parents provided at home guaranteed the child would do well in school. From the teacher's perspective, it was a perfect partnership. The spelling bee is a microcosm in which Indian values combine with American opportunity to produce a new generation of achievers. In another documentary on the subject called *Spelling the Dream*, the filmmaker Sam Rega said, "All of these children are Americans, they are part of the American dream, their families got here because of what our country allows. ... That is what people should remember."

Aside from the spelling bee, Indians have also won the last seven national geographic bees before that contest was discontinued. Indian kids also tend to outperform their peer groups in the Siemens Science Competition, the Intel Science Talent Search, and other contests. I was told by a couple of parents in Silicon Valley that the latest area of interest was robotics.

Time magazine's 2020 "Kid of the Year" issue featured Gitanjali Rao, a 15-year-old Indian American girl who invented a mobile device to test for lead in drinking water. The previous year, she was named in *Forbes*'s "30 under 30" list.

In an unusual pivot, six Indian American women were among the Miss World America contestants in 2020. I was initially surprised that Indian parents were willing to support what would normally be considered a frivolous pursuit, but when I read about the contestants, I discovered that the pattern among them remained consistent with the diaspora's aspirations. Serene Singh of Colorado was a Truman Scholar as well a Rhodes Scholar and was headed to Oxford University. Radhika Shah of Nevada was headed to Stanford and had been appointed by Governor Brian Sandoval as the youngest youth commissioner for the state. Manju Bangalore of Oregon was a physicist who has worked at the White House under President Obama on science policy. Educational achievement had remained a priority for each of them.

But are competitions a primer for success? Do the winners end up becoming stars later in life? Is the massive pressure and countless hours the child spends studying to win turn them into leaders or geniuses? It may be too early to tell, as most of the winners are too young to have maximized their potential and most of the winners are still in school, but a look at a few spelling bee winners who are now adults, don't indicate any unusual talents that resulted from being put under a period of prolonged, intense pressure. Rageshree Ramachandran and Nupur Lala, who won the contest in 1988 and 1999 respectively, are both doctors. Many of the male contestants studied engineering, although one played professional poker for a while before joining a start-up. They all have perfectly respectable careers, but it is too early to discern any pattern of achievement in later life that points to the discipline and work they put in earlier as a contributing factor. Most of the individuals I profiled in this book who achieved extraordinary success, have one striking characteristic in common. Their parents did not push them in the slightest when it came to their work and seemed quite hands-off. Their accomplishments were a result of their internal drive.

The psychologist Angela Duckworth believes that in order to achieve you have to be interested in or have a degree of passion for a subject: "Interest must come first. I think there are a lot of overeager, probably very well-intentioned parents out there who are kind of like chaining their kids to the piano bench in hopes that seventh hour of practice today is going to put them on course for Julliard or Harvard. And I think they're seriously getting things out of order." An example she uses is Srinath Mahankali, who won the 2013 spelling bee. He developed a passion for words and began memorizing winning words at the age of six, learning the diacritical marks in the dictionary that indicate pronunciation. His parents detected a talent and began to coach him, scouring words with interesting patterns or spellings for him to learn. Mahankali credits his parents for helping him win, grateful for all the hours they put in along with him.

Neil Kadakia, a contestant profiled in *Spellbound* who tripped up on the second round in the finals, had every conceivable support. *Spellbound* documents his father spending hours coaching him, hiring German and Latin tutors to help with additional vocabulary. He had even been taught to meditate to increase his powers of concentration. The young boy was under considerable pressure to perform. His father had engaged priests in India to pray for his success and members of their community in India were following his progress. Were he to win, many poor people in India would be fed in thanks. Despite all the tutors and training and meditation, one of the words he had the most trouble spelling during the contest was *Darjeeling*. He even had to request its origin. You could see the look of sheer embarrassment on his father's face as his son struggled with a word that should have been second nature to any Indian. Most Indians are tea drinkers and Darjeeling tea is usually a staple in their kitchen cabinet. Kadakia eventually spelled the word correctly, but it must have been his parents' moment of realization that despite their priests' prayers and maintaining close ties with India, they had raised an American kid who despite all his studying had no idea what or where Darjeeling was.

Many of the Indian parents raising this new generation of Americans are themselves products of the competitive pressure they endured in India. They arrived after 2000 and remain deeply influenced by their roots. Their attitudes toward education, competition, and its centrality to family life transported itself to the United States along with their spices, religion, and family values. Worried that their children will lose the "Indian work ethic" and "Indian family ties," they try from an early age to channel their children's energies into activities they consider productive or career-enhancing. Given their own rigorous training, the general perception is that the American education system is soft and lacking in discipline. Becoming adept at competing was an essential part of growing up in India. The parents not only prioritize education but are willing to spend an enormous amount of time with their children on it—just as their parents did for them in India. It is not uncommon for parents to enroll their kids in STEM classes before they even start preparing for their SATs.

Education forms the core of the pyramid of ingredients that has helped propel Indians towards the path of success in America but it is hardly unique to the Indian community. Chinese Americans and Jewish Americans have also internalized education as the path to success. What seems distinctive about Indians, particularly those who came to the United States after 2000 during the tech boom, is not only their obsession with education—which seems universal among Indians—but their laser focus on the STEM fields. After all, the dream of ambitious parents in India is for their child to get into an IIT because of the prestige that would accrue to the family and the child's potential earning power on graduation.[124]

Careers, finances and spouses are considered too important to be individual choices. Achievements and failures accrue to the family. Bill Gates, Steve Jobs, Mark Zuckerberg, and Peter Theil all dropped out of college. This would have been unacceptable to an Indian parent. Independence is not considered a desirable attribute among family members in an Indian household. Parents emphasize harmony within the family and prioritize the goals and aspirations of the group over the needs of the individual and prefer to control the lives of their children from birth through marriage.

The concept of *dharma*, or "duty," is a series of obligations between parents and their children. Its roots are derived from ancient religious texts. Most Indian parents consider it a sacred duty to provide for their children and guide them. If the children hold up their end of the bargain, it is understood that they will inherit their parents' homes, real estate, and wealth, as well as their practice or business if they have one. The children, in return, are expected to excel academically, obey and respect their elders and take care of them in their old age, and marry someone their parents approve of. Their ideal of family relationships is governed by collectivism and patriarchy.

The natural inclination of Indian parents is to shower their children with love. Parents are, if anything, faulted for not discipling children when they are young, but even though they are indulged at home, they expect nothing less than the highest scores from them in school. Low scores are viewed as a collective failure. One only has to visit various blogs on which Indian kids air their grievances to see how often children complain about their parents' expectations of straight A's—even an A-minus is considered unacceptable.[125]

According to an HSBC study on parents hopes and expectations with regards to their children's education, Indian parent's aspirations differed from those from other countries. 51 percent of the Indian parents chose successful careers followed by 49 percent choosing happiness in life and only 17 percent rated fulfilling their child's potential as an ultimate goal. By contrast, most parents in developed countries put a low priority on successful careers. Only a fifth of U.S. parents regarded successful careers as an ultimate goal, with the U.K. and Australia at 17 percent. China Taiwan and Hongkong were all below 20 percent. Being happy in life was prized by other countries. Indonesia 56 percent, France 86 percent, United Kingdom 78 percent and United Arab Emirates 77 percent.[126]

Steve Wozniak, who co-founded Apple, raised some hackles when he attended the ET Global Business Summit in New Delhi in 2018 and raised questions about the lack of Indian creativity. Asked about his views regarding India's prowess as a global force in tech, he said, "The culture here is one of success based upon academic excellence, studying, learning, practicing and having a good job and a great life. For upper India, not the lower ... but where is the creativity? The creativity gets left out when your behavior is too predictable and structured, everyone is similar. Look at a small country like New Zealand, the writers, singers, athletes; it's a whole different world."[127]

Wozniak admitted he did not know the culture of India well, but he did say he had not seen big advances in tech companies, even Infosys, a company he is familiar with, and which is regarded as one of India's most innovative and successful tech companies, with a market cap of $83 billion. Narayan Murthy, the founder of Infosys and father-in-law of former British Prime Minister Rishi Sunak, agrees with Wozniak. He voiced his concerns in his convocation address at the Indian Institute of Science. He pointed out that MIT and other Western institutions helped transform the world with inventions like the microchip, laser, and robotics. India, by comparison, had not produced any inventions that had become global household names or changed the world. The implication was that creativity was not fostered in Indian schools.

A four-month investigation by *The Indian Express* of India's top students who took the national board exams for class 10 and 12 between 1996 and 2015 further corroborated this view. Several of the students acknowledged that they were taught to work hard and focus on being goal oriented but were not taught critical thinking so important to modern science. Karuna Ganesh, a physician-scientist at Sloan Kettering Cancer Centre in New York said she only leant things pertinent to scientific inquiry when she came to the United States. Her views were echoed by several others.[128] The findings of the survey found that more than half the 'toppers' eventually moved overseas, with four out of five going to the United States Most left India with a degree from IIT and a majority of them specialized in STEM. Educators in India are aware of the deficiencies in the Indian system and are trying to address them but still have a long way to go.

One possible explanation for the systemic problem in the Indian educational system is Nikesh Arora's belief that Indian society is conditioned to minimize risk. He pointed that the educational system does not reward great thoughts—it encourages you to get things done.

Abraham Verghese, in an interview about his upbringing, talks about the relentless messaging that all Indian children receive growing up—and he was no exception. "You were either a doctor, an engineer, or a failure. It was that simple."

I have described the powerful forces in India that shaped the educated Indian immigrants who been arriving here since the 1990's as they are raising the new generation on Indian Americans. What keeps the overzealous Indian parent under control are the nurturing educators in the American system. Their approach tempers the ultra-competitive mindset that Indians have experienced themselves in India, teaching the parents to be involved in a more balanced and positive manner.

The generation born here—the older cohort who are in their forties and fifties—is not a monolith. They include Nikki Haley, Bobby Jindal, Neal Katyal, Atul Gawande (all born to the early immigrants who came prior to 1980) and have chosen a variety of careers. Many of them have intermarried and blended into the fabric of America. Their ties to India are more distant. But the generation born to those who immigrated after 1990 are more oriented to the cultural connections of their parents. They grew up with many more Indian American families around them, and their parents were able to stay closely connected to India due to improved technology and easy travel. But along with all the children from this group that will be heading to Ivy League schools to study STEM, there is increasing evidence on social media, that others will join non-profits, become activists, artists and musicians, reflecting the cultural influence of growing up in America and will find their place in the ever-evolving story of the American century.

Conclusion

I want to redefine genius... I want to define genius as something
hat you accomplish yourself as opposed to something that's given to you.
ANGELA DUCKWORTH

We all admire successful people, but those who become leaders or achieve celebrity status fascinate us. We wonder, what do they have that we don't? How can our children become like them? What are the secrets to their success? Are there any lessons we can learn from them that might help us duplicate their achievements?

Most of the Indians profiled in this book came from ordinary backgrounds. Armed with an education and a desire to succeed, they achieved extraordinary success combining grit, intellectual ability, and ingenuity. There is an Indian word for it: *jugaad*. It is a cross between ingenuity, creativity, and grit. Several people I interviewed mentioned it. Shantanu Narayen and Nikesh Arora both embraced the concept.

The individuals or the parents of those I have profiled did not come from money. Wealth in India in the sixties and seventies was a relative term. Few people in India owned a television set, a car, an air conditioner, or a gas stove—basic universal measures of belonging to the middle class. Ovens were unheard of and even a refrigerator or a phone line was only common in the big cities until the seventies. Basic amenities such as clean piped water and electricity were unreliable. Compared to living standards in the West, most of the people in India were poor.

Kanwal Rekhi mentions that his family lacked indoor plumbing growing up. The women in Suhas Patil's household sold their jewelry to finance the education of family members, and Chandrika Tandon was candid about growing up in a multigenerational home with very little disposable income. My family had indoor plumbing, but the municipality rationed water during the fifties and sixties. I remember we had to fill multiple buckets, as water was only supplied for a few hours each day.

The British left India impoverished when they departed in 1947, and the leaders of newly independent India adopted a socialist economic model. They hoped it would help eliminate poverty and mitigate against economic inequality, but the policies only succeeded in making everyone equally poor. Economic insecurity was deeply embedded in the Indian psyche.

In his book *Outliers*, Malcom Gladwell argues that despite all the stories one hears of someone making it from nothing, we sometimes fail to take into account the hidden privileges that highly motivated and successful individuals have access to: "People don't rise from nothing. We do owe something to parentage and patronage. The people who stand before kings may look like they did it all by themselves. But in fact, they are invariably the beneficiaries of hidden advantages and extraordinary opportunities and cultural legacies that allow them to learn and work hard and make sense of the world in ways others cannot."[129]

Caste privilege is not a hidden benefit, but a fact in plain sight that any Indian can identify, as Hindu last names contain a great deal of information. You can tell a person's caste, what language they are likely to speak, and what part of the country they are from, down to the state where they originated. It is like carrying your personal data on a placard around your neck. Although the immigrants and students who arrived between 1965 and 1985 did not come from wealth, 90 percent of these immigrants belonged to the privileged upper castes.

Indian society is a product of perhaps the longest experiment in social engineering in history, dating back over a thousand years to *Manusmriti*, an ancient religious Hindu text which encoded the caste system and embedded discrimination into social structures that persist even today, dividing society into five primary castes with specific occupations designated to each category. The privilege of learning was reserved for the upper castes. There was no mobility within castes. Brahmins were privileged over other castes when it came to education (Chandrika Tandon, Shantanu Narayen, Sundar Pichai, Siddhartha Mukherjee, and Atul Gawande are all Brahmins), with upper caste Kshatriya's included in the mix (Vinod Khosla, Nikesh Arora, Neal Katyal, and Deepak Chopra are all Punjabi

Kshatriyas). Sikhs and Muslims (Fareed Zakaria, Kanwal Rekhi, Nikki Haley) fall outside caste constraints as they are not Hindus.

British enthusiasm to "civilize" the natives fizzled when funds ran low and plans to expand education were scrapped. According to the historian Anil Seal, "In principle there maybe something to be said for educating mute, inglorious Miltons in the villages; in practice the pressing need was for clerks and public servants who could be hired at rates which the government could afford." There was a great demand from the local population to get an education, but as Indian nationalism grew, led by western-educated Indians, and calls for independence became a serious threat to British power, the government retreated from further expanding education, leaving it to the private sector. Indians suspected "that behind the reference to financial stringency lay the more sinister conclusion that the only good Indian was an uneducated one."[130] When the British left India in 1947, they had done little to "educate the natives," and the literacy rate was an appalling 12 percent. Although it has now risen to 76 percent, it is still below the global literacy rate of 86 percent, with men and the upper castes having greater access to education.

Education was the means by which all the people in this book and the many immigrants to America were able to avail themselves of the opportunities America had to offer. Education was opened up to all Indians after independence, and aggressive affirmative action programs were put in place. It was the override button—a way of circumventing class and caste by providing a path to a better future. Another critical benefit that was not to be underestimated, as Vinod Khosla made clear, was the level playing field provided by IIT and institutions like it. Admission was based on merit, and once you were accepted to a place like IIT, the fees were negligible. Unlike the United States, where obtaining scholarships was essential for Indian students to be able to consider going overseas to study, IIT and IIM was almost free thanks to subsidies put in place by the Indian government to encourage the study of science. It was an enormous hidden benefit. Chandrika Tandon specifically cites the subsidized tuition costs at the Indian Institute of Management as enabling her ability to study there, whereas Kanwal Rekhi's decision to attend Michigan Tech was entirely based on the scholarship he received from them.

The British had made English the official working language of the Indian government. It would turn out to be an exceptional gift, as English has become the dominant working language across the globe. From air traffic controllers to multinational corporations with far-flung offices, international communications are now generally conducted in English.

Due to the multitude of languages spoken within India and the fraught politics surrounding the elevation of any one language over another, English remained the default working language in India even after independence in 1947. This encouraged schools to continue teaching in English, resulting in a vast majority of India's educated population being fully conversant in the language. This has given Indian immigrants in the United States an advantage over immigrants from China and Latin America, because they are not only equipped with a good education but are proficient in English and have an innate self confidence that comes from belonging to a privileged class, all attributes which have helped them succeed.

Competitive ability is another ingredient that some of the CEOs pointed out that helps Indian Americans excel and reach the top. It is learned from a young age. When you are born in a country of 1.5 billion people, you are constantly jockeying for college placements, jobs, and resources. A simple daily event like using public transportation becomes a race. Overcrowded buses deliberately stop a few feet beyond the stop, and only the most agile passengers manage to get on. From school admissions to college, from government jobs to the private sector, everything is competitive—even obtaining gas or water connections, housing grants or surgical procedures in state hospitals. Nikesh Arora believes that there are so many things that are culturally ingrained into you when growing up in India, that it set him up much better to succeed in the United States. "We always had to make do with less and try to make the most of it. Some call it *jugaad*," he said. "There are so many people chasing the same dream—if you are not relentless and disciplined you are not going to get anywhere."

It is not unusual to have 100,000 applications for 20 places in a school or a similar ratio for job applicants. Everyday items that much of the world takes for granted assume gladiatorial dimensions in India. Some theorists call this grit and determination. For the coveted IIT entrance exam, in 2004, 1.17 million applicants applied for 17,385 seats making it harder to get into than Harvard or MIT.

Going overseas, especially to the United States, provided an escape hatch not just for students but for graduates as well. America provided Indian students with a key component that helped them realize their potential: opportunity.

Another common theory offered as an explanation for why Indians do well in America is that they are a population of outliers who have been pre-selected to succeed. The majority of Indians who come to the United States have already been through a rigorous vetting process in India and, having reached the top, they have gone through a second screening process in order to qualify for a graduate program in the United States or a H-1B visa, which has specific skill requirements. Almost all the first wave immigrants and a majority of the immigrants that entered after the nineties had to meet academic or technical requirements. By the time they arrive, they are not just qualified but highly motivated and determined. Indians who came to this country with advanced degrees were able to get well-paying jobs that helped them secure a place in America's middle class almost immediately, an accomplishment that other nationalities often do not reach until the first or second native-born generation.

If we follow the logic, then the success of these individuals lies in the decision they made to come to America. They were not content to live with the traditional confines of the land of their birth. They had the motivation and talent to take the risk of leaving all that was familiar behind, including their families and find their opportunities in America where they not only thrived but attained unimaginable success in Silicon Valley, medicine and other areas.

Indian American families have also found it easy to embrace American culture and assimilate. They celebrate Thanksgiving, Halloween, and even Christmas with enthusiasm, while continuing to worship at Hindu temples. Saris have given way to pantsuits and sweatpants and pizzas and hamburgers (or often veggie burgers) are a regular staple. These have now become common in India as well. Thanks to the internet, phone apps, and easy travel, people growing up in

India are familiar with American culture prior to their arrival. They likely listen to the same music and watch the same movies as their American cohorts. They also see no need to abandon their Indian food, music, or roots, as everything is now available in the United States. They often maintain a dual life—one with their American co-workers and friends, and one with their Indian network.

Bobby Jindal, who would become governor of Louisiana, began the process of assimilation by Americanizing his name from Piyush to Bobby. He then became a Catholic and took up shooting in order to appeal to his conservative Republican constituents. Nikki Haley, a presidential contender and former governor of South Carolina, married a white man and also converted to Christianity. Born a Sikh, she continued to occasionally attend Sikh religious services with her parents, placating all her gods. When Indians have encountered discrimination, they are told by their parents not to get distracted and to keep their focus on the ultimate goal. Only a handful of successful Indian Americans willingly admit that they had to manage discrimination on their climb up the ladder. Most either say it wasn't an issue or admit they pushed it aside just as their parents suggested they should. Perhaps this is because Indians recognize that they are themselves a deeply color-conscious society, where lighter skin is prized. One has only to look through the matrimonial ads to see the prejudices on full display, where every ad requests a "fair skinned" girl. People are willing to jettison caste constraints, and one often sees "caste no bar" as part of the description, but the color preference is seldom dropped.

It is notable that one of the reasons that Indians have assimilated so easily into the American way of life is the acceptability and adaptability of the Hindu religion. There is no central authority like the pope to rule on what it means to be a Hindu. You can pray to a stone (Lingum) or a monkey (Hanuman) or an elephant (Ganesh) or any number of gods and still be a Hindu. You can be a vegetarian or not, and while eating beef is one of the few don'ts, the practice is given a pass when overseas—in the way that crossing the ocean was considered a loss of caste. There are no strictures regarding abortion, prayer, fasting, or alcohol. Hinduism's flexible approach to life, in which responsibility lies with the individual, removes any social hesitations to assimilation.

Hinduism doesn't have one defining book like the Bible or Koran; it has a multitude of epics, treatises, essays, and philosophical works dating from 1500 BC and covering such subjects as the nature of God, science, medicine, and yoga. As a Hindu you can take your pick about which path to follow to get to your particular Nirvana. Hinduism is all about the individual and his or her personal quest. That is partly why the religion does not seek to convert. It doesn't truly matter what state others are in as long as you are on your path to enlightenment. A "live and let live" attitude defines Hindus. I belong to a long generation of Hindus on both sides of my family. The Hinduism I am familiar with is easygoing, tolerant of other people, and accepting. Recently, politicians in India seem to have introduced a more muscular form of Hinduism called Hindutva. It has been exported to the diaspora as well. I'm hoping it is a passing phase.

The graphic on facing page shows recent data from the 2020 US census that confirms the economic success of Indian Americans, states their average income as having risen above $133,000—well above the national average. Indian Americans are among the best educated and have the benefit of growing up in stable families where divorce rates are low (7 percent) compared to the rest of the country. Twenty-two percent live in multigenerational households, which tend to reinforce family unity, and more than 70 percent live with parents who are married.

Some of the main reasons for Indian American success is due to the factors discussed, but do the exceptional Indians have anything in common? Each of them described their path to success and a few things stand out.

Most of them had little parental pressure or involvement when it came to getting into the top educational institutions. The amount of time a parent spent on their children's career and education had little bearing on their academic performance.

Economic stability was another benefit that was of critical importance in a poor country.

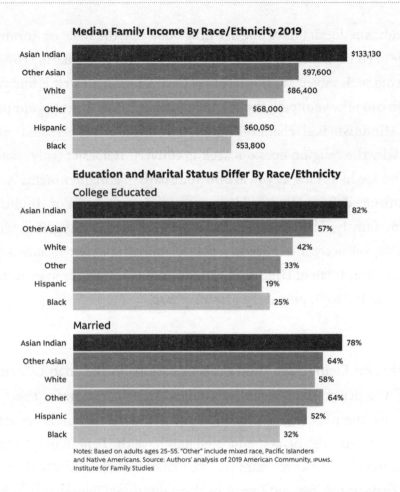

Median Family Income By Race/Ethnicity 2019

Race/Ethnicity	Median Family Income
Asian Indian	$133,130
Other Asian	$97,600
White	$86,400
Other	$68,000
Hispanic	$60,050
Black	$53,800

Education and Marital Status Differ By Race/Ethnicity

College Educated

Race/Ethnicity	College Educated
Asian Indian	82%
Other Asian	57%
White	42%
Other	33%
Hispanic	19%
Black	25%

Married

Asian Indian	78%
Other Asian	64%
White	58%
Other	64%
Hispanic	52%
Black	32%

Notes: Based on adults ages 25-55. "Other" include mixed race, Pacific Islanders and Native Americans. Source: Authors' analysis of 2019 American Community, IPUMS. Institute for Family Studies

A surprising number had fathers who had served in the Indian Armed Forces. Punjabis have traditionally been heavily recruited by the army. Their reputation as able fighters has deep historical roots. Kanwal Rekhi, Vinod Khosla, and Nikesh Arora are all Punjabis whose fathers served in the military. Although Ajay Banga is not profiled in the book, he was CEO of Mastercard and is now president of the World Bank and a high achieving Indian American whose Punjabi father was also a military man.

The army provided two important things to these achievers growing up: economic stability and adaptability. Economically, the army was a reliable employer; regardless of your status or position within the army, it provided income, housing, and health care, all critical benefits in a poor country. Military families tend to get moved around and both Khosla and Arora recall it made them adaptable to new circumstances. Discipline, an important life skill, was also valued in the home.

The others also in one way or another enjoyed relatively secure economic circumstances even if they were operating at a minimum level. Suhas Patil's father was an engineer and had a job at a steel mill with Tata, one of India's premiere companies. Satya Nadella's father worked for the government and the Krishnamurthy sisters' grandfather received a state pension. Although their father did not earn much, he was a bank employee with benefits. These were all "hidden privileges."

Siddhartha Mukherjee had just finished telling me a story about his grandmother's actions during the upheaval of partition in 1947. The family was from East Bengal, in what is now Bangladesh. They first moved to Calcutta, and later Mukherjee's father moved the family to Delhi when he started working, and that is where the family settled. Mukherjee wrote a moving piece in *The New Yorker* about the time he spent with his father in Delhi during the last few weeks of his father's life. He has established a start up in India that runs clinical trials for cancer treatments, he visits the research team often and seems to maintain his connections there.

I asked him if he felt Indian and was surprised when he said he felt somewhat nomadic. He had traveled from India to California to Oxford and back to the United States, but in terms of "feeling Indian," he said, "I feel Indian on Thursdays and other things on Fridays. I'm very comfortable in my Indian skin, but I have no shame or pride in discarding my Indian clothes, metaphorically or putting them on. I wear the clothes loosely. When I'm writing or working, I don't feel any need to super impose any identity on my work." Mukherjee did not feel either constrained or defined by his Indian identity. He slipped into American life with ease, and America has embraced him.

Almost every person I interviewed for the book expressed similar sentiments of having felt appreciated and given opportunities to shine in America. What comes through is that the story of their success is one that could not have unfolded in India or America alone. The cultural characteristics discussed laid the groundwork, but the networks of support the community developed in America such as TiE, AAPI, and Impact have contributed to supporting their ambitions along with America's merit based culture. It is through the alchemy of mixing one culture into the other that has produced a brilliant efflorescence from whose light we all benefit.

Acknowledgments

I could not have written the book without the cooperation of the people who are profiled and agreed to be interviewed for the book. They are all individuals with demanding schedules and burdened with requests. Time is one of their most precious commodities. Each one of them was gracious and willing to answer all my questions.

My background is in foreign policy and my knowledge of Silicon Valley and engineering was negligible when I started out. The vast network of IIT alumni from India and the United States are a well-knit group and they went out of their way to help me understand the "IIT club" as well as the Indians of Silicon Valley. Many of them had fascinating career stories that I wish could have included.

Anjali Joshi, B.J. Arun, Vish Mishra, Nikhil Jhaveri, Anu Basu and Professor Sidharth Sinha, all helped educate me about IIT, TiE, Silicon Valley, the role of Indians in it, and my many questions about tech.

A book like this would have been impossible to write without a network of well-wishers that were not just supportive but went out of their way to help connect me with people critical to the book. Two people who in particular deserve my gratitude are Sebastian Mallaby and Arun Kumar. Mallaby's many erudite books have educated me, and *Power Law* is a must-read for anyone who wants to understand the world of venture capital. Kumar, served as assistant secretary of commerce for global markets in the Obama administration and is the managing partner at Celesta Capital, a deep technology firm with companies in San Francisco and Bangalore. They both helped fill my information gap and were very generous in opening up their rolodex and connecting me with people in Silicon Valley.

Kanwal Rekhi introduced me to several people within the TiE family, and Nikesh Arora was very helpful in answering my many questions on tech and Silicon Valley, not related to his company.

My friend Mary Zients, who in her quiet and generous way, was supportive every step of the way, letting me use her office whenever I needed, and putting me in touch with people she felt should be part of the book. Her magnanimity is boundless.

I could not have had a more supportive team than HarperCollins. Their enthusiasm for my project was heartwarming and I especially owe Ananth Padmanabhan and Udayan Mitra my gratitude for their support. A special thanks to Paloma Dutta for getting my book across the finish line with all the patience and grace one could wish for.

A special thanks to my brilliant friend Peter Bergen for introducing me to my wonderful editor Paul Golob in New York, whose magic touch and insightful suggestions helped shape the book. Rafe Sagalyn, literary agent to many of my most illustrious friends in Washington, not only came up with the title, but generously gave of his time to help me think through the concept of the book in the beginning. Posey J. Chiddix took time out from her commitments at *The Spectator* and a tumultuous year at Columbia to assist on the book.

The encouragement and support of my family of writers and literary friends to write the book sustained me through my doubts. All their suggestions had an impact. They include Scott Moyers, Bea Moyers, John Burnham Schwartz, Jane Mayer, David Bradley, Katherine Bradley, Milan Vaishnav, Tresha Bergen, Somini Sengupta, Boykin Curry, Ela Jhaveri, Carole and Tim Geithner and Gahl Burt. I'd like to in particular thank Bill Hamilton, the former Washington editor of the *New York Times*, who spent time discussing my outline and making helpful suggestions when I was starting out. Rajiv Chandrasekaran, the former national editor of the *Washington Post*, provided helpful suggestions and wonderful anecdotes.

To Aurobind Patel whose aesthetic judgement is flawless and can turn any copy into a work of art. Thank You. To Saurav Das for executing a great design.

A special thanks to Kelly Anderson, who had to put up with endless conversations about my work on our morning walks and Ann T. Fleming, Robin Eidsmo and James Tooley for sending me information relevant to the people I was profiling.

My brother, Sanjiv Narula, who studied electrical engineering, patiently answered my questions about AI and other related questions I was too embarrassed to ask anyone else.

My circle of support who are always there to see me through my highs and lows, Jayati, Rima, Katherine, Gauri, and especially, my sister Tara Sinha, brilliant in her own right, made very insightful suggestions. She held my hand every day through my health challenge towards the end of the book and got me through, along with gentle Joanna Rosen and my two wonderful doctors, Kristian Thomas and Adam Skolnick.

My husband, Liaquat, was supportive of this book from the start, constantly sending me relevant articles and towards the end, always the most difficult time, came up with helpful suggestions that illuminated my way forward.

My faithful companion Monty who never left my side no matter how late I worked, curled up by my feet keeping watch over me. He is the embodiment of loyalty and love.

I owe the most to my two daughters, Shabu and Tara, to whom this book is dedicated.

Endnotes

1 Devesh Kapur, Nirvikar Singh, and Sanjoy Chakravorty, *The Other One Percent: Indians in America* (Oxford: Oxford University Press, 2016), 33-34.

2 *The Washington Post*. Ashley Parker, Josh Dawsey, Yasmin Abutaleb. March 24, 2020. Trump is in a tug-of-war with scientists over coronavirus policy.

3 There is limited data on the number of Indians during this period. But between 1900 and 1940, the estimates are between 2,031 and 5,850. There was a decline after this period due to discrimination. In 1960, there were only 12,296. See *The Other One Percent* for more details.

4 Jacoby, Dr. Harold S. "More Thind Against than Sinning," *The Pacific Historian*. Vol 11 Number 4. November 1958.

5 Asia Society Education. Asian Americans Then and Now.

6 Many of these early immigrants encountered racism. Articles about 'The Hindu invasion' began appearing in *The Pacific Monthly*. 300 workers quit Bellingham after the mill where they worked was surrounded by 500 men who pelted them with stones. They were accused of undercutting wages, insolence, and not assimilating. Familiar tropes that are used today against immigrants.

7 US Census.Gov.

8 Bay Area Census.Gov.

9 Walter Isaacson, *The Innovators* (New York: Simon & Schuster, 2014), 27.

10 The name "Silicon Valley" was conferred by journalist Don Hoefler in a series of articles first punished January 11, 1971 in a weekly electronics trade paper.

11 Sebastian Mallaby, *The Power Law: Venture Capital and the Making of the Future* (London: Penguin, 2022).

12 Deborah Perry Piscione, *Secrets of Silicon Valley* (New York: St. Martin's Press, 2013), 55.

13 National Bureau of Economic Research. Working paper 31308. Top Talent, Elite Colleges and Migration: Evidence from The Indian Institute of Technology. June 2023.

14 Marguerite Gong Hancock and Jeff Katz, "Oral History of Kanwal Rekhi," Computer History Museum, Dec. 20, 2017.

15 Ibid., 16.

16 National Bureau of Economic Research. Working paper 31308. Top Talent, Elite Colleges and Migration: Evidence from The Indian Institute of Technology. June 2023.

17 United States Census, 1970.

18 Sanjoy Chakravorty, Devesh Kapur, and Nirvikar Singh, *The Other One Percent: Indians in America* (Oxford: Oxford University Press, 2019), 29-34. US Census.Gov.

19 Adam Fischer. *The Valley of Genius*. 12. New York. 2018. Pg 48.

20 Fabless is when the fabrication and manufacturing is outsourced but the research and design is done in house. Nvidia and AMD are also Fabless semiconductor companies.

21 Source: "Venture Capital's Reckoning" *The Economist*, June 30th 2022 https://www.economist.com/leaders/2022/06/30/venture-capitals-reckoning

22 David Kirkpatrick, "Vinod Khosla Can See the Future. It Just Got Hazy for a Minute," *The Information*, Dec. 1, 2023.

23 *The New York Times.* Every generation gets the beach villain it deserves. August 30, 2018.

24 Rainer Zitelmann. CNBC. Make It. Bill Gates was an angry, difficult boss in early Microsoft days—here's why employees still liked him. February 24, 2020.

25 Daniels Fund. Alphabet and Google Deal with a Toxic Organizational Culture. 2020.

26 Daisuke Wakabayashi. *New York Times.* Google Executives See Cracks in Their Company's Success. June 2021

27 *New York Times.* Google calls in help from Larry Page and Sergey Brin. January 2023.

28 Satya Nadella, *Hit Refresh: The Quest to Rediscover Microsoft and Imagine a Better Future for Everyone* (New York: HarperCollins, 2017).

29 Ibid., 143.

30 Emily Jane Fox. Bill Gates admits he was a nightmare boss. *Vanity Fair.* Feb 1, 2016.

31 The "innovator's dilemma" was coined by Harvard professor Clayon Christensen. It is when established companies lose market share and begin to fail because they fail to seize the next wave, and younger, newer companies disrupt the market with newer technologies at the expense of the older, larger ones that are less nimble.

32 Ibid., 48.

33 Ibid., 66.

34 Ibid., 45-46.

35 *Statista.* Useful Microsoft Statistics 2022.

36 *Vanity Fair.* Emily Jane Fox. Feb 2016. Bill Gates admits he was a nightmare boss.

37 Jacob Morgan.

38 Statista 2024. Personal Computer Shipments Worldwide from 2006 to 2023.

39 Thomas Wilde, "Satya Nadella Says Microsoft is 'All in on Gaming' as it Teases New Hardware for Subscription Service," *GeekWire*, June 10, 2021.

40 Brad Smith and Carol Ann Browne, *Tools and Weapons: The Promise and the Peril of the Digital Age* (London: Penguin, 2019), 50.

41 *The Information.* July 1, 2024.

42 Aaron Holmes, "AI Agenda," *The Information*, Jan. 31, 2024.

43 *Fortune Magazine.* February 10, 2023.

44 HT News Desk, "SoftBank veteran Nikesh Arora now a billionaire CEO of Palto Alto Networks, has net worth of $1.5 billion," *Hindustan Times*, Jan. 3, 2024.

45 Sophie Shulman. Palo Alto Networks CEO: We will be the first $100 billion cyber company. 28/10/22. C-Tech. Calcalistech.

46 Nvidia, a chip company headed by Jensen Huang and has occasionally surpassed Microsoft but Microsoft has managed to hold its lead.

47 Indra Nooyi, *My Life in Full: Work, Family, and Our Future* (London: Penguin, 2021), 9.

48 Ibid., 22.

49 David M. Rubenstein, *How to Lead: Wisdom from the World's Greatest CEOs, Founders, and Game Changers* (New York: Simon & Schuster, 2020), 182.

50 Nooyi, *My Life in Full*, 22.

51 Rubenstein, *How to Lead*, 183.

52 Nooyi, *My Life in Full*, 62.

53 Shantanu Narayen, another South Indian Brahmin, was made CEO of Adobe the same year. Although it wasn't a consumer company, and part of the tech world, it was a Fortune 500 company.

54 Nooyi, *My Life in Full*, 256.

55 Ibid., 120.

56 Ibid., 253.

57 Josh Zeitz, "How LBJ pulled off the biggest government maneuver since D-Day," *Politico*, July 13, 2016.

58 Deepak Chopra and Sanjiv Chopra, *Brotherhood: Dharma, Destiny, and the American Dream* (Boston: Houghton Mifflin Harcourt, 2013), 135.

59 Vietnam Veterans of America, "Vietnam War Statistics." During which 58, 220 people died, 75,000 were severely disabled.

60 Dr. Bibuthi Mishra.

61 Chopra, *Brotherhood*, 147.

62 Spencer Furey, "White Picket Fences and the 'Worst City in America': Suburbanization and White Flight in the United States and Newark, New Jersey, 1930-2010," Topics in Digital History, Dartmouth, Oct. 31, 2016.

63 World War II veterans were 87.2 percent caucasian. Vietnam War veterans were 88 percent Caucasian.

64 Abraham Verghese, "The Cowpath to America," *The New Yorker*, June 23, 1997.

65 Dr. Gauri Gandhi.

66 American Immigration Council, "Foreign-Trained Doctors are Critical to Serving Many United States Communities," Jan. 17, 2018.

67 Abraham Verghese, *My Own Country: A Doctor's Story* (New York: Vintage, 1995), 18.

68 Zofeen Maqsood, "Indian doctors integral to US Corona battle," *The American Bazaar*, March 19, 2020.

69 Chopra, *Brotherhood*, 138.

70 There have been several other advocates for integrative medicine, but the two most famous are Dr. Andrew Weil and Dr. Deepak Chopra.

71 Chopra, *Brotherhood*.

72 Ibid., 205.

73 Ibid., 209.

74 Isaac Chotiner, "Deepak Chopra Has Never Been Sick," *The New Yorker*, Oct. 17, 2019.

75 Hans A. Baer, "The Work of Andrew Weil and Deepak Chopra: Two Holistic Health/New Age Gurus: A Critique of the Holistic Health/New Age Movements," *Medical Anthropology Quarterly* 17, no. 2 (June 2003): 233-250.

76 Verghese, *My Own Country*, 117.

77 Rajiv Chandrashekeran.

78 Ibid., 5.

79 Siddhartha Mukherjee, *The Gene: An Intimate History* (New York: Scribner, 2016), 457.

80　Ibid., 477.

81　Charles McGrath, "Atul Gawande Rocks in the O.R.," *New York Times*, April 3, 2007.

82　Atul Gawande, *The Checklist Manifesto: How to Get Things Done Right* (New York: Metropolitan Books, 2009), 87.

83　Elizabeth Gudrais, "The Unlikely Writer," *Harvard Magazine*, September-October 2009.

84　During the 2008 presidential campaign, Murthy founded Doctors for Obama as a way of engaging physicians in the political process. Once President Obama was elected, the group became Doctors for America, a nonprofit advocating for health care reform.

85　Steve Straehley. AllGov. Surgeon General of the United States: who is Vivek Murthy. Dec 25, 2014.

86　J. Sellers Hill, "United States Surgeon General Vivek Murthy '98 Guided by 'Inspiration in the Moment,'" *The Harvard Crimson*, June 2, 2023.

87　Franklin Foer, *The Last Politician: Inside Joe Biden's White House and the Struggle for America's Future* (London: Penguin, 2023), 41.

88　Vivek Murthy, *Together: The Healing Power of Human Connection in a Sometimes Lonely World* (New York: HarperCollins, 2020), 281.

89　Yale School of Medicine, "Alum's appointment as surgeon general a 'home run,'" *Yale Medicine Magazine* (Spring 2015).

90　Murthy, *Together*, 13.

91　Ibid.

92　Ibid., xxii.

93　CDC, "Suicide Data and Statistics."

94　Lakshmi Vijayakumar, "The national suicide prevention strategy in India: Context and considerations for urgent action," *The Lancet Psychiatry* 9, no. 2 (Dec. 8, 2021): 160-168.

95　Nicholas Kristof, "We Know the Cure for Loneliness. So Why Do We Suffer?" *New York Times*, Sept. 6, 2023.

96　Hillary Rodham Clinton, "The Weaponization of Loneliness," *The Atlantic*, Aug. 7, 2023.

97　Murthy, *Together*, 221.

98　David West, "Social media can put young people in danger, United States surgeon general warns," *NPR*, May 23, 2023.

99　In 2007, Murthy tried his hand at entrepreneurship. He co-founded Trial Networks, which optimizes the quality and efficiency of clinical trials.

100　Amanda Marcotte, "Church membership is in a freefall, and the Christian right has only themselves to blame," *Salon*, April 2, 2021.

101　Jake Meador, "The Misunderstood Reason Millions of Americans Stopped Going to Church," *The Atlantic*, July 29, 2023.

102　Marion Maneker, "Man of the World," *New York Magazine*, April 11, 2003.

103　Fareed Zakaria, *The Future of Freedom: Illiberal Democracy at Home and Abroad* (New York: W. W. Norton, 2003), 17.

104　Peter Osnos, "Fareed Zakaria and the Perils of Modern-Day Punditry," *The Atlantic*, Aug. 21, 2012.

105　Judge Luttig was a Reagan appointee and a respected intellectual among conservatives.

106　Katyal filed the case initially in 2003 and it got to the trial court in 2004, the court of appeals in 2005, and the Supreme Court in 2006.

107 Senator Graham had introduced a bill that set guidelines for the detainees held at Guantanamo limiting their access to US courts as they were considered enemy combatants.

108 Jonathan Mahler, *The Challenge: Hamdan v. Rumsfeld and the Fight over Presidential Power* (New York: Farrar, Straus and Giroux, 2008).

109 Joan Biskupic, Janet Roberts, and John Shiffman, "The Echo Chamber," *Reuters*, Dec. 8, 2014.

110 Shivani Vohra, "A Conversation With: Nikki Haley," *New York Times*, April 4, 2012.

111 Nikki Haley, *Can't Is Not an Option: My American Story* (New York: Sentinel, 2012), 169.

112 Nikki Haley, *With All Due Respect: Defending America with Grit and Grace* (New York: St. Martin's Press, 2019), 23.

113 Ibid., 11.

114 Ibid., 13-35.

115 Michael Kranish, "Nikki Haley let the Confederate flag fly until a massacre forced her hand," *The Washington Post*, May 27, 2023.

116 Kavya Gupta, "How Nikki Haley Built an $8 Million Fortune (And Helped Bail out Her Parents)," *Forbes*, April 8, 2023.

117 Matt Egan, "Ro Khanna to Big Oil: 'Spare us the spin' and just be human," *CNN*, Oct. 28, 2021.

118 Holly Otterbein and Adam Wren, "Ro Khanna says he's looking at the Senate. His allies are talking about the White House," *Politico*, Jan. 12, 2023.

119 The Patriot Act, enacted by Congress 45 days after the 9/11 attack, empowered law enforcement to conduct surveillance on American citizens to find terrorists and often targeted innocent citizens.

120 Raif Karerat, "Ro Khanna launches his 3rd bid to become a Congressman and unseat 'the dozer' Mike Honda," *The American Bazaar*, June 2, 2015.

121 Issie Lapowsky, "A Silicon Valley Lawmaker's $1 Trillion Plan to Save Trump Country," *WIRED*, March 30, 2017.

122 Since we spoke, in June 2024, The United States Supreme Court ruled in favor of Starbucks and against the workers in the case of employees arguing for the right to unionize.

123 Feliks Garcia, "National Spelling Bee Crowns Youngest Champion in History," *The Independent*, May 27, 2016.

124 Sandipan Deb Super Failure: Horrors of IIT Dream. *Live Mint*. July 23, 2019.

125 Saranya Misra. Indian parents are different than American parents. *Your Teen- for parents*. June 13, 2017.

126 Pyaralal Raghavan. Indian parents have very high expectations about their children's education and careers. *Times of India* July 18, 2015.

127 *The Economic Times*, Feb. 25, 2018.

128 Chopra, Ritika. Tracking India's Toppers: *The Indian Express*. Dec 29, 2020.

129 Gladwell, *Outliers*, 19.

130 Anil Seal, *The Emergence of Indian Nationalism: Competition and Collaboration in the Later Nineteenth Century* (Cambridge: Cambridge University Press, 1968), 16-17, 21.

131 Anil Seal, *The Emergence of Indian Nationalism: Competition and Collaboration in the Later Nineteenth Century* (Cambridge: Cambridge University Press, 1968), 16-17, 21.

Bibliography

Chakravorty, Sanjoy, Devesh Kapur, and Nirvikar Singh. *The Other One Percent: Indians in America*. Oxford: Oxford University Press, 2019.

Chopra, Deepak, and Sanjiv Chopra. *Brotherhood: Dharma, Destiny, and the American Dream*. Boston: New Harvest, 2013.

Chopra, Deepak. *Abundance: The Inner Path to Wealth*. New York: Harmony Books, 2022.

Chopra, Deepak. *Ageless Body, Timeless Mind: The Quantum Alternative to Growing Old*. New York: Three Rivers Press, 1993.

Chopra, Deepak. *Metahuman: Unleashing Your Infinite Potential*. New York: Harmony Books, 2019.

Chopra, Deepak. *Quantum Healing: Exploring the Frontiers of Mind/Body Medicine*. New York: Bantam Books, 1989.

Chopra, Deepak. *The Seven Spiritual Laws of Success: A Practical Guide to the Fulfillment of Your Dreams*. San Rafael: Amber-Allen Publishing, 1994.

Chopra, Deepak. *Total Meditation: Practices in Living the Awakened Life*. New York: Harmony Books, 2020.

Christensen, Brenda H. *The $8 Man: From India to North America, Immigrants Who Came with Nothing and Changed Everything*. Self-published, 2017.

Christensen, Clayton M. *The Innovator's Dilemma: When New Technologies Cause Great Firms to Fail*. Boston: Harvard Business Review Press, 1997.

Epstein, David. *Range: Why Generalists Triumph in a Specialized World*. New York: Riverhead Books, 2021.

Fisher, Adam. *Valley of Genius: The Uncensored History of Silicon Valley*. New York: Twelve, 2018.

Gawande, Atul. *Being Mortal: Medicine and What Matters in the End*. New York: Metropolitan Books, 2017.

Gawande, Atul. *Complications: A Surgeon's Notes on an Imperfect Science*. New York: Metropolitan Books, 2003.

Gawande, Atul. *The Checklist Manifesto: How to Get Things Right*. New York: Metropolitan Books, 2011.

Gladwell, Malcolm. *Outliers: The Story of Success*. Boston: Little, Brown and Company, 2008.

Grove, Andrew S. *Only the Paranoid Survive: How to Exploit the Crisis Points That Challenge Every Company*. New York: Crown Currency, 1999.

Haley, Nikki. *With All Due Respect: Defending America with Grit and Grace*. New York: St. Martin's Press, 2019.

Haley, Nikki. *Can't Is Not an Option: My American Story*. New York: Sentinel, 2012.

Isaacson, Walter. *Elon Musk*. New York: Simon & Schuster, 2023.

Isaacson, Walter. *Steve Jobs*. New York: Simon & Schuster, 2021.

Isaacson, Walter. *The Innovators: How a Group of Hackers, Geniuses, and Geeks Created the Digital Revolution*. New York: Simon & Schuster, 2015.

Khandelwal, Madhulika S. *Becoming American, Being Indian*. Ithaca: Cornell University Press, 2002.

Kissinger, Henry A., Eric Schmidt, and Daniel Huttenlocher. *The Age of AI: And Our Human Future*. Boston: Little, Brown and Company, 2021.

Lal, Vinay. *The Other Indians: A Political and Cultural History of South Asians in America*. Edited by Russell C. Leong and Don T. Nakanishi. Los Angeles: UCLA Asian American Studies Press, 2008.

Mahler, Jonathan. *The Challenge: Hamdan v. Rumsfeld and the Fight Over Presidential Power*. New York: Farrar, Straus and Giroux, 2008.

Mallaby, Sebastian. *The Power Law: Venture Capital and the Making of the New Future*. New York: Penguin Press, 2022.

Mukherjee, Siddhartha. *The Emperor of All Maladies: A Biography of Cancer*. New York: Scribner, 2010.

Mukherjee, Siddhartha. *The Gene: An Intimate History*. New York: Scribner, 2016.

Mukherjee, Siddhartha. *The Song of the Cell: An Exploration of Medicine and the New Human*. New York: Scribner, 2022.

Murthy, Vivek H. *Together: The Healing Power of Human Connection in a Sometimes Lonely World*. New York: HarperCollins, 2020.

Nadella, Satya, Greg Shaw, and Jill Tracie Nichols. *Hit Refresh: The Quest to Rediscover Microsoft's Soul and Imagine a Better Future for Everyone*. New York: HarperCollins, 2019.

Nooyi, Indra. *My Life in Full: Work, Family, and Our Future*. New York: Portfolio, 2021.

Piscione, Deborah Perry. *Secrets of Silicon Valley: What Everyone Else Can Learn from the Innovation Capital of the World*. New York: St. Martin's Press, 2013.

Rubenstein, David M. *How to Lead: Wisdom from the World's Greatest CEOs, Founders, and Game Changers*. New York: Simon & Schuster, 2020.

Saxenian, AnnaLee. *Regional Advantage: Culture and Competition in Silicon Valley and Route 128*. Cambridge: Harvard University Press, 1996.

Smith, Brad, and Carol Ann Browne. *Tools and Weapons: The Promise and the Peril of the Digital Age*. New York: Penguin Press, 2019.

Swisher, Kara. *Burn Book: A Tech Love Story*. New York: Simon & Schuster, 2024.

The Encyclopedia of the Indian Diaspora. Edited by Brij V. Lal, Peter Reeves, and Rajesh Rai. Honolulu: University of Hawai'i Press, 2006.

Verghese, Abraham. *Cutting for Stone*. New York: Alfred A. Knopf, 2009.

Verghese, Abraham. *My Own Country: A Doctor's Story*. New York: Vintage, 1995.

Verghese, Abraham. *The Covenant of Water*. New York: Grove Atlantic, 2023.

Wadhwa, Vivek, Ismail Amla, and Alex Salkever. *From Incremental to Exponential: How Large Companies Can See the Future and Rethink Innovation*. Oakland: Berrett-Koehler Publishers, 2020.

Zakaria, Fareed. *In Defense of a Liberal Education*. New York: W. W. Norton & Company, 2015.

Zakaria, Fareed. *Ten Lessons for a Post-Pandemic World*. New York: W. W. Norton & Company, 2020.

Zakaria, Fareed. *The Future of Freedom: Illiberal Democracy at Home and Abroad*. New York: W. W. Norton & Company, 2003.

Zakaria, Fareed. *The Post-American World: And the Rise of the Rest*. New York: W. W. Norton & Company, 2008.

Index

About the Author

Meenakshi Narula Ahamed is a freelance journalist and the author of *A Matter of Trust: India–US Relations from Truman to Trump*, a sweeping narrative history of the turbulent seventy-year relationship between the two countries.

Ahamed's writing has been published in the *New York Times*, *Washington Post*, *Atlantic*, CNN, *Wall Street Journal*, *Seminar*, and *Asian Age*. She has worked at the World Bank in Washington, DC, and for NDTV, and has served on the boards of Doctors without Borders, Drugs for Neglected Diseases, and the Vellore Christian Medical College Foundation.

Ahamed was born in Calcutta and received an MA from the Johns Hopkins School of Advanced International Studies. She divides her time between New York, Los Angeles, and New Delhi.

HarperCollins *Publishers* India

At HarperCollins India, we believe in telling the best stories and finding the widest readership for our books in every format possible. We started publishing in 1992; a great deal has changed since then, but what has remained constant is the passion with which our authors write their books, the love with which readers receive them, and the sheer joy and excitement that we as publishers feel in being a part of the publishing process.

Over the years, we've had the pleasure of publishing some of the finest writing from the subcontinent and around the world, including several award-winning titles and some of the biggest bestsellers in India's publishing history. But nothing has meant more to us than the fact that millions of people have read the books we published, and that somewhere, a book of ours might have made a difference.

As we look to the future, we go back to that one word— a word which has been a driving force for us all these years.

Read.